THE
TEMPLE
CLASSICS

THE VITA NUOVA
AND
CANZONIERE
OF
DANTE ALIGHIERI

Dante's Dream
By Dante Gabriel Rossetti

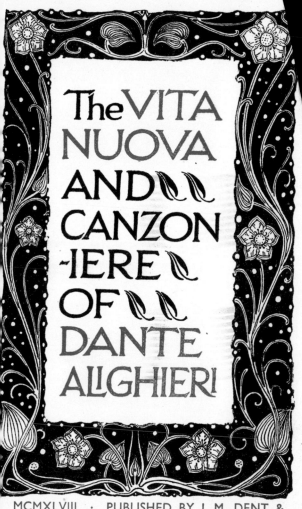

The VITA NUOVA AND CANZONIERE OF DANTE ALIGHIERI

MCMXLVIII · PUBLISHED BY J. M. DENT & SONS LTD., ALDINE HOUSE, LONDON W.C.

A

.§ I. In quella parte del libro della mia
memoria, dinanzi alla quale poco si potrebbe
leggere, si trova una rubrica, la quale dice :
incipit Vita Nova. Sotto la quale rubrica io
trovo scritte le parole, le quali è mio intendimento d' assemprare in questo libello, e se non
tutte, almeno la loro sentenzia.

§ II. Nove fiate già, appresso al mio nasci-
mento, era tornato lo cielo della luce quasi ad
un medesimo punto, quanto alla sua propria
girazione, quando alli miei occhi apparve prima
la gloriosa donna della mia mente, la quale fu
chiamata da molti Beatrice, i quali non sapeano
che si chiamare.

Ella era già in questa vita stata tanto, che
nel suo tempo lo cielo stellato era mosso verso
la parte d' oriente delle dodici parti l' una d'
un grado ; sì che quasi dal principio del suo
anno nono apparve a me, ed io la vidi quasi
alla fine del mio nono. Ella apparvemi vestita
di nobilissimo colore umile ed onesto sanguigno,
cinta ed ornata alla guisa che alla sua giovanissima etade si convenia. In quel punto dico
veracemente che lo spirito della vita, lo quale
dimora nella segretissima camera del cuore,
cominciò a tremare sì fortemente, che apparia

§ I. In that part of the book of my memory before which little could be read is found a rubric which saith : *Incipit Vita Nova*. Beneath which rubric I find written the words which it is my purpose to copy in this little book, and if not all, at least their substance.

§ II. Nine times already since my birth had the heaven of light returned almost to one and the same point in relation to its own proper revolution, when the glorious lady of my mind first appeared to mine eyes, who was called *Beatrice* by many that knew not what they were calling her.

She had already been so long in this life that, in her time, the heaven of the stars had moved one twelfth part of a degree towards the East ; so that almost from the beginning of her ninth year she appeared to me and I beheld her almost at the end of my ninth. She appeared to me clothed in most noble hue, a subdued and modest crimson, cinctured and adorned after the fashion that was becoming to her most tender age. At that point I verily declare that the vital spirit which dwelleth in the most secret chamber of the heart began to tremble so mightily that it was horribly

3

ne' menomi polsi orribilmente; e tremando disse queste parole : *Ecce Deus fortior me, qui veniens dominabitur mihi.*

In quel punto lo spirito animale, il quale dimora nell' alta camera, nella quale tutti li spiriti sensitivi portano le loro percezioni, si cominciò a maravigliare molto, e parlando spezialmente allo spirito del viso, disse queste parole : *Apparuit jam beatitudo vestra.*

In quel punto lo spirito naturale, il quale dimora in quella parte, ove si ministra lo nutrimento nostro, cominciò a piangere, e piangendo disse queste parole : *Heu miser ! quia frequenter impeditus ero deinceps.* D' allora innanzi dico ch' Amore signoreggiò l' anima mia, la quale fu sì tosto a lui disposata, e cominciò a prendere sopra me tanta sicurtade e tanta signoria, per la virtù che gli dava la mia imaginazione, che mi convenia fare compiutamente tutti i suoi piaceri. Egli mi comandava molte volte che io cercassi per vedere quest' angiola giovanissima: ond' io nella mia puerizia molte fiate l' andai cercando; e vedeala di sì nobili e laudabili portamenti, che certo di lei si potea dire quella parola del poeta Omero : "Ella non pareva figliuola d' uomo mortale, ma di Dio." Ed avvegna che la sua immagine, la quale continuamente meco stava, fosse baldanza d' amore a signoreggiarmi, tuttavia era di sì nobile virtù, che nulla volta sofferse, che Amore mi reggesse senza il fedele consiglio della ragione in quelle cose, là dove cotal consiglio fosse utile a udire. E però che soprastare alle passioni ed atti di tanta gioventudine pare alcuno parlare

apparent in the least of my pulses, and trembling, it said these words: *Ecce Deus fortior me, qui veniens dominabitur mihi.*

At that moment the animal spirit which dwelleth in the high chamber to which all the spirits of sense carry their perceptions, began to marvel much, and speaking especially to the spirits of sight said these words: *Apparuit jam beatitudo vestra.*

At that moment the natural spirit which dwells in that part where our nourishment is distributed began to weep, and weeping said these words: *Heu miser ! quia frequenter impeditus ero deinceps.* From thenceforward I say that Love held lordship over my soul, which was so early bounden unto him, and he began to hold over me so much assurance and so much mastery through the power which my imagination gave to him, that it behoved me to do all his pleasure perfectly. He commanded me many times that I should seek to behold this most youthful angel: wherefore in my childhood often did I go seeking her ; and I beheld her of so noble and laudable bearing that assuredly of her might be said those words of the poet Homer: "She seemed not the daughter of a mortal man but of God." And although her image that continually abode with me, were Love's exultancy to master me, nevertheless it was of so noble a virtue that no time did it suffer Love to rule over me without the faithful counsel of reason, in those things where such counsel were useful to hear. And since to dwell on things suffered and done in so young an age hath an appearance

fabuloso, mi partirò da esse; e trapassando
molte cose, le quali si potrebbero trarre dall'
esemplo onde nascono queste, verrò a quelle
parole, le quali sono scritte nella mia memoria
sotto maggiori paragrafi.

§ III. Poichè furono passati tanti dì, che
appunto erano compiuti li nove anni appresso l'
apparimento soprascritto di questa gentilissima;
nell' ultimo di questi dì avvenne, che questa
mirabile donna apparve a me vestita di colore
bianchissimo, in mezzo di due gentili donne, le
quali erano di più lunga etade; e passando per
una via, volse gli occhi verso quella parte ov' io
era molto pauroso; e per la sua ineffabile
cortesia, la quale è oggi meritata nel grande
secolo, mi salutò virtuosamente tanto, che mi
parve allora vedere tutti i termini della
beatitudine.

L' ora, che lo suo dolcissimo salutare mi
giunse, era fermamente nona di quel giorno: e
perocchè quella fu la prima volta che le sue
parole si mossero per venire a' miei orecchi, presi
tanta dolcezza, che come inebriato mi partii
dalle genti, e ricorso al solingo luogo d'una mia
camera, e puosimi a pensare di questa cortesissima.

E pensando di lei, mi sopraggiunse un soave
sonno, nel quale m' apparve una maravigliosa
visione: che mi parea vedere nella mia camera una
nebula di colore di fuoco, dentro alla quale io di-
scernea una figura d' uno signore, di pauroso aspetto
a chi lo guardasse. E pareami con tanta letizia
quanto a sè, che mirabil cosa era: e nelle sue
parole dicea molte cose, le quali io non intendea

of speaking idle tales I will turn me from them ;
and passing by many things which might be
drawn from the copy whence these are derived,
I will come to those words that are written in
my memory under more weighty paragraphs.

§ III. After so many days had passed, that
the nine years were precisely completed since
the above written appearance of this most gentle
one, and on the last of those days, it came to
pass that this wondrous lady appeared to me
clothed in hue of purest white in the midst of
two gentle ladies who were of fuller age ; and
passing by the way she turned her eyes towards
that part where I was right fearful ; and of her
ineffable courtesy which now is rewarded in the
greater world, gave me a salutation of such virtue,
that methought I beheld the uttermost bounds of
blessedness.

The hour when her most sweet salutation
.eached me was assuredly the ninth of that day :
and inasmuch as that was the first time that
her words set forth to come to mine ears, such
sweetness possessed me that as one drunken I
departed from all people and withdrew to the
solitude of a chamber of mine and set me a-
thinking of this most courteous one.

And as I thought of her, a gentle sleep fell
upon me wherein a wondrous vision appeared to
me : for methought I saw in my chamber a
cloud of the hue of flame, within which I discerned the figure of a lord, of fearful aspect to
one who should look on him. And he seemed
to me of such gladness as to himself that a
wondrous thing it was ; and in his words he said

se non poche, tra le quali io intendea queste:
Ego dominus tuus. Nelle sue braccia mi parea
vedere una persona dormire nuda, salvo che
involta mi parea in un drappo sanguigno
leggermente; la quale io riguardando molto
intentivamente, conobbi ch' era la donna della
salute, la quale m' avea lo giorno dinanzi degnato
di salutare. E nell' una delle mani mi parea che
questi tenesse una cosa, la quale ardesse tutta; e
pareami che mi dicesse queste parole: *Vide cor
tuum.* E quando egli era stato alquanto, pareami
che disvegliasse questa che dormia; e tanto si
sforzava per suo ingegno, che le facea mangiare
quella cosa che in mano gli ardeva, la quale ella
mangiava dubitosamente. Appresso ciò, poco
dimorava che la sua letizia si convertia in
amarissimo pianto: e così piangendo si ricogliea
questa donna nelle sue braccia, e con essa mi
parea che se ne gisse verso il cielo: ond' io
sostenea si grande angoscia, che lo mio deboletto
sonno non potè sostenere, anzi si ruppe, e fui
disvegliato. Ed immantinente cominciai a
pensare; e trovai che l' ora, nella quale m' era
questa visione apparita, era stata la quarta della
notte: sì che appare manifestamente, ch' ella
fu la prima ora delle nove ultime ore della
notte.

E pensando io a ciò che m' era apparito,
proposi di farlo sentire a molti, i quali erano
famosi trovatori in quel tempo: e conciòfosse-
cosach' io avessi già veduto per me medesimo
l' arte del dire parole per rima, proposi di fare
un sonetto, nel quale io salutassi tutti i fedeli d'
Amore, e pregandoli che giudicassero la mia

many things which I understood not save a few, among which I understood these : *Ego dominus tuus.* In his arms methought I saw one sleeping, naked, save that she seemed to me wrapped lightly in a crimson drapery ; whom, gazing at very intently, I knew to be the lady of the salutation, who the day before had deigned to salute me. And in one of his hands methought he held a thing that was all aflame ; and methought he said to me these words : *Vide cor tuum.* And when he had tarried a while, methought he awoke her who slept and so wrought he by his art that he made her eat of that thing that was aflame in his hand, whereof she ate afeared. Thereafter, short time he abode ere his gladness was changed to bitterest weeping : and thus weeping he gathered this lady up in his arms and with her methought he went away heavenward : whereat I sustained so great anguish that my feeble little sleep could not endure, but broke and I was awake. And straightway I began to ponder and found that the hour in which this vision had appeared to me had been the fourth hour of the night : so that it manifestly appeareth that it was the first of the last nine hours of the night.

And pondering on what had appeared to me, I purposed to make it known to many who were famous rhymers of that time : and forasmuch as I had of myself already learned the art of saying words in rhyme, I purposed to make a sonnet in which I should salute all Love's lieges and praying them that they would interpret my

*A

visione, scrissi loro ciò ch' io avea nel mio sonno
veduto; e cominciai allora questo sonetto:

A ciascun' alma presa, e gentil core,
    Nel cui cospetto viene il dir presente,
    A ciò che mi riscrivan suo parvente,
    Salute in lor signor, cioè Amore.

Già eran quasi ch' atterzate l' ore
    Del tempo che ogni stella n'è lucente,
    Quando m' apparve Amor subitamente,
    Cui essenza membrar mi dà orrore.

Allegro mi sembrava Amor, tenendo
    Mio core in mano, e nelle braccia avea
    Madonna, involta in un drappo dormendo.

Poi la svegliava, e d' esto core ardendo
    Lei paventosa umilmente pascea:
    Appresso gir ne lo vedea piangendo.

*Questo sonetto si divide in due parti: nella
prima parte saluto, e domando risponsione; nella
seconda significo a che si dee rispondere. La
seconda parte comincia quivi:* Già eran.

A questo sonetto fu risposto da molti e di
diverse sentenze, tra li quali fu risponditore
quegli, cui io chiamo primo de' miei amici; e
disse allora un sonetto lo quale comincia: *Vedesti
al mio parere ogni valore.* E questo fu quasi il
principio dell' amistà tra lui e me, quando egli
seppe ch' io era quegli che gli avea ciò mandato.

Lo verace giudicio del detto sogno non fu
veduto allora per alcuno, ma ora è manifesto alli
più semplici.

vision, I wrote to them what I had seen in my sleep; and then I began this sonnet:

To every captive soul and gentle heart, into whose presence come the present rhymes, that they may write me back their opinion—Greeting in their lord, to wit, Love.

Already nigh a third of the hours of the time that every star is bright to us, had passed, when suddenly Love appeared to me, the memory of whose being maketh me shudder.

Gladsome Love seemed to me, holding my heart in his hand, and in his arms he had my lady, wrapped in a drapery and sleeping.

Then he awakened her and of this flaming heart, she fearful, did humbly eat: afterwards I beheld him go his way a-weeping.

This sonnet divides into two parts: in the first part I make salutation and ask an answer; in the second I signify whereto answer should be made. The second part begins here: Already.

To this sonnet answer was made by many and in divers senses, among which he was an answerer whom I call chief of my friends; and he then composed a sonnet which begins: *Thou didst behold to my seeming all excellency.* And this was as 'twere the beginning of the friendship between him and me, when he knew that I was he who had sent him this.

The true interpretation of the said dream was not then seen by any one, but now it is manifest to the most simple.

§ IV. Da questa visione innanzi cominciò il
mio spirito naturale ad essere impedito nella sua
operazione, perocchè l' anima era tutta data nel
pensare di questa gentilissima ; ond' io divenni
in picciolo tempo poi di sì frale e debole condizione, che a molti amici pesava della mia vista :
e molti pieni d' invidia si procacciavano di sapere
di me quello ch' io voleva del tutto celare ad
altrui. Ed io accorgendomi del malvagio do-
mandare che mi faceano, per la volontà d'
Amore, il quale mi comandava secondo il consiglio della ragione, rispondea loro, che Amore
era quegli che così m' avea governato : dicea d'
Amore, perocchè io portava nel viso tante delle
sue insegne, che questo non si potea ricoprire. E
quando mi domandavano : Per cui t' ha così
distrutto questo Amore ? ed io sorridendo li
guardava, e nulla dicea loro.

§ V. Un giorno avvenne, che questa gentilissima sedea in parte, ove s' udiano parole
della Regina della gloria, ed io era in luogo, dal
quale vedea la mia beatitudine : e nel mezzo di
lei e di me, per la retta linea, sedea una gentile
donna di molto piacevole aspetto, la quale mi
mirava spesse volte, maravigliandosi del mio
sguardare, che parea che sopra lei terminasse ;
onde molti s' accorsero del suo mirare. Ed in
tanto vi fu posto mente, che, partendomi da
questo luogo, mi sentii dire appresso : Vedi come
cotale donna distrugge la persona di costui. E
nominandola, intesi che diceano di colei, che in
mezzo era stata nella linea retta che movea dalla
gentilissima Beatrice, e terminava negli occhi

§ IV. From this vision forward my natural spirit began to be imped ed in its action because my mind was wholly given to thinking of this most gentle lady ; wherefore in short time after I became of so frail and weak a state that the sight of me weighed upon many of my friends ; and many full of spite sought to learn from me what my will was wholly to conceal from others. And I, perceiving the malicious questioning they made of me, by Love's will, who commanded me according to the counsel of reason, answered them, that Love was he who had thus dealt with me : I spake of Love because I bore in my countenance so many of his tokens that this much could not be hidden. And when they asked me : Through whom hath this Love thus wasted thee ? then I, smiling, gazed at them and nothing said.

§ V. One day it came to pass that this most gentle lady sat in a place where words of the Queen of glory were being heard, and I was in a place from which I could behold my beatitude ; and in the midway between her and me in a direct line sat a gentle lady of most pleasing mien, who gazed at me many times, marvelling at my look which seemed to find its end in her ; whereby many became aware of her gazing. And so far was heed given thereto, that departing from this place I heard say behind me : Behold how such a lady wasteth this man's person. And by their naming her, I learned that they were speaking of her who had been in the middle of the direct line which started from the most gentle Beatrice and ended in mine eyes.

miei.   Allora mi confortai molto, assicurandomi
che il mio segreto non era comunicato, lo giorno,
altrui per mia vista.

Ed immantinente pensai di fare di questa gentile
donna schermo della veritade, e tanto ne mostrai
in poco di tempo, che il mio segreto fu creduto
sapere dalle più persone che di me ragionavano.
Con questa donna mi celai alquanti mesi ed
anni ; e per più fare credente altrui, feci per lei
certe cosette per rima, le quali non è mio intendimento di scrivere qui, se non in quanto
facessero a trattare di quella gentilissima Beatrice ;
e però le lascierò tutte, salvo che alcuna cosa ne
scriverò, che pare che sia loda di lei.

§ VI. Dico che in questo tempo, che questa
donna era schermo di tanto amore, quanto dalla
mia parte, mi venne una volontà di voler ricordare
il nome di quella gentilissima, ed accompagnarlo
di molti nomi di donne, e specialmente del nome
di questa gentildonna.   E presi i nomi di sessanta
le più belle della cittad, ove la mia donna fu
posta dall' altissimo sire, e composi una epistola
sotto forma di serventese, la quale io non scriverò :
e non n' avrei fatto menzione se non per dire
quello che, componendola, maravigliosamente
addivenne, cioè che in alcuno altro numero non
sofferse il nome della mia donna stare, se non in
sul nove, tra' nomi di queste donne.

§ VII. La donna, con la quale io avea tanto
tempo celata la mia volontà, convenne che si
partisse della sopradetta cittade, e andasse in
paese lontano : per che io, quasi sbigottito della

Then I comforted me greatly being assured that my secret had not been made common that day to others by my look.

And straightway I thought to make this gentle lady a screen of the truth, and such shew did I make thereof in a short time, that my secret was thought to be known by most of the persons who were talking of me. Some months and years I concealed me with this lady, and to make folk more credulous I composed for her certain little things in rhyme which it is not my purpose to write here, save in so far as they served to treat of that most gentle Beatrice; and therefore I will pass them all by, save that I will write thereof something that may seem to be in praise of her.

§ VI. I say that at this time when this lady was a screen of Love so great as that on my part, there came to me a desire that I should record the name of that most gentle one and accompany it with many names of ladies, and in especial with the name of this gentle lady: so I took the names of sixty, the fairest ladies of the city where my lady was placed by the most high Lord, and I composed an epistle in the form of a *serventese* which I will not write down, nor would I have made mention of it were it not to tell of what came wondrously to pass in composing it, namely that in no other number did it suffer the name of my lady to remain than in the ninth among the names of those ladies.

§ VII. It behoved the lady with whom I had so long hidden my desire, to depart from the aforesaid city and to go into a far country: wherefore I, as though dismayed at the fair defence

bella difesa che mi era venuta meno, assai me ne
disconfortai più che io medesimo non avrei
creduto dinanzi.   E pensando che, se della sua
partita io non parlassi alquanto dolorosamente,
le persone sarebbero accorte più tosto del mio
nascondere, proposi di farne alcuna lamentanza
in un sonetto, il quale io scriverò; perciocchè la
mia donna fu immediata cagione di certe parole,
che nel sonetto sono, siccome appare a chi lo
intende: e allora dissi questo sonetto:

O voi, che per la via d'Amor passate,
 Attendete, e guardate
 S'egli è dolore alcun, quanto il mio, grave:
 E priego sol, ch' udir mi sofferiate;
 E poi immaginate
 S' io son d' ogni tormento ostello e chiave.

Amor, non già per mia poca bontate,
 Ma per sua nobiltate,
 Mi pose in vita sì dolce e soave,
 Ch' io mi sentia dir dietro spesse fiate:
 Deh! per qual dignitate
 Così leggiadro questi lo cor have!

Ora ho perduta tutta mia baldanza,
 Che si movea d' amoroso tesoro;
 Ond' io pover dimoro
 In guisa, che di dir mi vien dottanza.

Sicchè, volendo far come coloro,
 Che per vergogna celan lor mancanza,
 Di fuor mostro allegranza,
 E dentro dallo cor mi struggo e ploro.

Questo sonetto ha due parti principali: chè nella
prima intendo chiamare i fedeli d' Amore per quelle

which had failed me, was much disquieted,
more than I myself would have believed
before. And thinking that if I spake not
somewhat sorrowfully of her departure, folk
would the sooner be aware of my concealment, I
purposed to utter some lamentation in a sonnet
which I shall write down, for that my lady
was the immediate cause of certain words which
are in the sonnet, as is apparent to him who understandeth it: so then I composed this sonnet:

O ye who on Love's way pass by, behold and see
    if there be any sorrow heavy as is mine, and
    I pray only that ye bear to hear me; and
    then imagine if I am the hostel and key of
    every torment.

Love, not indeed for my small goodness, but of
    his nobleness, placed me in a life so sweet and
    calm that I heard say behind me oft-times:
    through what worthiness hath this man his
    heart so glad!

Now have I lost all my exultancy, which sprang
    from a treasure of love; wherefore I remain
    poor in such wise that fear cometh upon
    me to tell thereof.

So that I, who would do as they that hide for
    shame their lack, make outward show of
    joy and in my heart do pine away and
    weep.

*This sonnet hath two chief parts; for in the first
my intent is to call Love's lieges by those words of*

parole di Geremia profeta : O vos omnes, qui transitis per viam, attendite et videte, si est dolor sicut dolor meus ; *e pregare che mi sofferino d'udire. Nella seconda narro là ove Amore m' avea posto, con altro intendimento che l' estreme parti del sonetto non mostrano : e dico ciò che io ho perduto. La seconda parte comincia quivi :* Amor, non già.

§ VIII. Appresso il partire di questa gentil-donna, fu piacere del signore degli angeli di chiamare alla sua gloria una donna giovane e di gentile aspetto molto, la quale fu assai graziosa in questa sopraddetta cittade ; lo cui corpo io vidi giacere senza l' anima in mezzo di molte donne, le quali piangevano assai pietosamente. Allora, ricordandomi che già l' avea veduta fare compagnia a quella gentilissima, non potei soste-nere alquante lagrime ; anzi piangendo mi proposi di dire alquante parole della sua morte in guiderdone di ciò, che alcuna fiata l' avea veduta con la mia donna. E di ciò toccai alcuna cosa nell' ultima parte delle parole che io ne dissi, siccome appare manifestamente a chi le intende : e dissi allora questi due sonetti, dei quali comincia il primo *Piangete amanti ;* il secondo *Morte villana.*

Piangete, amanti, poichè piange Amore,
    Udendo qual cagion lui fa plorare :
    Amor sente a pietà donne chiamare,
    Mostrando amaro duol per gli occhi fuore :

Perchè villana Morte in gentil core
    Ha messo il suo crudele adoperare,
    Guastando ciò che al mondo è da lodare
    In gentil donna, fuora dell' onore.

Jeremiah the prophet: O vos omnes, qui transitis per viam, attendite et videte, si est dolor sicut dolor meus; *and pray that they bear to hear me. In the second part I relate where Love had placed me, with other meaning than the last parts of the sonnet show: and I tell what I have lost. The second part begins here:* Love, not indeed.

§ VIII. After the departure of this noble lady it was the pleasure of the lord of the angels to call unto his glory a lady, young and of most gentle mien, who was of much favour in the aforesaid city, whose body I beheld lying bereft of its soul in the midst of many ladies that wept very piteously. Then remembering that once I had seen her bearing that most gentle lady company, I could not restrain some tears; but rather weeping did purpose to say some words of her death in guerdon of my having some times seen her with my lady. And I touched somewhat on that in the last part of the words which I composed, even as manifestly appeareth to him who understands them: and I then composed these two sonnets, the first of which begins: *Wail ye lovers;* the second *Churlish Death.*

Wail ye lovers (since love wails), when ye hear what cause maketh him to weep. Love heareth ladies uttering piteous cries, showing forth bitter grief through their eyes;

because churlish Death hath wrought his cruel work in a gentle heart, wasting all, save honour, which the world should praise in gentle lady.

Udite quant' Amor le fece orranza;
  Ch' io 'l vidi lamentare in forma vera
  Sovra la morta immagine avvenente;

E riguardava inver lo ciel sovente,
  Ove l' alma gentil già locata era,
  Che donna fu di sì gaia sembianza.

Questo primo sonetto si divide in tre parti.
Nella prima chiamo e sollecito i fedeli d' Amore
a piangere, e dico che lo signore loro piange, e che
udendo la cagione perch' e' piange, si acconcino più
ad ascoltarmi; nella seconda narro la cagione, nella
terza parlo d' alcuno onore, che Amore fece a
questa donna. La seconda parte comincia quivi.
Amor sente; *la terza quivi:* Udite.

Morte villana, di pietà nemica,
  Di dolor madre antica,
  Giudizio incontrastabile, gravoso,
  Poic' hai data materia al cor doglioso,
  Ond' io vado pensoso,
  Di te biasmar la lingua s' affatica.

E se di grazia ti vo' far mendica,
  Convenesi ch' io dica
  Lo tuo fallir, d' ogni torto tortoso;
  Non però che alla gente sia nascoso,
  Ma per farne cruccioso
  Chi d' Amor per innanzi si nutrica.

Dal secolo hai partita cortesia,
  E, ciò che 'n donne è da pregiar, virtute;
  In gaia gioventute
  Distrutta hai l' amorosa leggiadria.

Hear what great honour Love did to her, for I
beheld him in bodily form, lamenting o'er the
dead, comely image ;

and gazing oft heavenward, where the gentle
soul was already placed, that was mistress
of so winsome a vesture.

*This first sonnet divides into three parts. In
the first I call and solicit Love's lieges to weep,
and I say that their lord weepeth, and that hearing
the cause why he weeps, they may bestir themselves
more to listen to me; in the second part I relate
the reason ; in the third, I speak of a certain
honour that Love did to this lady. The second part
begins here*: Love heareth ; *the third*: Hear.

Churlish Death, of pity the foe, of sorrow the
ancient mother, Judgement ineluctible, heavy;
since thou hast given matter to the sorrowing
heart wherefore I pensive go, my tongue
wearieth itself in chiding thee.

And if of mercy I would beggar thee, it behoves
that I tell of thy iniquity, guilty thou of every
guilt ; not because it is hidden from folk, but
to kindle his wrath thereat who henceforth
shall be nurtured of Love.

From the world thou has reft courtesy and—
that thing of price in woman—virtue : in
winsome youth hast thou amorous grace destroyed.

Più non vo' discovrir qual donna sia,
　Che per le proprietà sue conosciute :
　Chi non merta salute,
　Non speri mai d'aver sua compagnia.

*Questo sonetto si divide in quattro parti ; nella
prima chiamo la Morte per certi suoi nomi propri ;
nella seconda parlando a lei, dico la ragione perch'
io mi movo a biasimarla ; nella terza la vitupero ;
nella quarta mi volgo a parlare a indiffinita persona,
avvegnachè quanto al mio intendimento sia diffinita.
La seconda parte comincia quivi :* Poic'hai data ;
la terza quivi : E se di grazia ; *la quarta quivi :*
Chi non merta.

§ IX. Appresso la morte di questa donna
alquanti dì, avvenne cosa, per la quale mi convenne partire della sopradetta cittade, ed ire
verso quelle parti, ov' era la gentil donna ch' era
stata mia difesa, avvegnachè non tanto lontanto
fosse lo termine del mio andare, quanto ella era.
E tuttochè io fossi alla compagnia di molti, quanto
alla vista, l' andare mi dispiacea sì, che quasi li
sospiri non poteano disfogare l' angoscia, che il
cuore sentia, però ch' io mi dilungava dalla mia
beatitudine.　E però lo dolcissimo signore, il
quale mi signoreggiava per virtù della gentilissima
donna, nella mia immaginazione apparve come
peregrino leggermente vestito, e di vili drappi.
Egli mi parea sbigottito, e guardava la terra, salvo
che talvolta mi parea, che li suoi occhi si volges-
sero ad uno fiume bello, corrente e chiarissimo, il
quale sen gia lungo questo cammino là ove io
era.

　A me parve che Amore mi chiamasse, e

No more will I disclose what lady she may be
    than by her known qualities. Let him who
    merits not salvation ne'er hope to have her
    company.

*This sonnet divides into four parts : in the first
I call Death by certain names proper to her ; in
the second speaking to her I tell the reason why I
am moved to chide her ; in the third I upbraid her ;
in the fourth I turn to speak to a person undefined,
albeit defined in respect to my own meaning.
Th.. second part begins here :* Since thou hast
given ; *the third here :* And if of mercy ; *the
fourth here :* Let him who merits not.

§ IX. Some days after the death of this
lady a thing befell wherefore it behoved me
to depart from the aforesaid city and go towards those parts, where abode that gentle
lady who had been my defence ; although the
end of my journey was not so far as she dwelt.
And albeit that, so far as seemed, I was in the
company of many, yet did the journey so mislike
me, that hardly could my sighs give vent to the
anguish which my heart felt, for that I was
faring farther from my beatitude. And so the
most sweet lord who held mastery over me by
the virtue of the most gentle lady, appeared in
my fancy as a pilgrim lightly clad and in coarse
apparel. He seemed to me dismayed, and he
gazed upon the ground, save that from time to
time methought his eyes turned to a river, fair,
swift and very clear, which flowed alongside this
road whereon I was.

Methought Love called on me, and said to me

dicessemi queste parole: Io vengo da quella
donna, la quale è stata lunga tua difesa, e so che
il suo rinvenire non sarà; e però quel cuore ch'io ti
facea avere da lei, io l'ho meco, e portolo a
donna la quale sarà tua difensione come questa
era (e nomollami si ch'io la conobbi bene); ma
tuttavia di queste parole, ch'io t'ho ragionate, se
alcune ne dicessi, dille per modo che per loro
non si discernesse lo simulato amore che hai
mostrato a questa, e che ti converrà mostrare ad
altrui.   E, dette queste parole, disparve tutta
questa mia immaginazione subitamente, per la
grandissima parte, che mi parve ch'Amore mi
desse di sè: e quasi cambiato nella vista mia,
cavalcai quel giorno pensoso molto, e accompagnato da molti sospiri.   Appresso lo giorno
cominciai questo sonetto:

Cavalcando l'altr'ier per un cammino,
    Pensoso dell'andar, che mi sgradia,
    Trovai Amor nel mezzo della via,
    In abito leggier di peregrino.

Nella sembianza mi parea meschino
    Come avesse perduto signoria;
    E sospirando pensoso venia,
    Per non veder la gente, a capo chino.

Quando mi vide, mi chiamò per nome,
    E disse: Io vegno di lontana parte,
    Ov'era lo tuo cor per mio volere;

E recolo a servir novo piacere.
    Allora presi di lui sì gran parte,
    Ch'egli disparve, e non m'accorsi come.

these words : I come from that lady who hath long been thy defence and I know that her return is not to be, and therefore I have with me, that heart which I made thee have for her, and bear it to a lady who shall be thy defence even as this one was, (and he named her to me so that I knew her well) ; but yet if thou tell any of these words which I have spoken to thee, tell them in such wise that the simulated love be not discerned by them, which thou hast shown to her and which it will behove thee to show to another. And, these words said, all this my fantasy vanished suddenly by reason of the great portion of himself that methought Love gave me : and as though transformed in my appearance, I rode that day very pensive and accompanied by many sighs. The day following I began this sonnet :

Riding the other day by a road and brooding on the journey, which misliked me, I met Love in the midst of the way in the light dress of a wayfarer.

In his appearance methought him wretched as if he had lost lordship ; and sighing he went pensive, with downcast brow in order not to see the folk.

When he beheld me he called me by name and said : I come from a far country where was thy heart by my will ;

and I am bringing it to serve a new delight. Then I took of him so great a part, that he vanished and I perceived not how.

Questo sonetto ha tre parti : nella prima parte dico siccome io trovai Amore, e qual mi parea ; nella seconda dico quello ch' egli mi disse, avvegnachè non compiutamente, per tema ch'io avea di discovrire lo mio segreto ; nella terza dico com' egli disparve. La seconda comincia quivi : Quando mi vide ; *la terza quivi :* Allora presi.

§ X. Appresso la mia tornata, mi misi a cercare di questa donna, che lo mio signore m'avea nominata nel cammino de'sospiri. Ed acciocchè il mio parlare sia più breve, dico che in poco tempo la feci mia difesa tanto, che troppa gente ne ragionava oltra li termini della cortesia ; onde molte fiate mi pesava duramente. E per questa cagione (cioè di questa soverchievole voce, che parea che m' infamasse viziosamente) quella gentilissima, la quale fu distruggitrice di tutti i vizii e regina delle virtù, passando per alcuna parte mi negò il suo dolcissimo salutare, nel quale stava tutta la mia beatitudine. Ed uscendo alquanto del proposito presente, voglio dare ad intendere quello che il suo salutare in me virtuosamente operava.

§ XI. Dico che quando ella apparia da parte alcuna, per la speranza dell' ammirabile salute nullo nemico mi rimanea, anzi mi giungea una fiamma di caritade; la quale mi facea perdonare a chiunque m' avesse offeso : e chi allora m' avesse addimandato di cosa alcuna, la mia risponsione sarebbe stata solamente, *Amore*, con viso vestito d' umiltà. E quando ella fosse alquanto propinqua al salutare, uno spirito d' Amore, distruggendo tutti gli altri spiriti sensitivi, pingea fuori i deboletti spiriti del viso,

*This sonnet hath three parts : in the first part
I tell how I met Love and in what guise he appeared
to me ; in the second I tell what he said, albeit not
fully for the fear that I had of discovering my
secret ; in the third I tell how he vanished. The
second begins here :* When he beheld me ; *the
third here :* Then I took.

§ X. After my return I set me to seek this
lady that my lord had named to me in the way
of sighs. And that my speech be the briefer, I
say that in short time I made her so much my
defence that too many folk spoke of it beyond
the bounds of courtesy ; so that many times it
weighed heavily upon me. And for this cause,
(that is to say this outrageous rumour, which
seemed to defame me of vice), that most gentle
one who was the destroyer of all vice and
queen of the virtues, as she passed a certain way
denied me her most sweet salutation in which
lay all my beatitude. And digressing somewhat
from my present purpose, I would give to understand what her salutation wrought in me by its
virtue.

§ XI. I say that when she appeared from
any direction, by the hope of her wondrous
salutation no enemy was left to me, but rather
a flame of charity possessed me which made me
pardon whomsoever had offended me ; and to him
who had then asked of me concerning any
matter, my answer would have been simply :
Love ! with a countenance clothed in humility.
And if she were somewhat nigh to giving her
salutation, a spirit of Love, destroying all the
other spirits of sense, thrust forth the feeble

e dicea loro : « Andate ad onorare la donna
vostra ; » ed egli si rimanea nel loco loro. E
chi avesse voluto conoscere Amore, far lo potea
mirando lo tremore degli occhi miei. E quando
questa gentilissima donna salutava, non che
Amore fosse tal mezzo che potesse obumbrare a
me la intollerabile beatitudine, ma egli quasi per
soverchio di dolcezza divenia tale, che lo mio
corpo, lo quale era tutto sotto il suo reggimento,
molte volte si movea come cosa grave inanimata.
Sicchè appare manifestamente che nella sua salute
abitava la mia beatitudine, la quale molte volte
passava e redundava la mia capacitade.

§ XII. Ora, tornando al proposito, dico che
poichè la mia beatitudine mi fu negata, mi giunse
tanto dolore, che partitomi dalle genti, in solinga
parte andai a bagnare la terra d' amarissime
lagrime : e poichè alquanto mi fu sollenato questo lagrimare, misimi nella mia camera là ove
potea lamentarmi senza essere udito. E quivi,
chiamando misericordia alla donna della cortesia,
e dicendo : « Amore, aiuta il tuo fedele » m' ad-
dormentai come un pargoletto battuto lagrimando.

Avvenne quasi nel mezzo del mio dormire, che
mi parea vedere nella mia camera lungo me
sedere un giovane vestito di bianchissime vestimenta, e pensando molto, quanto alla vista sua. Mi
riguardava là ov' io giacea, e quando m' avea
guardato alquanto, pareami che sospirando mi
chiamasse, e discessemi queste parole : *Fili mi,*
tempus est ut prætermittantur simulata nostra.
Allora mi parea ch' io 'l conoscessi, perocchè
mi chiamava così, come assai fiate nelli miei
sonni m' avea già chiamato.

little spirits of sight and said to them: "go and honour your lady," and he remained in their place. And whoso had desired to know Love could know him by gazing at the tremour of mine eyes. And when this most gentle lady gave salutation, so far from Love being such a medium as might dull the unbearable beatitude, he seemed rather to become such by surfeit of sweetness, that my body, which was wholly under his rule, many times fell like a heavy lifeless thing. So that it plainly appears that my beatitude lay in her salutation which many times exceeded and overflowed my capacity.

§ XII. Now returning to my purpose, I say that after my beatitude was denied to me, so much grief possessed me that having parted me from all folk I went to a solitary place to bathe the earth with bitterest tears: and after this weeping was somewhat assuaged in me I betook me to my chamber where I might lament unheard. And there craving pity of the mistress of courtesy, and saying: "Love help thy liege," I fell asleep like a little beaten, sobbing child.

It came to pass, like as in the midst of my sleep, that methought I saw a youth arrayed in pure white garments, sitting alongside me in my chamber, and deep in thought in so far as his appearance went. He gazed at me where I lay and when he had gazed at me a while, methought he called on me, sighing, and said these words to me: *Fili mi, tempus est ut prætermittantur simulacra nostra.* Then methought I knew him, because he called me, even as in my dreams erewhile he had many times called me.

E riguardandolo mi parea che piangesse pietosamente, e parea che attendesse da me alcuna
parola : ond' io assicurandomi, cominciai a
parlare così con esso : Signore della nobiltade,
perchè piangi tu ? E quegli mi dicea queste
parole : *Ego tamquam centrum circuli, cui simili*
modo se habent circumferentiæ partes ; tu autum non
sic. Allora pensando alle sue parole, mi parea
che mi avesse parlato molto oscuro, sì che io mi
sforzava di parlare, e diceagli queste parole :
Ch' è ciò, signore, che tu mi parli con tanta
scuritade ? E quegli mi dicea in parole volgari :
Non dimandar più che utile ti sia.

E però cominciai con lui a ragionare della
salute, la quale mi fu negata, e domandailo della
cagione ; onde in questa guisa da lui mi fu
risposto : Quella nostra Beatrice udìo da certe
persone, di te ragionando, che la donna, la quale
io ti nominai nel camino de' sospiri, ricevea da
te alcuna noia. E però questa gentilissima,
la quale è contraria di tutte le noie, non degna
salutare la tua persona, temendo non fosse noiosa.
Onde conciossiacosachè veracemente sia concos-
ciuto per lei alquanto lo tuo segreto per lunga
consuetudine, voglio che tu dica certe parole
per rima, nelle quali tu comprenda la forza ch'
io tegno sovra te per lei, e come tu fosti suo
tostamente dalla tua puerizia. E di ciò chiama
testimonio colui che 'l sa, e come tu preghi lui
che gliele dica : ed io, che sono quello, volentieri le ne ragionerò ; e per questo sentirà ella
la tua volontade, la quale sentendo, conoscerà le

And gazing at him methought he wept piteously and was awaiting some word from me; wherefore reassuring myself I began thus to speak with him: Lord of all nobleness, wherefore weepest thou? And he said these words to me: *Ego tamquam centrum circuli, cui simili modo se habent circumferentiæ partes; tu autem non sic* Then pondering over his words, methought he had spoken to me very darkly so that I forced myself to speak and said these words to him: Why is this, my lord that thou speakest so darkly to me? And he said to me in the vulgar tongue: Ask no more than may be for thy good.

And therefore I began to speak with him of the salutation which was denied to me and I asked him the cause; whereon in this wise was answer made to me by him: This our Beatrice hath heard from certain persons who were discoursing of thee, that the lady whom I named to thee in the way of sighs, had suffered some vexation through thee, and therefore this most gentle one, who is contrary to all vexations, deigned not to salute thy person fearing lest it be vexful. Wherefore inasmuch as somewhat of thy secret is verily known by her through long wont, I desire that thou compose certain words in rhyme, wherein thou shalt include the power that I hold over thee through her and how thou wast hers, right from thy very boyhood. And of that call thou him to witness who knoweth it; and how thou prayest him that he tell it her, and I, who am he, will gladly speak to her thereof; and by this she shall perceive thy desire, perceiving which, she will

parole degl' ingannati. Queste parole fa che
sieno quasi uno mezzo sì che tu non parli a lei
immediatamente, chè non è degno. E non le
mandare in parte alcuna senza me, ove potessero
essere intese da lei, ma falle adornare di soave
armonia, nella quale io sarò tutte le volte che
farà mestieri.

E dette queste parole, disparve e lo mio sonno
fu rotto. Ond' io ricordandomi, trovai che
questa visione m' era apparita nelle nona ora
del dì; e anzi che io uscissi di questa camera,
proposi di fare una ballata, nella quale seguitassi
ciò che 'l mio signore m' avea imposto, e feci
questa ballata:

Ballata, io vo' che tu ritruovi Amore,
 E con lui vadi a madonna davanti,
 Sicchè la scusa mia, la qual tu canti,
 Ragioni poi con lei lo mio signore.

Tu vai, ballata, sì cortesemente,
 Che sanza compagnia
 Dovresti avere in tutte parti ardire:
 Ma, se tu vuogli andar sicuramente,
 Ritrova l' Amor pria;
 Chè forse non è buon sanza lui gire:
 Perocchè quella, che ti debbe udire,
 Se, com' io credo, è invêr di me adirata,
 E tu di lui non fussi accompagnata,
 Leggeramente ti faria disnore.

Con dolce suono, quando se' con lui,
 Comincia este parole
 Appresso ch' averai chiesta pietate:
 Madonna, quegli, che mi manda a vui,
 Quando vi piaccia, vuole,

understand the words of the beguiled ones.
And look that these words be as it were a
medium, so that thou speak not to her directly,
for it is not meet.   And send them not without
me, to any place where they may be heard by
her ; but have them adorned with sweet music
wherein I will be every time that is needful.

And having said these words, he vanished and
my sleep was broken.   Wherefore I, remembering me, found that this vision had appeared to
me in the ninth hour of the day ; and before I
issued from this chamber I purposed to make a
ballad in which I should follow out what my
lord had imposed on me, and I made this ballad :

Ballad, I will that thou seek out Love and with
    him go before my lady, so that my lord may
    then plead to her my excuse, which thou
    singest.

Ballad, thou goest so courteously that thou
    oughtest without escort to be bold in every
    place : But if thou wouldest fare securely,
    seek Love first, for haply it is not well to go
    without him ; because if she who must hear
    thee is, as I believe, angered against me and
    thou wast not companied by him, lightly would
    she scorn thee.

With sweet melody (when thou art with him)
    begin these words, after thou hast craved pity :
    " Madonna, he who sendeth me to you desireth,
    when it may please you, that if he has

B

Sed egli ha scusa, che la m'intendiate.
Amore è quei, che per vostra beltate
Lo face, come vuol, vista cangiare:
Dunque, perchè gli fece altra guardare,
Pensatel voi, dacch' e' non mutò 'l core.

Dille: Madonna, lo suo cuore è stato
Con sì fermata fede,
Ch' a voi servir lo pronta ogni pensiero:
Tosto fu vostro, e mai non s' è smagato.
Sed ella non tel crede,
Di', che 'n domandi Amore, s' egli è vero:
Ed alla fine falle umil preghiero:
Lo perdonare se le fosse a noia,
Che mi comandi per messo ch' i' moia:
E vedrassi ubbidire al servitore.

E di' a colui ch' è d' ogni pietà chiave,
Avanti che sdonnei,
Chè le saprà contar mia ragion buona:
Per grazia della mia nota soave
Rimanti qui con lei,
E del tuo servo, ciò che vuoi, ragiona;
E s'ella per tuo prego gli perdona,
Fa' che gli annunzi un bel sembiante pace.
Gentil ballata mia, quando ti piace,
Muovi in tal punto, che tu n'aggi onore.

*Questa ballata in tre parti si divide: nella
prima dico a lei ov'ella vada, e confortola perocchè vada più sicura; e dico nella cui compagnia
si metta, se vuole securamente andare e senza
pericolo alcuno; nella seconda dico quello, che a lei
s'appartiene di fare intendere; nella terza la
licenzio del gire quando vuole, raccomandando lo*

excuse, you may hear it from me.   Love is
he that for your beauty maketh him to change
countenance at his will.   Conceive then why
he made him look upon another, since he
hath not changed his heart."

Say to her: "Madonna his heart hath been of
faith so steadfast that every thought spurs him
to serve you: early was he yours and ne'er
hath faltered."   If she believe thee not, bid
her ask of Love if it be true; and at the end,
make her a humble supplication that if to
pardon be irksome to her, she command me
by a messenger to die, and behold, her servant
shall obey.

And ere thou take leave of Madonna, say to him
who unlocketh all pity (for he will know how
to plead my good cause to her): By the grace
of my sweet music, tarry thou with her and of
thy servant speak, what thou wilt; and if she
at thy prayer do pardon him, see that a gracious
mien announce peace to him.   Gentle ballad
mine, when it may please thee, fare forth in
such wise that thou mayst have honour.

*This ballad is divided into three parts: in the
first I tell her whither she is to go and I comfort
her in order that she may fare more securely and I
say in whose company she is to place herself if she
would fare securely and without any peril: in the
second I say what it appertaineth to her to make
known; in the third I speed her on her journey*

suo dolce movimento nelle braccia della fortuna.
La seconda parte comincia quivi: Con dolce
suono; *la terza quivi:*   Gentil ballata.

Potrebbe già l'uomo opporre contra me e dire,
che non sapesse a cui fosse il mio parlare in seconda
persona, perocchè la ballata non è altro, che queste
parole ch' io parlo: e però dico che questo dub-
bio io lo intendo solvere e dichiarare in questo libello
ancora in parte più dubbiosa: ed allora intenderà
chi qui dubbia, o chi qui volesse opporre in questo
modo.

§ XIII. Appresso questa soprascritta visione,
avendo già dette le parole, che Amore m'avea
imposto di dire, m'incominciarono molti e diversi
pensamenti a combattere e a tentare, ciascuno
quasi indefensibilmente: tra' quali pensamenti
quattro m'ingombravano più il riposo della vita.
L'uno dei quali era questo: buona è la signoria
d' Amore, perocchè trae lo intendimento del suo
fedele da tutte le vili cose.   L' altro era questo:
non buona è la signoria d' Amore, perocchè
quanto lo suo fedele più fede gli porta, tanto più
gravi e dolorosi punti gli conviene passare.
L' altro era questo: lo nome d' Amore è sì
dolce a udire, che impossibile mi pare, che la
sua operazione sia nelle più cose altro che dolce,
conciossiacosachè i nomi seguitino le nominate
cose, siccome è scritto: *Nomina sunt consequentia*
rerum.   Lo quarto era questo: la donna per
cui Amore ti stringe così, non è come le altre
donne, che leggermente si mova del suo core.
E ciascuno mi combattea tanto, che mi facea
stare come colui, che non sa per qual via pigli il

when she will, commending her sweet movements to
the arms of fortune. The second part begins here :
With sweet melody, *the third here :* Gentle ballad.

Now a man might object against me and say that
he knew not to whom my words in the second
person were addressed, since the ballad is none
other than these words that I am speaking : and
therefore I say that I intend to solve this difficulty
and make it clear in this little book in a still more
difficult passage, and then he who is in a difficulty
here or who would here make this manner of
objection, shall understand it.

§ XIII. After this above written vision, when
I had already said those words which Love had
charged me to say, many and divers thoughts began to assail and tempt me, each one almost
irresistibly, among which thoughts four seemed
most to disturb my life's repose. The first
whereof was this : The lordship of Love is good
since it draweth the mind of his liege from all
evil things. The next was this : The lordship
of Love is not good since the more faith his
liege beareth him, the more heavy and more
grievous straits must he pass. The next was
this : The name of Love is so sweet to hear
that it seemeth to me impossible that its action in
most things be other than sweet, in as much as
names are sequent to the things named, even as it
is written : *Nomina sunt consequentia rerum.* The
fourth was this : The lady for whom Love
constraineth thee thus is not as other ladies that
her heart be lightly moved. And each assailed
me so, that it made me stand like one who knowe-
eth not by which path to take his way, and who

suo cammino, e che vuole andare, e non sa onde
si vada.   E se io pensava di voler cercare una
comune via di costoro, cioè là ove tutti si
accordassero, questa via era molto inimica verso
di me, cioè di chiamare e mettermi nelle braccia
della pietà.   Ed in questo stato dimorando, mi
giunse volontà di scriverne parole rimate; e
dissine allora questo sonetto :

Tutti li miei pensier parlan d' amore,
   Ed hanno in lor sì gran varïetate,
   Ch' altro mi fa voler sua potestate,
   Altro folle ragiona il suo valore :

Altro sperando m' apporta dolzore :
   Altro pianger mi fa spesse fïate ;
   E sol s' accordano in chieder pietate,
   Tremando di paura ch' è nel core.

Ond' io non so da qual materia prenda ;
   E vorrei dire, e non so ch' io mi dica :
   Così mi trovo in amorosa erranza.

E se con tutti vo' fare accordanza,
   Convenemi chiamar la mia nemica,
   Madonna la pietà, che mi difenda.

*Questo sonetto in quattro parti si può dividere :
nella prima dico e propongo, che tutti i miei pensieri
sono d' Amore, nella seconda dico che sono diversi,
e narro la loro diversitade ; nella terza dico in che
tutti pare che s' accordino ; nella quarta dico che,
volendo dire d'Amore, non so da quale pigli
materia ; e se la voglio pigliare da tutti, conviene
che io chiami la mia nemica, madonna la pietà.*

fain would go, yet knoweth not whither to turn. And if I thought that I would seek a way common to all, namely, where all might be in accord, this way was most inimical to me, namely to call upon and yield me to the arms of pity. And as I abode in this state, a desire came upon me to write words in rhyme concerning it and I then composed this sonnet:

All my thoughts speak of love and have in them such great diversity, that one maketh me desire his power: another argues his influence madness:

Another with hope bringeth me joy: another maketh me weep many a time; and they only accord in craving pity, trembling at the fear that is in my heart.

Wherefore I know not from which to draw my argument, and I would speak, yet know not what to say: Thus I find me in amorous bewilderment.

And if I would make accord with all, it behoveth me to call on my enemy, my lady Pity, that she defend me.

This sonnet can be divided into four parts: in the first I say and propound that all my thoughts are of love; in the second I say that they are divers and I recount their diversity; in the third I say in what they all seem to accord; in the fourth I say that desiring to speak of Love I know not from which to draw my argument, and if I would draw it from all it behoveth me to call on

Dico madonna, quasi per isdegnoso modo di parlare.
La seconda comincia quivi : Ed hanno in lor ;
la terza : E sol s' accordan ; *la quarta :*
Ond' io.

§ XIV. Appresso la battaglia delli diversi
pensieri, avvenne che questa gentilissima venne
in parte, ove molte donne gentili erano adunate ;
alla qual parte io fui condotto per amica persona,
credendosi fare a me gran piacere in quanto mi
menava là ove tante donne mostravano le loro
bellezze. Ond' io quasi non sapendo a che
fossi menato, e fidandomi nella persona, la quale
un suo amico all' estremità della vita condotto
avea, dissi : Perchè semo noi venuti a queste
donne ? Allora quegli mi disse : Per fare sì ch'
elle sieno degnamente servite.

E lo vero è, che adunate quivi erano alla
compagnia d' una gentildonna, che disposata era
lo giorno ; e però secondo l' usanza della
sopradetta cittade, conveniva che le facessero
compagnia nel primo sedere alla mensa che facea
nella magione del suo novello sposo. Sì che io,
credendomi far il piacere di questo amico, proposi di stare al servizio delle donne nella sua
compagnia. E nel fine del mio proponimento
mi parve sentire un mirabile tremore incom-
inciare nel mio petto dalla sinistra parte, e
stendersi di subito per tutte le parti del mio
corpo. Allora dico che poggiai la mia persona
simulatamente ad una pintura, la quale circondava
questa magione ; e temendo non altri si fosse
accorto del mio tremare, levai gli occhi, e

mine enemy, my lady Pity. I say my lady, as it were in a disdainful way of speaking. The second part begins here: And have in them; *the third:* And they only accord; *the fourth:* Wherefore I know not.

§ XIV. After the battle of the divers thoughts, it came to pass that this most gentle one came to a place where many gentle ladies were assembled; to which place I was conducted by one, my friend, who thought to do me great pleasure in so much as he was leading me where so many ladies were displaying their loveliness. Wherefore, as one not knowing to what I was being led, and trusting me to this person who had conducted his friend to the verge of life, I said: Why are we come to these ladies? Then he said to me. To look to it that they be worthily served.

And true it is that they were assembled there in the company of a gentle lady who had been wedded that day; and therefore, according to the usage of the aforesaid city, it behoved them to hold her company at the first sitting that she made at the table in the mansion of her new spouse. So that thinking to do pleasure to this my friend, I purposed to stay in his company at the service of the ladies. And finally, being thus minded, methought I felt a wondrous tremour begin at the left side of my breast and quickly spread over all parts of my body. Then I say that I covertly leaned my person against a painting which surrounded this hall, and fearing lest any one might be aware of my tremour I raised mine

*B

mirando le donne, vidi tra loro la gentilissima
Beatrice.   Allora furono sì distrutti li miei
spiriti per la forza che Amore prese veggendosi
in tanta propinquitade alla gentilissima donna,
che non mi rimase in vita più che gli spiriti del
viso ; ed ancor questi rimasero fuori de' loro
strumenti, perocchè Amore volea stare nel loro
nobilissimo luogo per vedere la mirabile donna :
e avvegna ch' io fossi altro che prima, molto mi
dolea di questi spiritelli, che si lamentavano
forte, e diceano : Se questi non ci sfolgorasse
così fuori del nostro luogo, noi potremmo stare
a vedere la meraviglia di questa donna, così
come stanno gli altri nostri pari.

Io dico che molte di queste donne, accor-
gendosi della mia trasfigurazione, si cominciaro
a maravigliare ; e ragionando si gabbavano di me
con questa gentilissima : onde di ciò accor-
gendosi l' amico mio di buona fede, mi prese
per la mano, e traendomi fuori della veduta di
queste donne, mi domandò che io avessi.
Allora riposato alquanto, e risurti li morti
spiriti miei, e li discacciati rivenuti alle loro
possessioni, dissi a questo mio amico queste
parole : Io ho tenuti i piedi in quella parte della
vita, di là dalla quale non si può ire più per
intendimento di ritornare.

E partitomi da lui, mi ritornai nella camera
delle lagrime, nella quale, piangendo e ver-
gognandomi, fra me stesso dicea : Se questa
donna sapesse la mia condizione, io non credo
che così gabbasse la mia persona, anzi credo che
molta pietà ne le verrebbe.   E in questo pianto
stando, proposi di dir parole, nelle quali a lei

eyes and gazing on those ladies beheld the most
gentle Beatrice in the midst of them. Then
were my senses so destroyed by the might which
Love assumed on beholding himself so nigh unto
the most gentle lady, that no more than the
spirits of sight remained alive; and even these
were left outside their organs because Love would
dwell in their most noble place to behold the
wondrous lady: and although I was other than
before, much did I grieve for these little spirits
who were lamenting loudly and saying: If he
there had not thus hurled us out of our place we
could stay beholding the marvel of this lady,
even as do the others our likes.

I say that many of these ladies perceiving
how I was transformed, began to marvel; and
discoursing, did make mockery of me with this
most gentle one: whereupon my innocent friend
perceiving this, took me by the hand and drawing
me forth from the sight of these ladies, asked
what ailed me. Then being somewhat restored
and my dead senses risen again and the expelled
returned into possession, I said these words to
this my friend: I have set my feet in that
region of life beyond which one cannot go with
intent to return.

And having departed from him I went back
to my chamber of tears, wherein, weeping and
ashamed, I said within myself: If this lady
knew my state I believe she would not thus
mock at my person, rather do I believe that
great pity of it would possess her. And as I
was thus weeping, I purposed to say words in

parlando significassi la cagione del mio trasfigura-
mento, e dicessi che io so bene ch' ella non è
saputa, e che se fosse saputa, io credo che pietà
ne giungerebbe altrui : e proposi di dirle, de-
siderando che venissero per avventura nella sua
audienza ; e allora dissi questo sonetto :

Coll' altre donne mia vista gabbate,
   E non pensate, donna, onde si mova,
   Ch' io vi rassembri sì figura nova,
   Quando riguardo la vostra beltate.

Se lo saveste, non potria pietate
   Tener più contra me l' usata prova ;
   Ch' Amor, quando sì presso a voi mi trova,
   Prende baldanza e tante sicurtate,

Che fiere tra' miei spirti paurosi
   E quale ancide, e qual caccia di fuora,
   Sicch' ei solo rimane a veder vui :

Ond' io mi cangio in figura d' altrui,
   Ma non sì, ch' io non senta bene allora
   Gli guai de' discacciati tormentosi.

*Questo sonetto non divido in parti, perchè la
divisione non si fa, se non per aprire la sentenzia
della cosa divisa : onde, conciossiacosachè per la
ragionata cagione assai sia manifesto, non ha mestieri
di divisione.*

*Vero è che tra le parole, ove si manifesta la
cagione di questo sonetto, si trovano dubbiose parole;
cioè quando dico, ch' Amore uccide tutti i miei
spiriti, e li visivi rimangono in vita, salvo che*

which speaking to her I should signify the cause of my transformation and say that I know verily that it is not known, and that if it were known, I believe that folk would be moved to pity of it, and I purposed to say these words desiring that perchance they might come to her hearing; and then I composed this sonnet:

With the other ladies you mock at my aspect and
  think not, lady, whence it cometh that I have
  the semblance of so strange a figure to you
  when I behold your beauty.

If you knew it, pity could no more maintain
  against me her wonted obduracy; for Love,
  when he findeth me so nigh unto you, exultant
  grows and taketh such assurance

that he smiteth among my afflicted senses and
  this he slayeth and that he chases forth, so
  that he alone remaineth to behold you.

Wherefore I change me to an alien semblance, yet
  am not so changed but that I truly hear then the
  lamentations of the outcast and tormented spirits.

I divide not this sonnet into parts because a division is only made to explain the meaning of the thing divided: wherefore insomuch as this is very manifest from the occasion of the sonnet that hath been set forth above, it hath no need of division.

True it is that among the words wherein the occasion of this sonnet is made manifest, dubious words are found; namely where I say that Love slays all my senses and the visual spirits remain

*fuori degli strumenti loro. E questo dubbio è
impossibile a solvere a chi non fosse in simil grado
fedele d' Amore; ed a coloro che vi sono è manifesto ciò che solverebbe le dubitose parole : e però non
è bene a me dichiarare cotale dubitazione, acciocchè
lo mio parlare sarebbe indarno, ovvero di
soperchio.*

§ XV. Appresso la nuova trasfigurazione mi
giunse un pensamento forte, il quale poco si
partia da me ; anzi continuamente mi riprendea,
ed era di cotale ragionamente meco : Posciachè
tu pervieni a così schernevole vista quando tu
se' presso di questa donna, perchè pur cerchi di
vederla ? Ecco, che se tu fossi domandato da
lei, che avresti tu da rispondere ? ponendo che
tu avessi libera ciascuna tua virtude, in quanto
tu le rispondessi. Ed a questo rispondea un
altro umile pensiero, e dicea : Se io non perdessi
le mie virtudi, e fossi libero tanto ch' io potessi
rispondere, io le direi, che sì tosto com' io
immagino la sua mirabil bellezza, sì tosto mi
giugne un desiderio di vederla, il quale è di
tante virtude, che uccide e distrugge nella
mia memoria ciò che contra lui si potesse
levare ; e però non mi ritraggono le passate
passioni da cercare la veduta di costei. Ond'
io, mosso da cotali pensamenti proposi di dire
certe parole, nelle quali, scusandomi a lei di
cotal riprensione, ponessi anche quello che
mi addiviene presso di lei ; e dissi questo
sonetto :

*alive save that they are outside their organs. And
this difficulty is impossible of solution to those who
are not in a like degree lieges unto Love, whereas
to those who are, that which would solve the
dubious words is manifest and therefore it is not
well for me to elucidate such difficulty, for that
my words would be in vain or else superfluous.*

§ XV. After the strange transformation a
potent thought possessed me which departed
little from me ; rather did it continually reprove
me, and such was its reasoning with me : Since
thou are reduced to so derisive an aspect when
thou are near this lady, wherefore dost thou still
seek to behold her ? Look ! if thou wert asked
by her what wouldst thou have to answer, assuming that thou hadst each of thy faculties free, so
far that thou mightest answer her ? And to
this another lowly thought made answer
and said : If I lost not my faculties and were
free so that I could answer, I would say to her
that as soon as I image forth her wondrous
beauty, so soon a desire posseses me to behold
her, which is of such power that it slays and
destroys in my memory all that could rise up
against it ; and therefore my past sufferings do
not restrain me from seeking the sight of her.
Wherefore moved by such thoughts I proposed
to say certain words, wherein making my excuse
unto her against such reproof I should set forth
also what happened to me when near her ; and
I composed this sonnet :

Ciò, che m' incontra nella mente more
    Quando vegno a veder voi, bella gioia,
    E quand' io vi son presso, sento Amore,
    Che dice : Fuggi, se 'l perir t' è noia.

Lo viso mostra lo color del core,
    Che, tramortendo, ovunque può s'appoi ;
    E per l' ebrietà del gran tremore
    Le pietre par che gridin : Moia, moia.

Peccato face chi allor mi vide,
    Se l' alma sbigottita non conforta,
    Sol dimostrando che di me gli doglia,

Per la pietà, che 'l vostro gabbo uccide,
    La qual si cria nella vista smorta,
    Degli occhi, c' hanno di lor morte voglia.

Questo sonetto si divide in due parti : nella prima dico la cagione, per che non mi tengo di gire presso a questa donna ; nella seconda dico quello che m' addiviene per andare presso di lei ; e comincia questa parte quivi : E quando vi son presso. *E anche questa seconda parte si divide in cinque, secondo cinque diverse narrazioni : chè nella prima dico quello che Amore, consigliato dalla ragione, mi dice quando le son presso ; nella seconda manifesto lo stato del core per esempio del viso ; nella terza dico, siccome ogni sicurtade mi vien meno ; nella quarta dico che pecca quegli che non mostra pietà di me, acciocchè mi sarebbe alcun conforto ; nell' ultima dico perchè altri dovrebbe aver pietà, cioè per la pietosa vista, che negli occhi mi giunge ; la qual vista pietosa è distrutta, cioè non pare altrui, per lo gabbare di questa donna, la quale trae a sua simile operazione coloro, che forse*

That which befalleth me, is effaced from memory when I set forth to behold you, beauteous Joy, and when I am nigh to you I hear Love say: Flee! if to perish be irksome to thee.

My countenance sheweth the hue of my heart, which, fainting, seeketh support, and with the great trembling inebriate, methinks the very stones cry out: Die! Die!

He who then beholds me, committeth sin if he comfort not the affrighted soul by shewing at least that he grieveth for me

because of the pity which your mocking slayeth, and which is begotten of the deathly hue of eyes that desire their death.

This sonnet divides into two parts: in the first I tell the reason why I withhold me not from approaching this lady; in the second I tell what befalleth me through approaching her, and I begin this part here: And when I am nigh to you. And the second part again divides into five according to five divers narrations; for in the first I tell what Love, counselled by reason, sayeth unto me when I am nigh to her; in the second I manifest the state of my heart by the index of the face; in the third I tell how that all confidence faileth me; in the fourth I say that he sins who sheweth not pity for me, in order that he might be of some comfort; in the last I tell why one ought to have pity, namely, for the piteous look that cometh over mine eyes, which piteous look is quenched, that is to say, appeareth not to others because of the mocking of this lady which draweth those to a like action who

vedrebbono questa pietà. *La seconda parte*
comincia quivi : Lo viso mostra ; *la terza :* E
per l' ebrietà ; *la quarta :* Peccata face ; *la*
quinta : Per la pietà.

§ XVI. Appresso ciò che io dissi questo
sonetto, mi mosse una volontà di dire anche
parole, nelle quali dicessi quattro cose ancora
sopra il mio stato, le quali non mi parea che fossero manifestate ancora per me. La prima delle
quali si è, che molte volte io mi dolea, quando
la mia memoria movesse la fantasia ad immaginare quale Amor mi facea : la seconda si è, che
Amore spesse volte di subito m'assalia sì forte,
che in me non rimanea altro di vita se non un
pensiero, che parlava di questa donna : la terza si
è, che quando questa battaglia d' Amore mi
pugnava così, io mi movea, quasi discolorito tutto,
per veder questa donna, credendo che mi difen-
desse la sua veduta da questa battaglia,
dimenticando quello che per appropinquare a
tanta gentilezza m' addivenia : la quarta si è,
come cotal veduta non solamente non mi difendea,
ma finalmente disconfiggea la mia poca vita ;
e pero dissi questo sonetto :

Spesse fiate venemi alla mente
 L'oscura qualità ch' Amor mi dona ;
 E vienmene pietà si, che sovente
 Io dico : ahi lasso ! avvien egli a persona ?

Ch' Amor m' assale subitamente
 Sì, che la vita quasi m'abbandona :
 Campami un spirto vivo solamente,
 E quei riman, perchè di voi ragiona.

haply might behold this piteous thing. The second part begins here : My countenance sheweth ; *the third :* And with the great trembling ; *the fourth :* He who then beholds ; *the fifth :* Because of that piteous look.

§ XVI. After I had composed this sonnet a desire stirred me to compose words also, in which I should tell of four things concerning my condition, which it seemed to me had not yet been made manifest by me. Whereof the first is, that oft-times I grieved when memory moved my fancy to imagine how Love dealt with me. The second is that Love did many times suddenly assail me so mightily that there remained naught in me of life save a thought that spake of this lady : the third is, that when this battle of love assailed me thus, I set forth as 'twere all pallid, to behold this lady, believing that the sight of her would defend me from this assault, forgetting what befell me through drawing nigh to such gentleness : the fourth is, how that such sight not only did not defend me but finally discomfited the small remnant of my life : and therefore I composed this sonnet :

Oft-times there cometh to my memory the dark condition that Love layeth on me ; and pity thereof toucheth me, so that oft I say : Ah me ! befalleth it thus to anyone ?

For Love assaileth me suddenly, so that life well-nigh forsakes me : one spirit alone escapeth alive within me and that remains, for that of you it speaketh.

Poscia mi sforzo, chè mi voglio aitare;
    E così smorto, e d' ogni valor vôto,
    Vegno a vedervi, credendo guarire:

E se io levo gli occhi per guardare,
    Nel cor mi si comincia uno tremoto,
    Che fa da' polsi l' anima partire.

Questo sonetto si divide in quattro parti, secondo che quattro cose sono in esso narrate : e perocchè sono esse ragionate di sopra, non m' intrametto se non di distinguere le parti per li loro cominciamenti : onde dico che la seconda parte comincia quivi : Ch' Amor; *la terza quivi :* Poscia mi sforzo ; *la quarta :* E se io levo.

§ XVII. Poichè io dissi questi tre sonetti, ne' quali parlai a questa donna, (però che furo narratorii di tutto quasi lo mio stato), credendomi tacere perocchè mi parea avere di me assai manifestato avvegnachè sempre poi tacessi di dire a lei, a me convenne ripigliare materia nova e più nobile che la passata. E perocchè la cagione della nova materia è dilettevolle a udire, la dirò quanto potrò più brevemente.

§ XVIII. Conciossiacosachè per la vista mia molte persone avessero compreso lo segreto del mio cuore, certe donne, le quali adunate s' erano, dilettandosi l'una nella compagnia dell' altra, sapeano bene lo mio cuore, perchè ciascuna di loro era stata a molte mie sconfitte. Ed io passando presso di loro, siccome dalla fortuna menato, fui chiamato da una di queste gentili

Then do I spur me, for fain would I aid me ; and thus pallid and void of all power, I come to behold you, thinking to be made whole.

And if I lift mine eyes to gaze, a quaking beginneth in my heart that maketh the soul to part from my pulses.

This sonnet divides into four parts according as four things are related in it : and since they are discoursed of above, I do not concern myself, save to distinguish the parts by their beginnings : wherefore I say that the second part begins here : For Love ; *the third here :* Then do I spur me ; *the fourth :* And if I lift.

§ XVII. After I had composed these three sonnets wherein I spake to this lady (for they were the reciters of wellnigh my whole condition), and when I thought to hold my peace, because meseemed to have manifested enough of myself, even though I should ever more refrain from addressing her, it behoved me to take up new matter and more noble than the past. And since the reason for that new matter is delightful to hear, I will, briefly as I may, discourse thereof.

§ XVIII. Insomuch as from my aspect the secret of my heart was understood by many persons, certain ladies, who had gathered together, each delighting in the company of other, knew my heart well because each of them had been at many of my discomfitures. And, passing near them as led by fortune, I was hailed by one of those gentle ladies, and she

donne; e quella, che m'avea chiamato, era donna
di molto leggiadro parlare. Sicchè quando io
fui giunto dinanzi da loro, e vidi bene che la
mia gentilissima donna non era tra esse, rassicur-
andomi le salutai, e domandai che piacesse loro.
Le donne erano molte, tra le quali n' avea certe
che si rideano tra loro. Altre v' erano, che
guardavanmi aspettando che io dovessi dire.
Altre v'erano, che parlavano tra loro, delle quali
una volgendo gli occhi verso me, e chiamandomi
per nome, disse queste parole: A che fine ami
tu questa tua donna, poichè tu non puoi la sua
presenza sostenere? Dilloci, chè certo il fine di
cotale amore conviene che sia novissimo.

E poichè m'ebbe dette queste parole, non
solamente ella, ma tutte le altre cominciaro ad
attendere in vista la mia risponsione. Allora
dissi loro queste parole: Madonne, lo fine del
mio amore fu già il saluto di questa donna, di
cui voi forse intendete; ed in quello dimorava
la mia beatitudine, chè era fine di tutti i miei
desiderii. Ma piochè le piacque di negarlo a
me, lo mio signore Amore, la sua mercede, ha
posta tutta la mia beatitudine in quello, che non
mi puote venir meno.

Allora queste donne cominciaro a parlare tra
loro; e siccome talor vedemo cader l' acqua
mischiata di bella neve, così mi parea vedere le
loro parole mischiate di sospiri. E poichè
alquanto ebbero parlato tra loro, mi disse anche
questa donna, che prima m' avea parlato, queste
parole: Noi ti preghiamo, che tu ne dica ove
sta questa tua beatitudine. Ed io rispondendole,
dissi cotanto: In quelle parole che lodano la

who had called me was a lady of most graceful speech. So that when I had arrived before them and saw that my most gentle lady was not among them, reassuring me I greeted them and asked what their pleasure might be. These ladies were many, amongst whom were certain who laughed amongst themselves. Others there were who gazed at me looking that I should speak. Others there were who spake among themselves, of whom one, turning her eyes towards me and calling me by name, said these words: To what end lovest thou this thy lady since thou canst not support her presence? Tell us, for certes it behoveth that the end of such love be strange indeed.

And after she had said these words to me, not only she but all the others began visibly to await my answer. Then I said these words to them: Ladies mine, the end of my love was once this lady's salutation of whom I ween ye are thinking; and therein dwelt my beatitude, for it was the end of all my desires. But since it hath pleased her to deny it to me, Love, my lord, by his grace, hath placed all my beatitude in that which cannot fail me.

Then these ladies began to speak among themselves; and even as sometimes we behold rain falling mingled with fair snow, even so methought I beheld their words mingled with sighs. And after they had spoken a while among themselves, the lady who first had spoken to me said these words also to me: We beseech thee to tell us where lieth this thy beatitude: And I answering them said simply: In those

donna mia. Ed elle rispose: Se tu ne dicessi
vero, quelle parole che tu n'hai dette notificando
la tua condizione, avresti tu operate con altro
intendimento.

Ond' io pensando a queste parole, quasi ver-
gognandomi mi partii da loro; e venìa dicendo
tra me medesimo: Poichè è tanta beatitudine in
quelle parole che lodano la mia donna, perchè
altro parlare è stato il mio? E però proposi di
prendere per materia del mio parlare sempre mai
quello che fosse loda di questa gentilissima; e
pensando a ciò molto, pareami avere impresa
troppo alta materia quanto a me, sicchè non
ardia di cominciare; e così dimorai alquanti dì
con desiderio di dire e con paura di cominciare.

§ XIX. Avvenne poi che, passando per un
cammino, lungo il quale correva un rio molto
chiaro d' onde, giunse a me tanta volontà di
dire, che cominciai a pensare il modo ch'io te-
nessi; e pensai che parlare di lei non si conveniva, se non che io parlassi a donne in seconda
persona; e non ad ogni donna, ma solamente a
coloro, che sono gentili, e non sono pure fem-
mine. Allora dico che la mia lingua parlò
quasi come per sè stessa mossa, e disse: *Donne,*
ch' avete intelletto d' amore. Queste parole io
riposi nella mente con grande letizia, pensando
di prenderle per mio cominciamento: onde poi
ritornato alla sopraddetta cittade, e pensando
alquanti dì, cominciai una canzone con questo
cominciamento, ordinata nel modo che si vedrà
di sotto nella sua divisione.

words that praise my lady. And she answered: If thou hadst spoken truly to us, thou wouldst have fashioned in other guise those words which thou didst say to us when thou didst signify thy condition to us.

Wherefore pondering on these words I departed from them as one shamed; and I went saying within myself: Since there is such beatitude in those words that praise my lady, why hath other speech been mine? And therefore I proposed to take evermore for the matter of my speech, that which should be praise of this most gentle lady; and pondering much on this, methought I had undertaken a matter too exalted for my strength, so that I dared not begin; and thus I tarried some days desiring to speak yet afeared to begin.

§ XIX. It then befell, that passing by a way along which there coursed a river of most clear waters, so great a desire to speak possessed me, that I began to ponder on the style I should use, and I thought that it was not fitting to speak of her except I spake to ladies in the second person, and not to every lady but to such only as are gentle and not mere women. Then I say that my tongue spake as if moved by itself and said: *Ladies, that have intelligence of love.* These words I treasured in my memory with great joy thinking to take them for my beginning; whereupon being afterward returned to the aforesaid city, and pondering for some days, I began a canzone with this beginning, ordered in that fashion which will be seen in its division below.

Donne, ch' avete intelletto d' amore,
   Io vo' con voi della mia donna dire;
   Non perch' io creda sue laude finire,
   Ma ragionar per isfogar la mente.
   Io dico che, pensando il suo valore,
   Amor sì dolce mi si fa sentire,
   Che, s' io allora non perdessi ardire,
   Farei parlando innamorar la gente.
   Ed io non vo' parlar sì altamente,
   Che divenissi per temenza vile;
   Ma tratterò del suo stato gentile
   A rispetto di lei leggeramente,
   Donne e donzelle amorose, con vui,
   Chè non è cosa da parlarne altrui.

Angelo chiama in divino intelletto,
   E dice: Sire, nel mondo si vede
   Meraviglia nell' atto, che procede
   Da un' anima, che fin quassù risplende.
   Lo cielo, che non have altro difetto
   Che d'aver lei, al suo Signor la chiede
   E ciascun santo ne grida mercede.
   Sola pietà nostra parte difende;
   Chè parla Iddio, che di madonna intende:
   Diletti miei, or sofferite in pace,
   Che vostra speme sia quanto mi piace
   Là, ov' è alcun che perder lei s' attende.
   E che dirà nell' Inferno a' malnati:
   Io vidi la speranza de' beati.

Madonna è desiata in l' alto cielo:
   Or vo' di sua virtù farvi sapere.
   Dico: qual vuol gentil donna parere
   Vada con lei; chè quando va per via,
   Gitta ne' cor villani Amore un gelo,

Ladies, that have intelligence of love, I would
  speak with you of my lady; not because I
  think to exhaust her praises, but to discourse
  for easement of my mind. I say, that pondering
  on her worth, Love maketh himself so sweetly
  felt within me that had I then not lost all my
  daring, I should enamour folk by my speech.
  And I will not speak so exaltedly that I
  should faint through fear; but lightly will I
  touch on her gentle state in respect of her,
  amorous dames and damsels, with you, for 'tis
  not a thing whereof to speak to others.

An angel crieth in its divine intelligence and
  saith: "Lord, in the world a marvel is displayed in act, emanating from a soul that
  shineth far as here on high. Heaven, that
  hath none other lack than to possess her,
  craveth her of its Lord and every saint crieth
  for the grace. Pity alone defendeth our
  cause; for God speaketh, intending my lady:
  Beloved mine, now suffer in peace that your
  hope be, so long as it pleaseth me, there,
  where is one who looketh for to lose her
  and who in Hell shall say to the damned:
  I have beheld the hope of the blessed.

My lady is desired in high heaven: now would
  I make you to know of her virtue. I say:
  whoso would seem a gentle lady let her go
  with her; for when she passeth by the way,
  Love casteth a chill into base hearts whereby

Per che ogni lor pensiero agghiaccia e père.
E qual soffrisse di starla a vedere
Diverria nobil cosa, o si morria:
E quando trova alcun che degno sia
Di veder lei, quei prova sua virtute;
Chè gli addivien ciò che gli dà salute,
E si l' umilia, che ogni offesa oblia.
Ancor le ha Dio per maggior grazia dato,
Che non può mal finir chi le ha parlato.

Dice di lei Amor : Cosa mortale
Come esser può si adorna e si pura?
Poi la riguarda, e fra sè stesso giura
Che Dio ne intende di far cosa nova.
Color di perle ha quasi in forma, quale
Conviene a donna aver, non fuor misura :
Ella è quanto di ben può far natura;
Per esempio di lei beltà si prova.
Degli occhi suoi, come ch' ella gli muova,
Escono spirti d' amore infiammati,
Che fieron gli occhi a qual, che allor gli guati,
E passan si che 'l cor ciascun ritrova.
Voi le vedete Amor pinto nel riso,
Ove non puote alcun mirarla fiso.

Canzone, io so che tu girai parlando
A donne assai, quando t' avrò avanzata:
Or t' ammonisco, perch' io t' ho allevata
Per figliuola d' Amor giovane e piana,
Che dove giugni, tu dichi pregando
Insegnatemi gir; ch' io son mandata
A quella, di cui loda io sono ornata.
E se non vogli andar siccome vana,
Non ristare ove sia gente villana :

every thought of theirs is frozen and perisheth.
And whoso should endure to stay and behold
her, would become a noble thing or else would
die : and when she findeth one worthy to
behold her, he proveth her virtue ; for this
befalleth him, that she giveth him salutation
and maketh him so humble that he forgetteth
every offence. Also hath God given her for
superior grace, that whoso hath spoken with her
cannot end ill.

Of her saith Love : How can mortal thing
so lovely be and pure ? Then gazeth he at
her, and within himself doth swear that God
intendeth to make in her what ne'er yet was.
Suffused is she with hue as of pearls, such as
beseemeth a lady to have, not beyond measure :
she is the utmost that Nature can create of
goodness : by her ensample beauty is proved.
From her eyes, whereso she turn them, issue
flaming spirits of Love that smite the eyes of
him who then doth look on them and pierce so,
that each one touches the heart. Ye see
Love painted on her lips where none can
gaze on her steadfastly.

Canzone, I know that thou shalt fare speaking
with many ladies after I have sped thee :
now I admonish thee, for that I have raised
thee up to be a daughter of Love young and
guileless, that where thou comest thou say
beseechingly: Teach me how to fare, for I am
sent to her with whose praises I am adorned.
And if thou wouldst not go like a vain thing,
tarry not where base folk be. Contrive, if

Ingégnati, se puoi, d' esser palese
Solo con donna o con uomo cortese,
Che ti merranno per la via tostana.
Tu troverai Amor con esso leì;
Raccomandami a lui come tu dèi.

*Questa canzone, acciocchè sia meglio intesa, la
dividerò più artificiosamente che le altre cose di
sopra, e però ne fo tre parti. La prima parte è
proemio delle seguenti parole ; la seconda è lo in-
tento trattato ; le terza è quasi una servigiale delle
precedenti parole. La seconda cominicia quivi:*
Angelo chiama; *la terza quivi:* Canzone, io so.
*La prima parte si divide in quattro : nella prima
dico a cui dir voglio della mia donna e perchè io
voglio dire ; nella seconda dico quale mi pare a me
stesso quand' io penso lo suo valore, e come io direi
se non perdessi l'ardimento ; nella terza dico come
credo dire, acciocchè io non sia impedito da viltà ;
nella quarta ridicendo ancora a cui intendo di dire,
dico la ragione per che dica loro. La seconda
cominicia quivi:* Io dico; *la terza quivi:* Ed io
non vo' parlar; *la quarta quivi:* Donne e
donzelle.

Poi quando dico Angelo chiama, *comincio a
trattare di questa donna ; e dividesi questa parte
in due. Nella prima dico, che di lei si comprende
in cielo ; nella seconda dico, che di lei si comprende
in terra, quivi:* Madonna è desiata.
*Questa seconda parte si divide in due ; che nella
prima dico di lei quanto dalla parte della nobilità
della sua anima, narrando alquante delle sue*

thou canst, to be revealed only to courteous
woman or man, who shall bring thee by the
speedier way. There with her shalt thou
find Love; commend me to him as is thy
duty.

*In order that this canzone be better understood
I will divide it with more art than the other com-
positions above and therefore I first make three
parts of it. The first part is a prelude to the
words that follow; the second is the subject
treated of, the third is as 'twere a servant to
the preceding words. The second begins here:* An
Angel crieth; *The third here:* Canzone, I know.
*The first part divides into four; in the first I say to
whom I would speak of my lady and wherefore I
would speak; in the second I say how I seem to
myself when I think on her worth, and how I
would speak if I lost not courage; in the third I
tell how I think to speak of her in order that I be
not hindered by faint-heartedness; in the fourth,
repeating again to whom it is my intent to speak, I
tell the reason wherefore I speak to them. The
second begins here:* I say; *the third:* And I
will not speak; *the fourth:* Amorous dames and
damsels.*

Then when I say: An Angel crieth; *I begin
to treat of this lady; and this part is divided into
two; in the first I tell what is understood of her
in heaven; in the second I tell what is understood of her on earth, here:* My lady is desired.

*This second part divides into two: for in the
first I speak of her as concerns her nobility of soul,
relating somewhat of the virtues that proceed*

virtudi che dalla sua anima procedono : nella
seconda dico di lei quanto dalla parte della nobilità
del suo corpo, narrando alquante delle sue bellezze,
quivi : Dice di lei Amor.

Questa seconda parte si divide in due ; *che nella*
prima dico d' alquante bellezze, che sono secondo
tutta la persona ; nella seconda dico d'alquante
bellezze, che sono secondo determinata parte della
persona quivi : Degli occhi suoi.

Questa seconda parte si divide in due ; *che*
nell' una dico degli occhi, che sono principio di
Amore ; nella seconda dico della bocca ch' è fine d'
Amore.   Ed acciocchè quinci si levi ogni vizioso
pensiero, ricordisi chi legge, che di sopra è scritto
che il saluto di questa donna, lo quale era opera-
zione della sua bocca, fu fine de' miei desiderii,
mentre che io lo potei ricevere.

Poscia quando dico : Canzone, io so, *aggiungo*
una stanza quasi come ancella delle altre, nella
quale dico quello, che da questa mia canzone
desidero.   E perocchè quest' ultima parte è lieve
ad intendere, non mi travaglio di più divisioni.

Dico bene, *che a più aprire lo intendimento di*
questa canzone si converrebbe usare più minute
divisioni ; ma tuttavia chi non è di tanto ingegno,
che per queste che son fatte la possa intendere, a
me non dispiace se la mi lascia stare : chè certo io
temo d'avere a troppi comunicato il suo intendi-
mento, pur per queste divisioni che fatte sono, s'egli
avvenisse che molti la potessero udire.

§ XX. Appresso che questa canzone fu
alquanto divolgata fra le genti, conciofosse-

from her soul; in the second
concerns the nobility of her body,
what of its beauties, here: Of her saith

This second part divides into two; for
first I speak of certain beauties that appertain to
whole person, in the second I speak of certain beauties
that appertain to a definite part of her person,
here: From her eyes.

This second part divides into two, for in the
one I tell of the eyes which are the beginning of
Love; in the second I tell of the mouth which is
the goal of Love. And in order that every
vicious thought may be eschewed, let him who
readeth remember what is written above, that the
salutation of this lady, which was of the acts of
her mouth, was the goal of my desires while I was
able to receive it.

Then when I say: Canzone, I know that thou,
I add a stanza, as 'twere a handmaid to the
others in which I tell what I desire of this my
Canzone, and since this last part is easy to
understand I do not weary me with more divisions;

I admit, indeed, that more minute divisions must
needs be employed to unfold the meaning of this
canzone further, but, nevertheless, whoso hath not
wit enough to be able to understand it by those
divisions that have been made, it displeaseth me
not if he let it be, for certes I fear I have com-
municated its meaning to too many, even by those
divisions that have been made, if it chanced that
many should hear it.

§ XX. After this canzone had been somewhat published among folk, forasmuch as a

e alcuno amico l' udisse, volontà lo
.sse a pregarmi ch' io gli dovessi dire che è
Amore, avendo forse, per le udite parole,
speranza di me oltrechè, degna. Ond' io pensando che appresso di cotal trattato, bello era
trattare alcuna cosa d' Amore, e pensando che
l'amico era da servire, proposi di dire parole,
nelle quali trattassi d' Amore; e dissi allora
questo sonetto:

Amore e cor gentil sono una cosa,
   Siccom 'il Saggio in suo dittato pone;
   E cosi senza l' un l' altro esser osa,
   Com' alma razional senza ragione.

Fagli natura, quando è amorosa,
   Amor per sire, e 'l cor per sua magione,
   Dentro allo qual dormendo si riposa
   Talvolta brieve, e tal lunga stagione

Beltate appare in saggia donna pui,
   Che piace agli occhi sì, che dentro al core
   Nasce un desio della cosa piacente:

E tanto dura talora in costui,
   Che fa svegliar lo spirito d' amore:
   E simil face in donna uomo valente.

*Questo sonetto si divide in due parti. Nella
prima dico di lui in quanto è in potenza; nella
seconda dico di lui in quanto di potenza si riduce
in atto. La seconda comincia quivi:* Beltate
appare. *La prima si divide in due: nella prima
dico in che soggetto sia questa potenza; nella
seconda dico come questo soggetto e questa potenza*

certain friend heard it, he was moved by a
desire to entreat me to tell him what Love is,
having perchance through the words he had
heard, a hope of me beyond my desert. Wherefore thinking that after such a composition it
was a fair thing to treat somewhat of Love, and
thinking that a friend should be served, I
purposed to say words wherein I should treat of
Love and I then composed this sonnet:

Love and a gentle heart are one same thing,
    even as the poet teacheth in his rhymes; and
    one without the other dare no more exist than
    a rational soul apart from reason.

Nature maketh them when in amorous mood,
    Love for lord, the heart for his dwelling-
    place, wherein slumbering he reposeth, it may
    be for brief, it may be for long season.

Beauty appeareth in wise lady then, which is so
    pleasing to the eyes that within the heart a
    desire is born for the pleasing thing.

And some whiles it so long endureth therein
    that it maketh the spirit of love to awaken:
    and the like doth man of worth in woman.

*This sonnet divides into two parts. In the
first I speak of Love as existing in potentiality; in
the second I speak of him as developed from
potentiality into actuality. The second begins here:*
Beauty appeareth. *The first divides into two:
in the first I say in what subject this potency
dwells; in the second I say how this subject and*

sieno prodotti in essere, e come l' uno guarda l'
altro, come forma materia. La seconda comincia
quivi : Fagli natura. *Poi quando dico :* Beltate
appare, *dico come questa potenza si riduce in atto ;*
e prima come si riduce in uomo, poi come si riduce
in donna, quivi : E simil face in donna.

§ XXI. Poichè trattai d' Amore nella sopra
scritta rima, vennemi volontà di dire anche in
lode di questa gentilissima parole, per le quali
io mostrassi come si sveglia per lei quest' amore,
e come non solamente lo sveglia là ove dorme,
ma là ove non è in potenza, ella mirabilmente
operando lo fa venire. E dissi allora questa
Sonetto :

Negli occhi porta la mia donna Amore ;
    Per che si fa gentil ciò ch' ella mira :
    Ov' ella passa, ogni uom vêr lei si gira,
    E cui saluta fa tremar lo core.

Sicchè, bassando il viso, tutto smuore,
    E d' ogni suo difetto allor sospira :
    Fuggon dinanzi a lei superbia ed ira :
    Aiutatemi, donne, a farle onore.

Ogni dolcezza, ogni pensiero umile
    Nasce nel core a chi parlar la sente ;
    Ond' è laudato chi prima la vide.

Quel ch' ella par quand' un poco sorride,
    Non si può dicer, nè tener a mente,
    Sì è nuovo miracolo gentile.

*this potency are brought into existence and how the
one is related to the other as form is to matter.
The second begins here :* Nature maketh them.
Then when I say, Beauty appeareth, *I say how
this potentiality is developed into actuality ; and
first how it is develpoed in man, then how it is
deveioped in woman, here :* And the like doth.

§ XXI. After I had treated of Love in the
aforewritten rhyme, a desire came upon me to
say also some words in praise of this most
gentle one, whereby I should show how this
Love is awakened by her and how not only doth
she awaken it where it slumbereth, but where it
exists not even potentially, she by her marvellous
working bringeth it forth. And then I composed
this sonnet :

In her eyes my lady beareth Love ; wherefore
    what she looketh upon is gentle made : where
    she passeth, every man turns him to her, and
    the heart of him whom she saluteth she
    maketh to tremble.

So that abasing his countenance all pale he
    groweth, and then doth sigh at his every
    fault. Pride and anger flee before her : Aid
    me ladies to do her honour.

All sweetness, every lowly thought springeth
    forth in his heart who heareth her speak ;
    wherefore praise is his who first beheld her.

What she seemeth when she smiles a little,
    cannot be told nor held in memory, a miracle
    is she so rare and gentle.

Questo sonetto ha tre parti. Nella prima dico siccome questa donna riduce in atto questa potenza, secondo la nobilissima parte degli occhi suoi : e nella terza dico questo medesimo secondo la nobilissima parte della sua bocca. E intra queste due parti ha una particella ch' è quasi domandatrice d' aiuto alla precedente parte ed alla seguente, e comincia quivi : Aiutatemi, donne. *La terza comincia quivi :* Ogni dolcezza.

La prima si divide in tre ; che nella prima dico come virtuosamente fa gentile ciò ch' ella vede ; e questo è tanto a dire, quanto adducere Amore in potenza là ove non è. Nella seconda dico, come riduce in atto Amore ne' cuori di tutti coloro cui vede. Nella terza dico quello che poi virtuosamente adopera ne' lor cuori. La seconda comincia : Ov' ella passa : *la terza :* E cui saluta.

Quando poscia dico : Aiutatemi, donne, *do ad intendere a cui la mia intenzione è di parlare, chiamando le donne che m' aiutino ad onorare costei.*
Poi quando dico : Ogni dolcezza, *dico quel medesimo ch' è detto nella prima parte, secondo due atti della sua bocca ; uno de' quali è il suo dolcissimo parlare, e l' altro lo suo mirabile riso ; salvo che non dico di questo ultimo come adoperi ne' cuori altrui, perchè la memoria non puote ritener lui, nè sue operazioni.*

§ XXII. Appresso ciò non molti dì passati (siccome piacque al glorioso Sire, lo quale non negò la morte a sè), colui ch' era stato genitore di tanta meraviglia, quanta si vedeva ch' era quella nobilissima Beatrice, di questa vita uscendo

This sonnet hath three parts. In the first I say how this lady evolves this potentiality into actuality according to that most noble part, her eyes: and in the third I tell of this same, according to that most noble part, her mouth. And between these two parts is a little part which is as 'twere a supplicant for aid for the part that precedes and for the part which follows, and it begins here: Aid me, ladies; *The third begins here:* All sweetness.

The first divides into three; in the first I tell how by her virtue she maketh gentle all that she beholdeth, and this is as much as to say, bringeth forth love into potentiality where he is not. In the second I say how she brings forth Love into actuality in the hearts of all whom she beholdeth. In the third I say what she then effects miraculously in their hearts. The second begins: Where she passeth; *the third:* And whom she saluteth.

When I say afterwards: Aid me, ladies, *I make it understood to whom my intention is to speak, calling on ladies that they aid me to honour her.*

Then when I say: All sweetness, *I say the self-same that has been said in the first part according to two acts of her mouth; one of which is her most sweet speech and the other her wondrous smile; save that I tell not of this latter how it operates in the hearts of men, because memory cannot retain it nor its effects*

§ XXII. After the passage of not many days (even as it pleased the glorious Lord who denied not death unto himself), he who had been the parent of so great a marvel as that most gentle Beatrice was seen to be, departing from this life, went verily

se ne gío alla gloria eternale veracemente. Onde,
conciossiachè cotale partire sia doloroso a coloro
che rimangono, e sono stati amici di colui che
se ne va, e nulla sia così intima amistà, come
quella da buon padre a buon figliuolo, e da buon
figliuolo a buon padre; e questa donna fosse in
altissimo grado di bontade, e lo suo padre
(siccome da molti si crede, e vero è) fosse buono
in alto grado; manifesto è, che questa donna
fu amarissimamente piena di dolore.

E conciossiacosachè, secondo l' usanza della
sopradetta cittade, donne con donne, e uomini con
uomini si adunino a cotale tristizia, molte donne
s'adunaro colà, ove questa Beatrice piangea
pietosamente: ond' io veggendo ritornare alquante
donne da lei, udii lor dire parole di questa gentilissima com' ella si lamentava. Tra le quali parole
udii come dicevano: Certo ella pianga sì che
qual la mirasse dovrebbe morire di pietade.
Allora trapassarono queste donne; ed io rimasi
in tanta tristizia, che alcuna lagrima talor bagnava
la mia faccia, ond' io mi ricopria con pormi
spesse volte le mani agli occhi. E se non fosse
ch' io attendea anche udire di lei (perocchè io
era in luogo onde ne giva la maggior parte delle
donne che da lei si partiano), io men sarei
nascoso incontanente che le lagrime m' aveano
assalito.

E però dimorando ancora nel medesimo
luogo, donne anche passaro presso di me, le quali
andavano ragionando e dicendo tra loro queste
parole: Chi dee mai esser lieta di noi, che
avemo udito parlare questa donna così pietosa-

to eternal glory. Wherefore inasmuch as such parting is grievous to those who are left behind and have been friends of him who passeth away, and since no friendship is so intimate as that borne by a good father to a good child, and by a good child to a good father, and since this lady was of surpassing goodness and her father (even as by many is believed, and truly), was good in a high degree, it is manifest that this lady was filled with bitterest grief.

And inasmuch as according to the use of the aforesaid city, women with women and men with men assemble at such mourning, many ladies were gathered where this Beatrice was weeping piteously : wherefore seeing some ladies return from her, I heard them speak words of this most gentle one how she was lamenting. Among which words I heard how they said : Certes she weepeth so that whoso should behold her must needs die of pity. Then these ladies passed by ; and I was left in such sadness that from time to time a tear would bathe my face, wherefore I did defend me by placing many times my hands before mine eyes. And were it not that I expected to hear further of her (because I was in a place by which the greater number of the ladies went that were parting from her), I should have hidden me immediately the tears had assailed me.

And therefore as I tarried yet in the same place, other ladies passed by near me, who went discoursing and saying among them these words : Who of us should e'er be joyous that have heard this lady speak so piteously ? After

*c

mente? Appresso costoro passarono altre, che
veniano dicendo: Questi che quivi è, piange
nè più nè meno come se l' avesse veduta, come
noi l' avemo. Altre poi diceano di me: Vedi
questo che non pare esso; tal è divenuto. E
così passando queste donne, udii parole di lei e
di me in questo modo che detto è.

Ond' io poi pensando, proposi di dire parole,
acciocchè degnamente avea cagione di dire, nelle
quali io conchiudessi tutto ciò che udito avea da
questa donne. E però che volentieri le avrei
domandate, se non mi fosse stata riprensione,
presi materia di dire, come si io le avessi
domandate, ed elle m'avessero risposto.

E feci due sonetti, che nel primo domando
in quel modo che voglia mi giunse di doman-
dare; nell' altro dico la loro risposta, pigliando
ciò ch' io udii da loro, siccome lo m' avessero
detto rispondendo. E cominciai il primo: *Voi,
che portate;* il secondo: *Se' tu colui.*

Voi, che portate la sembianza umile,
  Cogli occhi bassi mostrando dolore,
  Onde venite, chè 'l vostro colore
  Par divenuto di pietà simile?

Vedeste voi nostra donna gentile
  Bagnata il viso di pianto d' amore?
  Ditelmi, donne, chè mel dice il core,
  Perch' io vi veggio andar senz' atto vile.

E se venite da tanta pietate,
  Piacciavi di restar qui meco alquanto,
  E quel che sia di lei, nol mi celate:

those, others passed, who went saying: He who is here, weepeth neither more nor less than if he had beheld her even as we have done. Others then said of me: Behold this man who seemeth not himself, so changed is he. And thus while these ladies were passing, I heard words of her and of me in this manner that I have said.

Wherefore then pondering I purposed to say words (for worthy cause had I to speak), wherein I should include all that I had heard from these ladies. And forasmuch as I would fain have questioned them had it been no blame to me, I took the matter of my rhymes as if I had questioned and they had answered.

And I made two sonnets; in the first I ask after that fashion wherein the desire came upon me to ask; in the other I tell their answer using what I heard from them, even as if they had said it responsive to me. And the first begins. *Ye that bear*; the second: *Art thou he?*

Ye that bear a lowly mien, with eyes downcast
    betraying grief, whence come ye, for your hue
    seems grown to pity's semblance.

Did ye behold our gentle lady, her face wet
    with tears of love? Tell it me, ladies, for my
    heart telleth it me because I see you wend in
    no ungentle guise.

And if ye come from grief so piteous, deign tō
    tarry here with me awhile, and hide not from
    me how it fares with her.

Ch' io veggio gli occhi vostri c' hanno pianto,
 E veggiovi venir si sfigurate,
 Che 'l cor mi trema di vederne tanto.

Questo sonetto si divide in due parti. Nella
prima chiamo e dimando queste donne se vengono da
lei, dicendo loro ch' io il credo, perchè tornano
quasi ingentilite. Nella seconda le prego che mi
dicano di lei ; e la seconda comincia quivi : E se
venite.

Se' tu colui, c' hai trattato sovente
 Di nostra donna, sol parlando a nui ?
 Tu rassomigli alla voce ben lui,
 Ma la figura ne par d' altra gente.

Deh, perchè piangi tu sì coralmente,
 Che fai di te pietà venir altrui ?
 Vedestù pianger lei, che tu non pui
 Punto celar la dolorosa mente ?

Lascia piangere a noi, e triste andare,
 (E' fa peccato chi mai ne conforta),
 Che nel suo pianto l' udimmo parlare.

Ella ha nel viso la pietà sì scorta,
 Che qual l'avesse voluta mirare,
 Saria inanzi lei piangendo morta.

Questo sonetto ha quattro parti, secondo che
quattro modi di parlare ebbero in loro le donne per
cui rispondo. E perocchè di sopra sono assai
manifesti, non mi trametto di narrare la sentenzia
delle parti, e però le distinguo solamente. La
seconda comincia quivi : E perchè piangi tu ; *la*

For I see your eyes that have wept and I behold
   you come away so transformed, that my heart
   quakes only at glimpses thereof.

*This sonnet divides into two parts. In the
first I call and ask these ladies if they come from
her, saying unto them that so I believe because they
return as 'twere enobled. In the second I pray
them that they speak to me of her ; and the second
begins here :* And if ye come.

Art thou he that hath oft treated of our lady,
   speaking to us alone? Thou dost indeed
   resemble him by the voice, but thy form
   seemeth to us another's.

Nay, wherefore weepest thou so broken-heartedly,
   that thou bringest pity of thee upon others?
   Didst thou behold her weep, that thou can'st
   not conceal thy dolorous soul?

Leave weeping to us and sad faring (he doth
   sin who e'er would comfort us) that in her
   tears have heard her speak.

She in her countenance hath anguish so manifest,
   that whoso had dared to gaze on her would
   have fallen dead before her wailing.

*This sonnet hath four parts, according as the
ladies for whom I answer had among them four
modes of speaking. And since they are made clear
enough above, I do not concern myself to relate the
sense of the parts and therefore only indicate them.
The second begins here :* Nay, wherefore weepest

terza : Lascia piangere a noi ; *la quarta ;* Ell'
ha nel viso.

§ XXIII. Appresso ciò pochi dì, avvenne
che in alcuna parte della mia persona mi giunse
una dolorosa infermitade, ond' io soffersi per
molti dì amarissima pena ; la quale mi condusse
a tanta debolezza, che mi convenia stare come
coloro, i quali non si possono movere. Io dico
che nel nono giorno sentendomi dolore intollerabile, giunsemi un pensiero, il quale era della
mia donna. E quando ebbi pensato alquanto di
lei, io ritornai alla mia deboletta vita, e veggendo
come leggero era lo suo durare, ancora che sano
fosse, cominciai a piangere fra me stesso di tanta
miseria. Onde sospirando forte, fra me medesimo
dicea : Di necessità conviene, che la gentilissima
Beatrice alcuna volta si muoia.

E però mi giunse uno sì forte smarrimento,
ch' io chiusi gli occhi e cominciai a travagliare
come farnetica persona, ed immaginare in questo
modo : che nel cominciamento dell' errare che
fece la mia fantasia, mi apparvero certi visi di
donne scapigliate, che mi diceano : Tu pur
morrai. E dopo queste donne, m'apparvero
certi visi diversi ed orribili a vedere, i quali mi
diceano : Tu se' morto.

Così cominciando ad errare la mia fantasia,
venni a quello, che non sapea dove io fossi ; e
veder mi parea donne andare scapigliate piangendo
per via, maravigliosamente tristi ; e pareami
vedere il sole oscurare sì, che le stelle si mostravano d'un colore, che mi facea giudicare che
piangessero, e parevami che gli uccelli volando

thou? *the third*: Leave weeping to us; *the fourth*:
She in her countenance hath.

§ XXIII. A few days after this, it came to
pass that a grievous infirmity fell upon some part
of my body whereby for many days I suffered
most bitter pain; which brought me to such
weakness that it behoved me to lie like those
who cannot stir. I say that on the ninth day,
feeling within me pain intolerable, a thought
came to me that was of my lady. And when I
had pondered somewhat concerning her, I re-
verted to my poor feeble life, and seeing how
slender was its power to endure, even were I
whole, I began to weep within myself at such
misery. Wherefore sighing heavily I said
within myself: Of necessity the most noble
Beatrice must one day die.

And thereat so great bewilderment possessed
me, that I closed mine eyes and began to be in
travail, even as one delirious and to imagine in
this wise: that in the beginning of the wandering that my fancy made, certain faces of dishevelled women appeared to me who said to
me: Thou too shalt die. And after these
ladies, certain strange faces and horrible to
behold appeared to me, and said: Thou art
dead:

Thus my fancy beginning to wander, I came
to such a point that I knew not where I was,
and methought I beheld dishevelled ladies pass
by the way, weeping and wondrously sad; and
methought I beheld the sun grow dark, so that
the stars showed themselves of a hue that made
me judge they were weeping, and methought

cadessero morti, e che fossero grandissimi terre-
moti.   E maravigliandomi in cotale fantasia, e
paventando assai, imaginai alcuno amico, che mi
venisse a dire: Or non sai? la tua mirabile
donna è partita di questo secolo.   Allora incominciai a piangere molto pietosamente; e non
solamente piangea nella imaginazione, ma piangea
con gli occhi bagnandoli di vere lagrime.

Io imaginava di guardare verso il cielo, e
pareami vedere moltitudine di angeli, i quali
tornassero in suso ed avessero dinanzi loro una
nebuletta bianchissima: e pareami che questi
angeli cantassero gloriosamente; e le parole del
loro canto mi parea che fossero queste: *Osanna
in excelsis ;* ed altro non mi parea udire.   Allora
mi parea che il cuore, ov' era tanto amore, mi
dicesse: Vero è che morta giace la nostra donna.
E per questo mi parea andare per vedere lo
corpo, nel quale era stata quella nobilissima e
beata anima.   E fu sì forte la errante fantasia,
che mi mostrò questa donna morta: e pareami
che donne la coprissero la testa con un bianco
velo: e pareami che la sua faccia avesse tanto
aspetto d'umiltade, che parea che dicesse: Io
sono a vedere lo principio della pace.

In questa imaginazione mi giunse tanta umiltade
per veder lei, che io chiamava la Morte, e dicea:
Dolcissima Morte, vieni a me, e non m' esser
villana; perocchè tu dêi esser fatta gentile, in
tal parte se' stata! or vieni a me che molto ti
desidero: tu vedi ch'io porto già lo tuo colore.
E quando io avea veduto compiere tutti i dolorosi
mestieri, che alle corpora de' morti s'usano di

that birds on the wing fell dead and that there were great earthquakes. And, marvelling in such fantasy and much affrighted, I imagined that a certain friend came and said to me: Come, knowest thou not? thy wondrous lady hath departed from this world. Then I began to weep most piteously; and not only did I weep in imagination but I wept with mine eyes, wetting them with real tears.

I imagined that I gazed heavenward, and methought I beheld a multitude of angels who were returning upward and had a cloudlet exceeding white before them, and methought these angels sang gloriously and that the words of their song were these: *Osanna in excelsis*; and naught else meseemed to hear. Then methought my heart where dwelt love so great, said to me: True it is that our lady lieth dead. And at this methought I went and beheld the body wherein that most noble and blessed soul had been. And so strong was the errant fancy, that it showed to me this lady dead; and methought ladies covered her head with a white veil, and that her face had an aspect of humility so great that she seemed to be saying: Now do I behold the fount of peace.

In this vision there fell such great humility upon me through the sight of her, that I called on Death and said: Sweetest Death, come unto me and be not churlish to me; for needs must thou have become gentle, in such place hast thou been! Now come unto me who greatly desire thee: thou seest that I already wear thy hue. And when I had beheld all the mournful offices

fare, mi parea tornare nella mia camera, e quivi
mi parea guardare verso il cielo : e sì forte era
la mia imaginazione, che, piangendo, cominciai a
dire con vera voce : O anima bellissima, com'
è beato colui che ti vede! E dicendo queste
parole con doloroso singulto di pianto, e chiamando la Morte che venisse a me, una donna
giovane e gentile, la quale era lungo il mio letto,
credendo che il mio piangere e le mie parole
fossero lamento per lo dolore della mia infermità,
con grande paura cominciò a piangere. Onde
altre donne, che per la camera erano, s'accorsero
che io piangeva per lo pianto che vedeano fare
a questa : onde facendo lei partire da me, la
quale era meco di propinquissima sanguinità
congiunta, elle si trassero verso me per isvegliarmi,
credendo che io sognassi, e diceanmi : Non
dormir più, e non ti sconfortare. E parlandomi
così, cessò la forte fantasia entro quel punto ch'io
volea dire : O Beatrice, benedetta sii tu. E
già detto avea : O Beatrice. . . quando riscuo-
tendomi apersi gli occhi, e vidi ch' io era
ingannato ; e con tutto ch' io chiamassi questo
nome, la mia voce era sì rotta dal singulto del
piangere, che queste donne non mi poterono
intendere.

Ed avvegnachè io mi vergognassi molto,
tuttavia per alcuno ammonimento d' amore mi
rivolsi loro. E quando mi videro, cominciaro a
dire : Questi par morto ; e a dir fra loro :
procuriam di confortarlo. Onde molte parole
mi diceano da confortarmi ; e allora mi doman-

fulfilled which are wont to be done to the
bodies of the dead, methought I returned to my
chamber and there gazed heavenward : and so
strong was my imagination, that weeping, I
began to say with my real voice : O soul most
beauteous, how blessed is he that beholdeth
thee ! And as I uttered these words with
grievous sobbing and tears, and called on Death
that he might come to me, a young and gentle
lady who was beside my bed, believing that my
tears and my words were a lament for the pain
of my sickness, began to weep with great dread.
Whereupon other ladies who were about the
chamber perceived that I was weeping, by the
weeping which they beheld this lady make.
Wherefore causing her (who was joined to me
by most close kinship) to depart from me, they,
believing I was dreaming, drew towards me, in
order to awaken me, and they said to me :
Sleep no more, and be not discomforted. And
as they thus spake to me, the mighty vision
ceased at the moment when I was about to say :
O Beatrice blessed be thou ! And already I
had said : O Beatrice . . . when coming to myself I opened mine eyes and saw that I had been
beguiled ; and although I uttered this name my
voice was so broken by the convulsion of weeping, that these ladies could not understand me.

And albeit I was sore abashed, yet by some
admonition of love I turned me towards them.
And when they beheld me they began to say :
He seemeth dead ; and to say among them-
selves : let us take heed to comfort him.
Wherefore many words they said to comfort

davano di che io avessi avuto paura. Ond' io,
essendo alquanto riconfortato, e conosciuto il
falso imaginare, risposi loro: Io vi dirò quello
c'ho avuto. Allora cominciandomi dal principio, fino alla fine dissi loro ciò che veduto
avea, tacendo il nome di questa gentilissima.
Onde io poi, sanato di questa infermità, proposi
di dir parole di questo che m' era avvenuto,
perocchè mi parea che fosse amorosa cosa a
udire; e sì ne dissi questa canzone:

Donna pietosa e di novella etate,
    Adorna assai di gentilezze umane,
    Ch' era là ov'io chiamava spesso Morte,
    Veggendo gli occhi mei pien di pietate,
    Ed ascoltando le parole vane,
    Si mosse con paura a pianger forte;
    Ed altre donne, che si furo accorte
    Di me per quella che meco piangia,
    Fecer lei partir via,
    Ed appressàrsi per farmi sentire.
    Qual dicea: Non dormire;
    E qual dicea: Perchè sì ti sconforte?
    Allor lasciai la nova fantasia,
    Chiamando il nome della donna mia.

Era la voce mia sì dolorosa,
    E rotta sì dall' angoscia e dal pianto,
    Ch' io solo intesi il nome nel mio core;
    E con tutta la vista vergognosa,
    Ch' era nel viso mio giunta cotanto,
    Mi fece verso lor volgere Amore.

me; and then they questioned me of what I had
been afeard. Whereupon, being somewhat restored and having recognised the emptiness of my
dream, I answered: I will tell you how it
hath fared with me. Then I began to tell all
I had seen from the beginning to the end, but I
concealed the name of that most gentle one.
Wherefore being afterwards healed of this
infirmity, I proposed to say words concerning
what had befallen me, since methought it was a
lovesome thing to hear; and so I composed
thereon this Canzone:

A lady, compassionate and of tender age, much
    adorned with human excellencies, who was
    there where I oft called on Death, seeing
    mine eyes filled with anguish and hearing
    mine empty words, was moved by dread to
    weep aloud: and other ladies, who had be-
    come ware of me because of her that wept
    with me, made her to depart and drew nigh
    to me to recall me to my senses. One said:
    Sleep no more; and another said: Where-
    fore art thou so dismayed? Then calling on
    the name of my lady, I let my strange fancy go.

So sorrowful was my voice and so broken by
    the anguish and by the weeping, that I alone
    heard the name in my heart: and with all
    the shamed look that had so fallen upon my
    visage, Love made me turn towards them.

Egli era tale a veder mio colore,
Che facea ragionar di morte altrui:
Deh, confortiam costui,
Pregava l' una l' altra umilemente;
E dicevan sovente:
Che vedestù, che tu non hai valore?
E quando un poco confortato fui,
Io dissi: Donne, dicerollo a vui.

Mentre io pensava la mia frale vita,
E vedea 'l suo durar com' è leggiero,
Piansemi Amor nel core, ove dimora;
Per che l' anima mia fu sì smarrita,
Che sospirando dicea nel pensiero:
Ben converrà che la mia donna mora.
Io presi tanto smarrimento allora,
Ch' io chiusi gli occhi vilmente gravati;
Ed eran sì smagati
Gli spirti miei, che ciascun giva errando.
E poscia immaginando,
Di conoscenza e di verità fuora,
Visi di donne m' apparver crucciati,
Che mi dicen: Pur morràti, morràti.

Poi vidi cose dubitose molte
Nel vano immaginar, ov' io entrai;
Ed esser mi parea non so in qual loco,
E veder donne andar per via disciolte,
Qual lagrimando, e qual traendo guai,
Che di tristizia saettavan foco.
Poi mi parve vedere appoco appoco
Turbar lo Sole ed apparir la stella,
E pianger egli ed ella;
Cader gli augelli volando per l' âre,

Such was my hue to behold, that it made them discourse of death. Pray, comfort we him, one humbly entreated the other, and oft they said : What sawest thou, that thou hast lost all power ? And when I was somewhat comforted I said : Ladies, I will tell it you :

While I was pondering on my frail life and beheld its length how brief it is, Love wept in my heart where he abideth ; whereat my soul was so bewildered, that sighing I said in thought : Truly it shall come to pass that my lady shall die. Then did bewilderment so great seize me, that I closed mine eyes, basely weighed down, and so confounded were my spirits that each went forth a-wandering. And then, as I dreamed, bereft of sense and of truth, agonised faces of women appeared to me who said : Thou too shalt die, shalt die !

Then saw I dread things many, in the vain vision on which I entered ; and methought I was in a strange place and beheld dishevelled women going by the way, one a-weeping, another uttering lamentations that shot forth fiery shafts of grief. Then methought I beheld little by little the sun grow troubled, the stars appear, and him and them weep, birds flying in

E la terra tremare;
Ed uom m' apparve scolorito e fioco,
Dicendomi: Che fai? non sai novella?
Morta è la donna tua, ch' era sì bella.

Levava gli occhi miei bagnati in pianti,
E vedea (che parean pioggia di manna),
Gli angeli che tornavan suso in cielo,
Ed una nuvoletta avean davanti,
Dopo la qual gridavan tutti: Osanna;
E s' altro avesser detto, a voi dire' lo.
Allor diceva Amor: Più non ti celo;
Vieni a veder nostra donna che giace.
L' immaginar fallace
Mi condusse a veder mia donna morta;
E quando l' ebbi scorta,
Vedea che donne la covrian d' un velo;
Ed avea seco umiltà sì verace,
Che parea che dicesse: Io sono in pace.

Io diveniva nel dolor sì umile,
Veggendo in lei tanta umiltà formata,
Ch' io dicea: Morte, assai dolce ti tegno;
Tu dêi omai esser cosa gentile,
Poichè tu se' nella mia donna stata,
E dêi aver pietate, e non disdegno.
Vedi che sì desideroso vegno
D' esser de' tuoi, ch' io ti somiglio in fede
Vieni, chè 'l cor ti chiede.
Poi mi partia, consumato ogni duolo;
E quando io era solo,
Dicea, guardando verso l' alto regno:
Beato, anima bella, chi ti vede!
Voi mi chiamaste allor, vostra mercede.

the air fall, and the earth quake; and a man appeared to me pallid and faint, saying: What doest thou? knowest thou not the news? Dead is thy lady that was so fair.

Mine eyes I lifted wet with tears, and beheld (as 'twere a shower of manna) angels ascending heavenward and a cloudlet had they before them, following which all did shout Hosannah! and if aught else they had said I would tell it you. Then said Love: No more I hide from thee; come and behold our lady lying dead. The false vision led me to behold my lady dead, and when I had perceived her I saw that ladies were covering her with a veil, and with her was humility so true that methought she said: I am in peace.

I, in my grief waxed so humble, beholding imaged in her, humility so great, that I said: Death! very sweet I hold thee; henceforth thou needs must be a noble thing, since thou hast dwelt with my lady and must needs show pity and not disdain. Thou seest that I come so envious to be of thine, that I bear thy semblance faithfully. Come, for my heart calleth thee. Then, all mourning fulfilled, I departed; and when I was alone I said, gazing towards the realm on high: Blessed, fair soul is he that beholdeth thee! Ye did recall me then, of your grace.

*Questa canzone ha due parti : nella prima dico,
parlando a indiffinita persona, com' io fui levato d'
una vana fantasia da certe donne, e come promisi
loro di dirla : nella seconda dico, com' io dissi a
loro. La seconda comincia quivi :* Mentr' io
pensava. *La prima parte si divide in due : nella
prima dico quello che certe donne, e che una sola,
dissero e fecero per la mia fantasia, quanto è
dinanzi ch' io fossi tornato in verace cognizione ;
nella seconda dico quello che queste donne mi dissero,
poich' io lasciai questo farneticare ; e comincia
quivi :* Era la voce mia. *Poscia quando dico :*
Mentr' io pensava, *dico com' io dissi loro questa
mia imaginazione ; e intorno a ciò fo due parti.
Nella prima dico per ordine questa imaginazione ;
nella seconda, dicendo a che ora mi chiamaro, le
ringrazio chiusamente ; e questa parte comincia
quivi :* Voi mi chiamaste.

§ XXIV. Appresso questa vana imaginazione,
avvenne un dì, che sedendo io pensoso in alcuna
parte, ed io mi sentii cominciare un tremito nel
core, così come s' io fossi stato presente a questa
donna. Allora dico che mi giunse una imaginazione d'Amore : chè mi parve vederlo venire
da quella parte ove la mia donne stava ; e pareami
che lietamente mi dicesse nel cor mio : Pensa
di benedire lo dì ch' io ti presi, perocchè tu lo
dèi fare. E certo mi parea avere lo core così
lieto, che mi parea che non fosse lo core mio,
per la sua nova condizione.

E poco dopo queste parole, che 'l core mi
disse con la lingua d' Amore, io vidi venire verso
me una gentil donna, la quale era di famosa

This canzone hath two parts: in the first I say speaking to an indefinite person how I was roused from an empty dream by certain ladies and how I promised to tell it to them: in the second I say how I told it them. The second begins here: While I was pondering. *The first part divides into two: in the first part I tell what certain ladies, and what one alone said, because of my dream, all the time preceeding my return to real consciousness; in the second I tell what these ladies said to me after I had left this delirium: and it begins here:* So sorrowful was my voice. *Then when I say:* While I was pondering, *I say how I told this my vision to them; and concerning that I make two parts. In the first I tell of the vision in due order; in the second, saying at what point they awakened me, in conclusion, I thank them: and this part begins here:* Ye did recall me.

§ XXIV. After this my empty dream, it came to pass one day, that sitting pensive in a certain place, lo, I felt a tremour begin at my heart as if I had been in the presence of this lady. Then, I say there came to me a vision of Love: for methought I beheld him coming from that part where my lady was and methought he said joyously within my heart: Think to bless the day when I took thee captive, for thou hast cause so to do. And certes methought I had a heart so glad, that it seemed not mine own because of its changed state.

And shortly after these words which my heart said to me by the tongue of Love, I beheld a gentle lady coming towards me who was famed

beltade, e fu già molto donna di questo mio
primo amico. E lo nome di questa donna era
Giovanna, salvo che per la sua beltade, secondo
ch' altri crede, imposto l' era nome Primavera :
e così era chiamata. E appresso lei guardando,
vidi venire la mirabile Beatrice. Queste donne
andaro presso di me così l' una appresso l' altra,
e parvemi che Amore mi parlasse nel core, e
dicesse : Quella prima è nominata Primavera
solo per questa venuta d' oggi ; chè io mossi lo
impositore del nome a chiamarla *Primavera* cioè
prima verra, lo dì che Beatrice si mostrerà dopo
l' imaginazione del suo fedele. E se anco vuoli
considerare lo primo nome suo, tanto è quanto
dire Primavera, perchè lo suo nome Giovanna
è da quel Giovanni, lo quale precedette la verace
luce, dicendo : *Ego vox clamantis in deserto :*
parate viam Domini. Ed anche mi parve che
mi dicesse, dopo queste, altre parole, cioè : Chi
volesse sottilmente considerare, quella Beatrice
chiamerebbe Amore, per molta simiglianza che
ha meco. Ond' io poi ripensando, proposi de
scriverne per rima al primo mio amico (tacendo
certe parole le quali pareano da tacere), credendo
io che ancora il suo cuore mirasse la beltà di
questa Primavera gentile. E dissi questo sonetto :

Io mi sentii svegliar dentro allo core
   Uno spirto amoroso che dormia :
   E poi vidi venir da lungi Amore
   Allegro sì, che appena il conoscia ;

for her beauty and was erst the much-beloved mistress of this my first friend. And the name of this lady was Giovanna (Joan), save that for her beauty, as folk believe, the name Primavera (Spring) was given to her: and even so was she called. And looking beyond her I beheld the wondrous Beatrice coming. These ladies passed near me, thus one after the other and methought Love spoke within my heart and said: The first is named Primavera solely for this coming to-day; for I moved the giver of the name to call her *Primavera* which is to say *prima verra* (she will come first) on the day that Beatrice shall reveal herself after her liege's vision. And if thou wilt consider also her first name, it is as much as to say, Primavera, because her name Giovanna cometh from that Giovanni (John) who was the forerunner of the True Light, saying: *Ego vox clamantis in deserto parate viam Domini.* And further methought Love said other words to me after these, namely: He who should subtly consider would call Beatrice, Love, for the great similitude that she hath unto me. Wherefore pondering, I purposed to write of this in rhyme to my first friend (concealing certain words which it seemed fitting to conceal), believing that his heart did still gaze on the beauty of this gentle Primavera. And I composed this sonnet:

I felt a spirit of love that slept, awaken within my heart: and then I beheld Love coming from afar, so gladsome that scarce I knew him,

Dicendo : Or pensa pur di farmi onore ;
    E 'n ciascuna parola sua ridia.
    E, poco stando meco il mio signore,
    Guardando in quella parte, onde venia,

Io vidi monna Vanna e monna Bice
    Venire invêr lo loco là ov' i' era,
    L'una appresso dell' altra meraviglia :

E sì come la mente mi ridice,
    Amor mi disse : Questa è Primavera,
    E quella ha nome Amor, sì mi somiglia.

*Questo sonetto ha molte parti : la prima delle
quali dice, come io mi sentii svegliare lo tremore
usato nel core, e come parve che Amore m' apparisse
allegro da lunga parte ; la seconda dice, come, mi
parve che Amore mi dicesse nel core, e quale mi
parea ; la terza dice come, poi che questo fu
alquanto stato meco cotale, io vidi ed udii certe cose.
La seconda parte comincia quivi :* Dicendo : Or
pensa pur ; *ta terza quivi :* E poco stando. *La
terza parte si divide in due ; nella prima dico quello
ch' io vidi ; nella seconda dico quello ch' io udii ;
e comincia quivi :* Amor mi disse.

§ XXV. Potrebbe qui dubitar persona degna
di dichiararle ogni dubitazione, e dubitar potrebbe di ciò ch' io dico d'Amore, come se fosse
una cosa per sè, e non solamente sostanza intel-
ligente, ma come se fosse sostanza corporale.
La qual cosa, secondo verità, è falsa ; chè
Amore non è per sè siccome sostanza, ma è un
accidente in sostanza. E che io dica di lui

saying: Now think to do me honour, and in
each word of his he laughed. And as my
lord stayed awhile with me, gazing toward.
that place whence he came,

I beheld Monna Vanna and Monna Bice coming
towards the place where I was, one marvel
following the other:

And even as memory retelleth me, Love said to
me: This is Primavera, and that hath Love
for name, so like is she unto me.

*This sonnet hath many parts : whereof the first
telleth how I felt the wonted tremour stir within
my breast and how it seemed that Love appeared
to me gladsome from a far place ; the second telleth
what meseemed that Love said within my heart
and how he appeared to me ; the third tells how
after he had been awhile with me in such wise, I
saw and heard certain things. The second part
begins here : Saying : now think ; the third here :
And as my lord. The third part divides into
two ; in the first I tell what I saw ; in the
second I tell what I heard ; and it begins here :
Love said to me.*

§ XXV. Here a person worthy of having all
his difficulties made plain might be perplexed,
for he might be in a difficulty as to what I say
concerning Love, as if he were a thing in himself
and not only an intelligent being but a corporeal
being. Which thing according to truth, is false;
for Love exists not as a being in itself but is a
quality of a being. And that I speak of him as

come se fosse corpo, ed ancora come se fosse
uomo, appari per tre cose che io dico di lui.
Dico che 'l vidi di lungi venire; onde, conciossiacosachè *venire* dica moto locale (e local-
mente mobile per sè, secondo il Filosofo, sia
solamente corpo), appare che io ponga Amore
essere corpo. Dico anche di lui che rideva, ed
anche che parlava; le quali cose paiono esser pro-
prie dell' uomo, e specialmente esser risibile; e
però appare ch' io pongo lui esser uomo.

A cotal cosa dichiarare, secondo ch' è buono
al presente, prima è da intendere, che antica-
mente non erano dicitori d'Amore in lingua
volgare, anzi erano dicitori d'Amore certi poeti
in lingua latina: tra noi, dico, avvegna forse che
tra altra gente addivenisse e addivegna ancora
siccome in Grecia, non volgari ma litterati poeti
queste cose trattavano. E non è molto numero
d' anni passato, che apparirono prima questi
poeti volgari; chè dire per rima in volgare tanto
è quanto dire per versi in latino, secondo alcuna
proporzione. E segno che sia picciol tempo è,
che, se volemo cercare in lingua d' *Oco* e in
lingua di *Sì*, noi non troveremo cose dette anzi
lo presente tempo per centocinquanta anni. E
la cagione, per che alquanti grossi ebbero fama
di saper dire, è che quasi furono i primi, che
dissero in lingua di *Sì*. E lo primo, che
cominciò a dire siccome poeta volgare, si mosse
però che volle fare intendere le sue parole a

if he were a body and again as if he were a
human being, is apparent in three things which I say
of him. I say that I saw him coming from afar;
wherefore inasmuch as *coming* implies locomotion
(and as according to the Philosopher a body only
is *per se* capable of local movement), it appeareth
that I assume Love to be a body. I say also of
him that he laughed and also that he spoke; which
things seem to be proper to man and especially
the faculty of laughter; and therefore it
appeareth that I assume him to be man.

In order to make such things plain so far as
is meet for the present purpose, be it first understood that of old there were no versifiers of Love
in the vulgar tongue but rather certain poets of
Love in the latin tongue: I mean, among us,
though perchance among other folk it may have
happened and still happen, even as in Greece,
that literary and not vernacular poets treated of
these things. And not many years have past
since these poets in the common tongue appeared
for the first time; for, to compose in rhyme in
the common tongue is equivalent to composing
verses in latin, observing a certain measure.
And a token of the shortness of the time is,
that if we seek in the tongue of *Oc* and in the
tongue of *Sì* we shall find nothing composed
earlier than one hundred and fifty years before
the present time. And the reason why some
few rude rhymsters had a reputation for skill in
composing verses is, that they were almost the
first to compose in the tongue of *Sì*. And the
first that began to compose as a vernacular poet
was moved because he desired to make his words

D

donna, alla quale era malagevole ad intendere i
versi latini. E questo è contro a coloro, che
rimano sopra altra materia che amorosa; conciossiacosachè cotal modo di parlare fosse dal
principio trovato per dire d'Amore.

Onde, conciossiacosachè a' poeti sia conceduta
maggior licenza di parlare che alli prosaici
dicitori, e questi dicitori per rima non sieno
altro che poeti volgari, è degno e ragionevole,
che a loro sia maggior licenza largita di parlare,
che agli altri parlatori volgari: onde, se alcuna
figura o colore rettorico è conceduto alli poeti,
conceduto è a' rimatori. Dunque se noi
vedemo, che li poeti hanno parlato alle cose inanimate come se avessero senso e ragione, e fat-
tole parlare insieme; e non solamente cose vere,
ma cose non vere (cioè che detto hanno, di cose
le quali non sono, che parlano, e detto che molti
accidenti parlano, siccome fossero sostanze ed
uomini); degno è lo dicitore per rima fare lo
simigliante, non senza ragione alcuna, ma con
ragione, la quale poi sia possibile d' aprire per
prosa. Che i poeti abbiano così parlato, come
detto è, appare per Virgilio; il quale dice che
Giuno, cioè una dea nemica dei Troiani, parlò
ad Eolo signore delli venti, quivi nel primo dell'
Eneida: Æole, namque tibi etc., e che questo
signore le rispose quivi: *Tuus, o regina, quid
optes* etc. Per questo medesimo poeta parla la
cosa, che non è animata, alla cosa animata nel
terzo dell' *Eneida*, quivi: *Dardanidæ duri* etc.
Per Lucano parla la cosa animata alla cosa in-

intelligible to a lady who had difficulty in understanding latin verses. And this is directed against those who rhyme upon other matter than that of Love, inasmuch as such manner of speech was at the beginning invented to treat of Love.

Wherefore, inasmuch as greater license in speech is conceded to poets than to composers in prose and as they who compose in rhyme are no other than poets in vernacular, it is seemly and reasonable that greater license be vouchsafed to them than to other writers in the vulgar tongue : wherefore if any figure or rhetorical colour is conceded to the poets it is also conceded to the rhymers. Therefore if we see that the poets have spoken to inanimate things as if they had sense and reason and have made them speak together, and not only real things but unreal things (that is to say they have said of things which do not exist that they speak and have said that many qualities of things speak as if they were beings and men), the composer in rhyme has a right to do the like ; not indeed without some reason, but with a reason which it were possible afterwards to make clear in prose. That the poets have thus spoken as has been said, appears in Virgil, who saith that Juno, a goddess, to wit, hostile to the Trojans, spake to Eolus lord of the winds, here in the first book of the *Æneid* : *Æole, namque tibi* etc., and that this lord answered her here : *Tuus, o regina, quid optes* etc. In this same poet the thing that is inanimate speaks to the animate thing in the third book of the *Æneid* here : *Dardanidæ duri* etc. In Lucan the animate thing speaketh to the

animata, quivi: *Multum, Roma, tamen debes
civilibus armis*. Per Orazio parla l' uomo alla
sua scienza medesima, siccome ad altra persona;
e non solamente sono parole d' Orazio, ma
dicele quasi recitando le parole del buono Omero,
quivi nella sua *Poetria*: *Dic mihi, Musa virum*
etc. Per Ovidio parla Amore, come se fosse
persona umana, nel principio del libro che ha
nome *Rimedio d'Amore*, quivi: *Bella mihi, video,
bella parantur, ait*. E per questo puote essere
manifesto a chi dubita in alcuna parte di questo
mio libello.

E acciocchè non ne pigli alcuna baldanza
persona grossa, dico che nè li poeti parlavano
così senza ragione, nè que' che rimano deono
così parlare, non avendo alcuno ragionamento in
loro di quello che dicono; perocchè grande
vergogna sarebbe a colui, che rimasse cosa sotto
veste di figura o di colore rettorico, e poi
domandato non sapesse dinudare le sue parole da
cotal vesta, in guisa ch' avessero verace intendimento. E questo mio primo amico ed io ne
sapemo bene di quelli che così rimano stolta-
mente.

§ XXVI. Questa gentilissima donna, di cui
ragionato è nelle precedenti parole, venne in
tanta grazia delle genti, che quando passava per
via, le persone correano per vederla; onde
mirabile letizia me ne giungea. E quando ella
fosse presso ad alcuno, tanta onestà venia nel
core di quello, ch' egli non ardia di levare gli
occhi, nè di rispondere al suo saluto; e di questo
molti, siccome esperti, mi potrebbero testimoniare
a chi nol credesse. Ella coronata e vestita d'

inanimate thing here : *Multum, Roma, tamen
debet civilibus armis.* In Horace a man speaks
to his own poetic faculty even as to another
person ; and they are not the words of Horace
only but he says them as though reciting the
words of the good Homer, here in his *Poetria* :
Dic mihi Musa, virum, etc. In Ovid Love
speaketh, as he were a human being, in the
beginning of the book named *Remedy of Love*,
here : *Bella mihi, video, bella parantur ait.* And
by this may all be made clear to one who finds
a difficulty in certain parts of this my little book.

And in order that no witless person may take
any licence therefrom I say that neither did the
poets speak thus without reason, nor should they
who rhyme speak thus, without having some
interpretation in their own minds of what they
say ; for deep shame were it to him who should
rhyme under cover of a figure or of a rhetorical
colour and, afterwards, being asked, knew not
how to strip such vesture from his words, in
such wise that they should have a real meaning.
And this my first friend and I well know of
many who rhyme thus stupidly.

§ XXVI. This most gentle lady of whom
the preceding words were spoken came to such
favour among folk, that when she passed by the
way people ran to behold her, wherefore
wondrous joy possessed me thereat. And when
she was near to any one, modesty so great
possessed his heart that he dared not lift his
eyes nor respond to her salutations ; and of this
many even from experience could bear witness
for me, to him who should not believe it. She,

umiltà s' andava, nulla gloria mostrando di ciò
ch' ella vedeva ed udiva.   Dicevano molti, poichè passata era : Questa non è femina, anzi è
uno de' bellissimi angeli del cielo.   Ed altri
dicevano : Questa è una meraviglia ; che bene-
detto sia lo Signore che sì mirabilmente sa
operare ! Io dico ch' ella si mostrava sì gentile e
sì piena di tutti i piaceri, che quelli che la miravano
comprendevano in loro una dolcezza onesta e
soave tanto che ridire nol sapevano ; nè alcuno
era lo quale potesse mirar lei, che nel principio
non gli convenisse sospirare.   Queste e più
mirabili cose da lei procedeano virtuosamente.
Ond' io pensando a ciò, volendo ripigliare lo
stile della sua loda, proposi di dire parole, nelle
quali dessi ad intendere delle sue mirabili ed
eccellenti operazioni ; acciocchè non pure coloro
che la poteano sensibilmente vedere, ma gli altri
sapessono di lei quello che le parole ne possono
fare intendere.   Allora dissi questo sonetto :

Tanto gentile e tanto onesta pare
    La donna mia, quand' ella altrui saluta,
    Ch' ogni lingua divien tremando muta,
    E gli occhi non ardiscon di guardare.

Ella sen va, sentendosi laudare,
    Benignamente d' umiltà vestuta ;
    E par che sia una cosa venuta
    Di cielo in terra a miracol mostrare.

crowned and clad in humility went her way,
showing no pride at what she saw and heard.
Said many after she had passed: This is no
woman, rather is she one of the fairest angels of
heaven. And others said: this is a marvel and
blessed be the Lord who knoweth how to work
so wondrously! I say that she showed herself
so gentle and so filled with all winsomeness, that
they who gazed upon her, felt within them a
pleasant and modest sweetness, such that none
could tell it again, nor was any who could look
upon her without being first constrained to sigh.
These and more wondrous things proceeded
from her by her power. Wherefore, pondering
on this, and desiring to resume the manner of
her praise, I purposed to say words in which I
should make some of her wondrous and excellent
effects understood, in order that not only those
who could behold her with their bodily senses
but that others should know of her as much as
words can convey to the understanding. Then
I composed this sonnet:

So gentle and so modest my lady seems when
    she saluteth others, that every tongue grows
    tremblingly dumb, and eyes dare not to look
    on her.

She goeth her way, hearing her praises, benignly
    clothed in humility, and seemeth to be a thing
    come from heaven to earth, to show forth a
    miracle.

Mostrasi sì piacente a chi la mira,
    Che dà per gli occhi una dolcezza al core,
    Che intender non la può chi non la prova.

E par che della sua labbia si muova
    Uno spirto soave e pien d' amore,
    Che va dicendo all' anima: sospira.

    Questo sonetto è sì piano ad intendere, per quello che narrato è dinanzi, che non ha bisogno d' alcuna divisione; e però lasciando lui,

    § XXVII. Dico che questa mia donna venne in tanta grazia, che non solamente era ella onorata e laudata, ma per lei erano onorate e laudate molte. Ond' io veggendo ciò e volendo manifestare a chi ciò non vedea, proposi anche di dire parole, nelle quali ciò fosse significato: e dissi allora questo sonetto lo quale narra come la sua virtù adoperava nelle altre.

Vede perfettamente ogni salute
    Chi la mia donna tra le donne vede:
    Quelle, che van con lei, sono tenute
    Di bella grazia a Dio render mercede,

E sua beltata è di tanta virtute,
    Che nulla invidia all' altre ne procede,
    Anzi le face andar seco vestute
    Di gentilezza, d'amore e di fede.

La vista sua face ogni cosa umile,
    E non fa sola sè parer piacente,
    Ma ciascuna per lei riceve onore.

Herself she sheweth so winsome to him who gazeth on her, that through his eyes she giveth a sweetness to his heart, such that he who proveth it not, cannot understand it.

And it seemeth that from her countenance a spirit moveth, gentle and filled with love, that goeth saying to the soul : sigh !

This sonnet is so plain to the understanding from what is related above that it needeth not any division ; and therefore leaving it,

§ XXVII. I say that this my lady grew to such favour that not only was she honoured and praised but many ladies were honoured and praised through her. Wherefore I, seeing this and desiring to make it manifest to those who saw it not, purposed to say further words wherein this should be signified : and I then composed this sonnet, which relates how her virtue wrought in the other ladies.

He who beholdeth my lady among other ladies, beholdeth perfectly all saving power : they who go with her are holden to render thanks to God for his sweet grace.

And her beauty is of such virtue that no envy thereof is stirred in others, rather doth it make them go with her clad in gentleness, in love and in faith.

The sight of her maketh all things humble and maketh not only herself to seem lovely, but each one through her receiveth honour.

*D

Ed è negli atti suoi tanto gentile,
　　Che nessun la si può recare a mente,
　　Che non sospiri in dolcezza d' amore.

*Questo sonetto ha tre parti : nella prima dico
tra che gente questa donna più mirabile parea ;
nella seconda dico come era graziosa la sua compagnia ; nella terza dico di quelle cose ch' ella
virtuosamente operava in altrui. La seconda
comincia quivi ;* Quelle che van; *la terza quivi ;*
E sua beltate. *Quest' ultima parte si divide in
tre ; nella prima dico quello che operava nelle
donne, cioè per loro medesime ; nella seconda dico
quella che operava in loro per altrui ; nella terza
dico come non solamente nelle donne operava, ma
in tutte le persone, e non solmente nella sua presenza, ma, ricordandosi di lei, mirabilmente
operava. La seconda comincia quivi ;* La vista;
la terza quivi ; Ed è negli atti.

§ XXVIII. Appresso ciò, cominciai a pensare
un giorno sopra quello che detto avea della mia
donna, cioè in questi due sonetti precedenti ; e
veggendo nel mio pensiero ch' io non avea detto
di quello che al presente tempo adoperava in me,
parvemi difettivamente aver parlato ; e però proposi di dire parole, nelle quali io dicessi come
mi parea esser disposto alla sua operazione, e
come operava in me la sua virtude. E non
credendo ciò poter narrare in brevità di sonetto,
cominciai allora una canzone, la quale comincia :

Si lungamente m' ha tenuto Amore,
　　E costumato alla sua signoria,
　　Che sì com' egli m' era forte in pria,
　　Così mi sta soave ora nel core.

And in her bearing so gentle is she, that none
  can call her to memory and sigh not in the
  sweetness of love.

*This sonnet hath three parts : in the first I tell
among what folk this lady seemeth most wondrous ;
in the second I tell how gracious was her com-
panionship ; in the third I tell of those things which
she by her power wrought in others. The second
begins here :* They who go ; *the third here :* And
her beauty. *This last part divides into three : in
the first I tell of what she wrought in women, to
wit through themselves ; in the second I tell of what
she wrought in them through others ; in the third I
tell how it was not only in women that she wrought
but in all persons, and not only in her presence but
that by the remembrance of her she wrought
wondrously. The second begins here :* The sight ;
the third here : And in her bearing.

§ XXVIII. Thereafter I began to ponder
one day on what I had said of my lady, to wit
in these two preceding sonnets, and perceiving in
my thought that I had not told of what in the
present time she wrought in me, methought I
had spoken imperfectly ; and therefore I purposed to say words wherein I should tell how
I seemed to be to her power propense, and how
her virtue wrought in me. And believing that
I could not relate this in the brevity of a sonnet
I then began a canzone which beginneth :

So long hath Love held me, and so wonted to
  his mastery, that even as he was hard to me at
  first so now doth he dwell sweet in my breast.

Però quando mi toglie sì 'l valore,
Che gli spiriti par che fuggan via,
Allor sente la frale anima mia
Tanta dolcezza, che 'l viso ne smuore.
Poi prende Amore in me tanta virtute,
Che fa li miei sospiri gir parlando;
Ed escon fuor chiamando
La donna mia, per darmi più salute.
Questo m' avviene ovunque ella mi vede,
E sì è cosa umil, che non si crede.

§ XXIX. *Quomodo sedet sola civitas plena populo! facta est quasi vidua domina gentium.*

Io era nel proponimento ancora di questa canzone, e compiuta n' avea questa sovrascritta stanza, quando lo Signore della giustizia chiamò questa gentilissima a gloriare sotto l' insegna di quella reina benedetta Maria, lo cui nome fue in grandissima reverenza nelle parole di questa Beatrice beata.

Ed avvegnachè forse piacerebbe al presente trattare alquanto della sua partita da noi, non è mio intendimento di trattarne qui per tre ragioni: la prima si è, che ciò non è del presente proposito, se volemo guardare nel proemio, che precede questo libello; la seconda si è che, posto che fosse del presente proposito, ancora non sarebbe sufficiente la mia penna a trattare, come si converrebbe, di ciò; la terza si è che, posto che fosse l' uno e l' altro, non è convenevole a me trattare di ciò, per quello che, trattando, mi converrebbe essere lodatore di me medesimo (laqual cosa è al postutto sconvenevole e

Therefore, when he bereaveth me so of power that my spirits seem to flee away, then my frail soul feeleth such sweetness, that my visage pales thereat. Then Love takes such power over me that he maketh my sighs to go speaking, and they issue forth beseeching my lady to grant me yet further saving grace. This befalls every time she beholdeth me and is a thing so lowly that it passeth all belief.

§ XXIX. *Quomodo sedet sola civitas plena populo! facta est quasi vidua domina gentium.*

I was still at my purpose of this canzone and had finished thereof this aforewritten stanza, when the Lord of justice called this most gentle lady to dwell in glory under the ensign of that queen, the blessed Mary, whose name was in very great reverence on the lips of this blessed Beatrice.

And although perchance it were pleasing at present to treat somewhat of her departure from us, it is not my intent to treat thereof here for three reasons: the first is that it is not to the present purpose, if we have regard to the introduction which precedeth this little book; the second is that supposing it were to the present purpose, my pen would not yet be sufficient to treat thereof as were fitting; the third is that supposing both the one and the other were, it is not fitting in me to treat thereof, for that so doing it would behove me to be a praiser of myself, (which thing is unseemly and blameworthy

biasimevole a chi 'l fa), e però lascio cotale
trattato ad altro chiosatore.

Tuttavia, perchè molte volte il numero del
nove ha preso luogo tra le parole dinanzi, onde
pare che sia non senza ragione, e nella sua partita
cotale numero pare che avesse molto luogo,
conviensi qui dire alcuna cosa, acciocchè pare al
proposito convenirsi. Onde prima dirò come
ebbe luogo nella sua partita, e poi ne assegnerò
alcuna ragione, perchè questo numero fu a lei
cotanto amico.

§ XXX. Io dico che, secondo l' usanza
d'Arabia, l' anima sua nobilissima si partì nella
prima ora del nono giorno del mese; e secondo
l' usanza di Siria, ella si partì nel nono mese dell'
anno; perchè il primo mese è ivi Tisrin primo,
il quale a noi è Ottobre. E secondo l' usanza
nostra, elle si partì in quello anno della nostra
indizione, cioè degli anni Domini, in cui il
perfetto numero nove volte era compiuto in quel
centinaio, nel quale in questo mondo ella fu
posta: ed ella fu de' Cristiani del terzodecimo
centinaio. Perchè questo numero le fosse tanto
amico, questa potrebb' essere una ragione; conciossiacosachè, secondo Tolomeo e secondo la
cristiana verità, nove siano li cieli che si muovono,
e secondo comune opinione astrologica li detti
cieli adoperino quaggiù secondo la loro abitudine
insieme; questo numero fu amico di lei per dare
ad intendere, che nella sua generazione tutti e
nove li mobili cieli perfettissimamente s' aveano
insieme. Questa è una ragione di ciò; ma più

beyond all things in him who doeth it), and therefore I leave such treatise to other interpreter.

Yet, because many times the number nine hath found place among the preceding words, whereby it appeareth that it is not without reason, and in her departure such number appears to have much place, it is meet here to say something, inasmuch as it appeareth to be fitting to the purpose. Wherefore I will first tell what place it had in her departure and then I will assign some reason why this number was so friendly to her.

§ XXX. I say that according to the Arabian style her most noble soul departed in the first hour of the ninth day of the month; and according to the Syrian style, it departed on the ninth month of the year, because the first month there is Tisrin I. which with us is October. And according to our style, she departed in that year of our era, namely of the years of our Lord, wherein the perfect number was completed nine times in that century wherein she was placed in this world, and she was of the Christians of the thirteenth century. Why that number was so friendly to her, this might be a reason : inasmuch as according to Ptolemy and according to christian verity, nine are the heavens that move, and according to the general opinion of astrologers the said heavens operate here below according to their conjunctions, this number was friendly to her to give to understand, that at her birth the whole nine moving heavens were most perfectly related together. This is one reason for it : but thinking more

sottilmente pensando, e secondo la infallibile
verità, questo numero fu ella medesima; per
similitudine dico, e ciò intendo cosi : Lo numero
del tre è la radice del nove, perocchè senz' altro
numero, per sè medesimo moltiplicato, fa nove,
siccome vedemo manifestamente che tre via tre
fa nove. Dunque se il tre è fattore per sè
medesimo del nove, e lo fattore dei miracoli per
sè medesimo è tre, cioè Padre, Figliuolo e Spirito
santo, li quali sono tre ed uno, questa donna fu
accompagnata dal numero del nove a dare ad intendere, che ella era un nove, cioè un miracolo,
la cui radice è solamente la mirabile Trinitate.
Forse ancora per più sottil persona si vedrebbe
in ciò più sottil ragione ; ma questa è quella ch'
io ne veggio, e che più mi piace.

§ XXXI. Poichè la gentilissima donna fu
partita da questo secolo, rimase tutta la sopradetta
cittade quasi vedova e dispogliata di ogni
dignitade, ond' io, ancora lagrimando in questa
desolata cittade, scrissi a' principi della terra
alquanto della sua condizione, pigliando quello
cominciamento di Geremia : *Quomodo sedet sola
civitas !* E questo dico, acciocchè altri non si
meravigli, perchè io l'abbia allegato di sopra,
quasi come entrata della nuova materia che
appresso viene. E se alcuno volesse me
riprendere di ciò che non scrivo qui le parole che
seguitano a quelle allegate, scusomene, perocchè
lo intendimento mio non fu da principio di
scrivere altro che per volgare : onde, conciossiacosachè le parole, che seguitano a quelle che
sono allegate, sieno tutte latine, sarebbe fuori del
mio intendimento se io le scrivessi ; e simile

subtly and according to infallible truth, this number was her very self; by similitude I mean and I understand it thus: The number three is the root of nine because, without other number, multiplied by itself it makes nine, even as we see manifestly that three times three make nine. Therefore if three is the sole factor of nine and the sole factor of miracles is three, namely Father, Son and Holy Ghost, who are three and one, this lady was accompanied by the number nine to give to understand that she was a nine, that is, a miracle whose root is the wondrous Trinity alone. Perchance a more subtle person might see in it a yet more subtle reason; but this is what I see therein and what pleaseth me most.

§ XXXI. After the most gentle lady had departed from this world, all the aforesaid city was left as 'twere widowed and bereft of all worthiness; wherefore I, still weeping in this desolate city, wrote to the chief people of the land somewhat of its condition, taking that beginning of Jeremiah the prophet: *Quomodo sedet sola civitas!* And this I say, in order that folk may not marvel that I have cited it above, as 'twere the portal of the new matter that cometh after. And if any one should desire to reprove me because I do not here write the words that follow those cited, I excuse me herein:—that my intention was from the beginning not to write otherwise than in the vulgar tongue: wherefore, inasmuch as the words that follow those cited are all latin, it were beside my purpose if I wrote them: and a

intenzione so che ebbe questo mio amico, a cui
ciò scrivo, cioè ch' io gli scrivessi solamente in
volgare.

§ XXXII. Poichè gli occhi miei ebbero per
alquanto tempo lagrimato, e tanto affaticati erano
ch' io non potea disfogare la mia tristizia, pensai
di voler disfogarla con alquante parole dolorose;
e però proposi di fare una canzone, nella quale
piangendo ragionassi di lei, per cui tanto dolore
era fatto distruggitore dell' anima mia; e
cominciai allora: *Gli occhi dolenti* ec.

Acciocchè questa canzone paia rimanere viepiù
vedova dopo il suo fine, la dividerò prima ch' io la
scriva: e cotal modo terrò da qui innanzi. Io
dico che questa cattivella canzone ha tre parti: la
prima è proemio; nella seconda ragiono di lei;
nella terza parlo alla canzone pietosamente. La
seconda comincia quivi: Ita n' è Beatrice; *la terza*
quivi: Pietosa mia canzone. *La prima si divide*
in tre: nella prima dico per che mi muovo a dire;
nella seconda dico, a cui voglio dire; nella terza
dico, di cui voglio dire. La seconda comincia
quivi: E perchè mi ricorda; *la terza quivi:* E
dicerò. *Poscia quando dico:* Ita n' è Beatrice,
ragiono di lei, e intorno a ciò fo due parti. Prima
dico la cagione perchè tolta ne fu; appresso dico
come altri piange della sua partita, e comincia questa
parte quivi: Partissi della sua. *Questa parte si*
divide in tre: nella prima dico chi non la piange;
nella seconda dico chi la piange; nella terza
dico della mia condizione. La seconde comincia
quivi: Ma n' ha tristizia e doglia; *la terza:*

like intent I know had my friend to whom I am writing this, namely, that I should write to him only in the vulgar tongue.

§ XXXII. After mine eyes had for some time wept and were so weary that I could not ease my sorrow, I thought I would ease it in some dolorous words; therefore I purposed to make a canzone, wherein lamenting, I should discourse of her, through whom sorrow so great had been the destroyer of my soul; and then I began: *Sorrowing for pity*, etc.

In order that this canzone may appear far more widowed after its end, I will divide it before I write it: and such fashion will I hold to from this point forward. I say that this poor little canzone hath three parts: the first is the introduction; in the second I discourse of her; in the third I speak piteously to the Canzone. The second begins here: Gone is Beatrice; *the third here:* My piteous song. *The first divides into three: in the first I say wherefore I am moved to speak; in the second I say to whom I would speak; in the third I say of whom I would speak. The second beginneth here:* And because I remember; *the third:* And weeping I will tell. *Then when I say:* Gone is Beatrice, *I discourse of her, and of that I make two parts. First I tell the reason why she was taken from us, afterwards I say how folk wept at her departure, and this part begins:* From her fair body. *This part divides into three. In the first I tell who weepeth not for her; in the second I tell who weepeth for her; in the third I tell of my condition. The second begins here:* But he who beholdeth; *the*

Dannomi angoscia. *Poscia quando dico :* Pietosa
mia canzone, *parlo a questa mia canzone*
designandole a quali donne sen vada, e steasi con
loro.

Gli occhi dolenti per pietà del core
　　Hanno di lagrimar sofferta pena,
　　Sì che per vinti son rimasi omai.
　　Ora s'io voglio sfogar lo dolore,
　　Che appoco appoco alla morte mi mena
　　Convenemi parlar traendo guai.
　　E perchè mi ricorda ch' io parlai
　　Della mia donna, mentre che vivia,
　　Donne gentili, volentier con vui,
　　Non vo' parlarne altrui,
　　Se non a cor gentil che 'n donna sia ;
　　E dicerò di lei piangendo, pui
　　Che se n' è gita in ciel subitamente,
　　Ed ha lasciato Amor meco dolente.

Ita n' è Beatrice in l' alto cielo,
　　Nel reame ove gli angeli hanno pace,
　　E sta con loro ; e voi, donne, ha lasciate.
　　Non la ci tolse qualità di gelo,
　　Nè di calor, siccome l' altre face ;
　　Ma sola fu sua gran benignitate.
　　Chè luce della sua umilitate
　　Passò li cieli con tanta virtute,
　　Che fe maravigliar l' eterno Sire,
　　Sì che dolce desire
　　Lo giunse di chiamar tanta salute,
　　E fella di quaggiuso a sè venire ;
　　Perchè vedea ch' esta vita noiosa
　　Non era degna di sì gentil cosa.

third, Sighs give me great anguish. *Then when
I say :* My piteous song, *I speak to this my
canzone, pointing out to her, what ladies she may
go to and with them may abide.*

Sorrowing for pity of my heart, mine eyes
have suffered such pain of weeping that now
they lie vanquished. Now if I would ease
my sorrow that little by little bringeth me
unto death, it behoves me to speak uttering
lamentations. And because I remember
that I spake of my lady, while she lived,
gentle ladies, willingly with you, I would
not speak of her to other, save to a gentle
heart that in woman may be. And weeping,
will tell of her, since she hath passed straightway to heaven and hath left Love with me
sorrowing.

Gone is Beatrice into high heaven, to the realm
where the angels are in peace and abideth
with them ; and you, ladies, hath she left.
Not her from us, excess of cold did take, nor
yet of heat, even as it doth the others, but
'twas alone her great benignness; for the
light of her humility pierced the heavens
with such power that it made the eternal
Lord to marvel, so that sweet desire came
upon him to summon perfection so great, and
he made her come unto himself from here
below, because he saw that this weariful
life was unworthy of a thing so gentle.

Partissi della sua bella persona
   Piena di grazia l' anima gentile,
   Ed èssi gloriosa in loco degno.
   Chi non la piange, quando ne ragiona,
   Core ha di pietra sì malvagio e vile,
   Ch' entrar non vi può spirito benegno.
   Non è di cor villan sì alto ingegno,
   Che possa immaginar di lei alquanto,
   E però non gli vien di pianger voglia:
   Ma n' ha tristizia e doglia
   Di sospirare e di morir di pianto,
   E d' ogni consolar l' anima spoglia,
   Chi vede nel pensiero alcuna volta
   Qual ella fu, e com' ella n' è tolta.

Dannomi angoscia li sospiri forte,
   Quando il pensiero nella mente grave
   Mi reca quella che m' ha il cor diviso:
   E spesse fiate pensando la morte,
   Me ne viene un desio tanto soave,
   Che mi tramuta lo color nel viso.
   Quando l' immaginar mi tien ben fiso,
   Giugnemi tanta pena d' ogni parte,
   Ch' i' mi riscuoto per dolor ch' io sento
   E si fatto divento,
   Che dalle genti vergogna mi parte.
   Poscia piangendo, sol nel mio lamento
   Chiamo Beatrice; e dico: Or, se' tu morta!
   E mentre ch'io la chiamo, mi conforta.

Pianger di doglia e sospirar d' angoscia
   Mi strugge il core ovunque sol mi trovo,
   Sì che ne increscerebbe a chi 'l vedesse.

From her fair body the gentle soul departed, full of grace and dwells in glory in a worthy place. Whoso weeps not for her when he discourseth of her, hath a heart of stone so evil and base that no spirit benign can enter there. The churlish heart hath never wit so high that can imagine aught of her and therefore no desire to weep cometh upon it: but he who in thought but once beholdeth what she was and how she is taken from us, hath grief and sorrow thereat, yea, even to sigh and die of weeping, and strippeth his soul of all consolation.

Sighs give me great anguish, when in my heavy memory, thought recalls to me her who hath cleft my heart, and oft-times thinking of Death, there cometh upon me a desire so sweet that it changeth the hue of my countenance. When the vision holdeth me right steadfastly, pain so great seizeth me on every side that I return to myself through the sorrow I feel, and so changed become that shame sundereth me from all people. Then weeping, I call alone on Beatrice in my lamentation, and say: Now art thou dead! And while I call on her, am comforted.

Tears of sorrow and sighs of anguish desolate my heart, wheresoe'er I find me alone, so that he should have ruth who beheld it.

E qual è stata la mia vita, poscia
Che la mia donna andò nel secol novo,
Lingua non è che dicer lo sapesse :
E però, donne mie, per ch' io volesse,
Non vi saprei ben dicer quel ch' io sono ;
Sì mi fa travagliar l' acerba vita ;
La quale è sì invilita,
Che ogni uom par che mi dica: Io t'abbandono,
Vedendo la mia labbia tramortita.
Ma qual ch' io sia, la mia donna sel vede,
Ed io ne spero ancor da lei mercede.

Pietosa mia canzone, or va piangendo ;
E ritrova le donne e le donzelle,
A cui le tue sorelle
Erano usate di portar letizia ;
E tu, che sei figliuola di tristizia,
Vattene sconsolata a star con elle.

§ XXXIII. Poichè detta fu questa canzone, si
venne a me uno, il quale, secondo li gradi dell'
amistade, era amico a me immediatamente dopo
il primo : e questi fu tanto distretto di sanguinità con questa gloriosa, che nullo più presso l'
era. E poiche fu meco a ragionare, mi pregò
che io gli dovessi dire alcuna cosa per una donna
che s' era morta ; e simulava sue parole, acciocchè paresse che dicesse d' un' altra, la quale
morta era cortamente : ond' io accorgendomi che
questi dicea solo per quella benedetta, dissi di
fare ciò che mi domandava lo suo prego. Ond'
io poi pensando a ciò, proposi di fare un sonetto,
nel quale mi lamentassi alquanto, e di darlo a

And what my life hath been since my lady
passed into the new world, tongue is not that
could tell: and therefore ladies mine, even if I
would, myself could not well tell what I am,
so my bitter life maketh me travail; which is
so base become that every man seemeth to say
to me on beholding my pallid face: I forsake
thee. But what I may be, my lady's self
doth see, and I yet hope guerdon of it from
her.

My piteous song, now go thy weeping way;
and find the dames and damsels to whom
thy sisters were wont to bring gladness; and
thou that art sorrow's child, go hence disconsolate to abide with them.

§ XXXIII. After this canzone had been
composed there came to me one who, according
to the degrees of friendship, is my friend immediately after the first; and he was so closely united
in kinship to this glorious lady that none was
nearer to her. And after he had been discoursing with me, he prayed me that I should compose
him something for a lady who had died; and he
dissimulated his words in order that it might
appear that he spoke of another who had shortly
died; wherefore perceiving that he was speaking
solely because of this blessed one, I said I would
do what his prayer asked of me. Wherefore
pondering on this, I purposed to make a sonnet
in which I should mourn somewhat, and give it

questo mio amico, acciocchè paresse, che per lui l' avessi fatto; e dissi allora: *Venite a intendere* ec.

Questo sonetto ha due parti : nella prima chiamo li fedeli d' Amore che m' intendano ; nella seconda narro della mia misera condizione. La seconda comincia quivi : Li quali sconsolati.

Venite a intender li sospiri miei,
    O cor gentili, chè pietà il desia ;
    Li quali sconsolati vanno via,
    E s' e' non fosser, di dolor morrei ;

Perocchè gli occhi mi sarebbon rei
    Molte fiate più ch' io non vorria,
    Lasso ! di pianger sì la donna mia,
    Ch' io sfogherei lo cor, piangendo lei.

Voi udirete lor chiamar sovente
    La mia donna gentil, che se n' è gita
    Al secol degno della sua virtute ;

E dispregiar talora questa vita,
    In persona dell' anima dolente,
    Abbandonata dalla sua salute.

§ XXXIV. Poichè detto ebbi questo sonetto, pensando chi questi era, cui lo intendeva dare quasi come per lui fatto, vidi che povero mi pareva lo servigio e nudo a così distretta persona di questa gloriosa. E però innanzi ch' io gli dessi il soprascritto sonetto, dissi due stanze di una canzone; l' una per costui veracemente, e l' altra per me, avvegnachè paia l' una e l' altra per una persona detta, a chi non guarda sottil-

to this my friend in order that it should appear
that I had done it for him; and I composed
then this sonnet: *Come and hear* etc.

*This sonnet hath two parts: in the first I call
upon Love's lieges that they hear me; in the second
I relate my wretched condition. The second begins
here:* Which go forth disconsolate.

Come and hear my sighs ye gentle hearts, (for
 pity asketh it), which go forth disconsolate;
 and were it not for them I should die of
 grief;

because mine eyes would be my debtors, many
 more times than I would desire, woe is me!
 for such due weeping for my lady that I might
 ease my heart, bewailing her.

Ye will hear them oft call upon my gentle lady,
 who hath gone to the world worthy of her
 virtue,

and disprize sometimes this life, in the person
 of the sorrowing soul, forsaken by its salvation.

§ XXXIV. After I had composed this
sonnet, thinking who he was to whom I intended
to give it as though written in his name, I
perceived that this seemed but poor and naked
service for a person so closely akin to this
glorious lady. And therefore ere I gave him
the above written sonnet, I composed two
stanzas of a canzone; one for him truly, the
other for myself, although to one who looketh not
subtly, both seem to be composed for one person.

mente. Ma chi sottilmente le mira vede bene
che diverse persone parlano; in ciò che l' una
non chiama sua donna costei, e l' altra sì, come
appare manifestamente. Questa canzone e
questo sonetto gli diedi, dicendo io che per lui
solo fatto l' avea.

La canzone comincia : Quantunque volte, *ed
ha due parti : nell' una cioè nella prima stanza, si
lamenta questo mio caro amico, distretto a lei ; nella
seconda mi lamento io cioè nell' altra stanza che
comincia :* E' si raccoglie. *E così appare che
in questa canzone si lamentano due persone l' una
delle quali si lamenta come fratello, l' altra come
servitore.*

Quantunque volte, lasso ! mi rimembra
  Ch' io non debbo giammai
  Veder la donna, ond' io vo sì dolente,
  Tanto dolore intorno al cor m' assembra
  La dolorosa mente,
  Ch' io dico : Anima mia, che non ten vai ?
  Chè li tormenti, che tu porterai
  Nel secol che t' è già tanto noioso,
  Mi fan pensoso di paura forte ;
  Ond' io chiamo la Morte,
  Come soave e dolce mio riposo ;
  E dico : Vieni a me ! con tanto amore,
  Ch' io sono astioso di chiunque muore.

E' si raccoglie negli miei sospiri
  Un suono di pietate,
  Che va chiamando Morte tuttavia.
  A lei si volser tutti i miei desiri,
  Quando la donna mia
  Fu giunta dalla sua crudelitate :

But whoso considereth them subtly, perceiveth well that different persons are speaking; in that one calleth her not his lady and the other doth, even as manifestly appears. This canzone and this sonnet gave I him, saying, that solely for him I had made them.

The canzone begins : How many times so'er, *and hath two parts : in one, namely, in the first stanza, this my friend dear to me, and close akin to her mourneth ; in the second it is I who mourn, namely, in the other stanza that begins :* There gathers. *And thus it appeareth that in the canzone two persons mourn, one of whom mourns as a brother, the other as a servant.*

How many times so'er, alas ! I remember that never more shall I behold the lady for whom I go thus sorrowing, such grief my grieving mind gathereth about my heart, that I say : My soul, why departest thou not ? for the torments thou shalt endure in the world that is now so hateful to thee, make me pensive with great fear; wherefore I call on Death as my sweet and gentle rest and say : Come unto me ! with love so great that envious am I of whosoever dieth.

There gathers in my sighs a sound of anguish that goeth forth calling on Death evermore. To him turned all my desires when my lady was smitten by his cruelty : because her

Perchè il piacere della sua beltate
Partendo sè dalla nostra veduta,
Divenne spiral bellezza grande,
Che per lo cielo spande
Luce d' amor, che gli angeli saluta,
E lo intelletto loro alto e sottile
Face maravigliar ; tanto è gentile !

§ XXXV. In quel giorno, nel quale si com-
piva l' anno, che questa donna era fatta de'
cittadini di vita eterna, io mi sedea in parte,
nella quale ricordandomi di lei, disegnava un
angelo sopra certe tavolette : e mentre io 'l
disegnava, volsi gli occhi, e vidi lungo me
uomini a' quali si convenia di fare onore. E'
riguardavano quello ch' io facea ; e secondo che
mi fu detto poi, egli erano stati già alquanto
anzi che io me n' accorgessi. Quando li vidi,
mi levai, e salutando loro dissi : Altri era testè
meco, e perciò pensava. Onde partiti costoro,
ritornaimi alla mia opera, cioè del disegnare
figure d' angeli : facendo ciò, mi venne un pensiero di dire parole per rima, quasi per annovale
di lei, e scrivere a costoro, li quali erano venuti
a me : e dissi allora questo sonetto, che comincia
Era venuta, lo quale ha due cominciamenti ; e
però lo dividerò secondo l' uno e l' altro.

Dico che secondo il primo, questo sonetto ha tre
parti : nella prima dico, che questa donna era già
nella mia memoria ; nella seconda dico quello che
Amore però mi facea ; nella terza dico degli effetti
d'Amore. La seconda comincia quivi ; Amor

winsome beauty withdrawing itself from our sight, became a great spiritual loveliness, which through heaven sheds a light of love, that saluteth the angels and maketh their high and rare intelligence to marvel; so gentle it is!

§ XXXV. On that day in which the year was completed when this lady was made of the citizens of life eternal, I was sitting in a place wherein, remembering her, I was drawing an angel upon certain tablets: and while I was drawing I turned mine eyes and beheld alongside me men to whom honour was due. And they were looking at what I was doing and, according as was told to me afterwards, they had been there already some while before I perceived them. When I beheld them I arose, and greeting them said: Someone was but now with me and therefore was I in thought. Wherefore they being departed I returned to my work, namely, to the drawing of figures of angels. While doing this a thought came to me to compose words in rhyme as for her anniversary and to write to those who had come to me: and I then composed this sonnet which begins: *There had come*, which hath two beginnings: and therefore I will divide it according to both:

I say that according to the first beginning this sonnet hath three parts; in the first I say that this lady was already in my mind; in the second I tell what Love therefore did to me; in the third I tell of the effects of Love. The second begins here;

che; *la terza quivi* : Piangendo usciano. *Questa*
parte si divide in due : nell' una dico che tutti i
miei sospiri usciano parlando ; nell' altra dico come
alquanti diceano certe parole diverse dagli altri.
La seconda comincia quivi : Ma quelli. *Per*
questo medesimo modo si divide secondo l'altro
cominciamento, salvo che nella prima parte dico
quando questa donna era così venuta nella mia
mente, e ciò non dico nell' altro.

Primo cominciamento

Era venuta nella mente mia
   La gentil donna, che per suo valore
   Fu posta dall' altissimo signore
   Nel ciel dell' umiltate, ov è Maria.

Secondo cominciamento

Era venuta nella mente mia
   Quella donna gentil, cui piange Amore,
   Entro quel punto, che lo suo valore
   Vi trasse a riguardar quel ch' io facia.

Amor, che nella mente la sentia,
   S' era svegliato nel distrutto core,
   E diceva a' sospiri : Andate fuore ;
   Per che ciascun dolente sen partia.

Piangendo usciano fuori del mio petto
   Con una voce, che sovente mena
   Le lagrime dogliose agli occhi tristi.

Ma quelli, che n' uscian con maggior pena,
   Venien dicendo : O nobile intelletto,
   Oggi fa l' anno che nel ciel salisti.

Love who; *the third here*; Wailing they issued. *This part divides itself into two; in one I say that all my sighs issued forth speaking; in the other I tell how some of them said certain words different from the others. The second begins here; But they. In the same manner it is divided according to the other beginning, save that in the first part I tell when this lady had come into my memory and this I say not in the other.*

First Beginning

There had come into my mind the gentle lady, who for her worth was placed by the most high Lord in the heaven of peace, where Mary is.

Second Beginning

There had come into my mind that gentle lady, whom Love bewaileth, at the very moment when her virtue drew you to look at that which I was doing.

Love, who perceived her in my mind, was wakened in my wasted heart and said to my sighs: Fare forth; wherefore each one departed sorrowing.

Wailing they issued forth from my breast with a voice that oft bringeth grievous tears to my sad eyes.

But they that issued thence with greatest smart came saying: O noble intellect, to-day maketh a year since thou didst ascend to heaven.

E

§ XXXVI. Poi per alquanto tempo, concio-
fossecosachè io fossi in parte, nella quale mi
ricordava del passato tempo, molto stava pensoso,
e con dolorosi pensamenti tanto che mi faceano
parere di fuori d'una vista di terribile sbigotti-
mento.   Ond' io, accorgendomi del mio travagliare, levai gli occhi per vedere s' altri me
vedesse.   Allora vidi una gentil donna giovane e
bella molto, la quale da una fenestra mi riguardava molto pietosamente quant' alla vista; sicchè
tutta la pietade pareva in lei accolta.   Onde,
conciossiacosachè quando i miseri veggono di
loro compassione altrui, più tosto si muovono a
lagrimare, quasi, come di sè stessi avendo pietade,
io sentii allora li miei occhi cominciare a voler
piangere; e però, temendo di non mostrare la
mia vile vita, mi partii dinanzi dagli occhi di
questa gentile; e dicea poi fra me medesimo:
E' non può essere, che con quella pietosa donna
non sia nobilissimo amore.   E però proposi di
dire un sonetto, nel quale io parlassi a lei, e
conchiudessi in esso tutto ciò che narrato è in
questa ragione.   E però che questa ragione è
assai manifesta, nol dividerò.

Videro gli occhi miei quanta pietate
    Era apparita in la vostra figura,
    Quando guardaste gli atti e la statura,
    Ch' io facia pel dolor molte fiate.

Allor m' accorsi che voi pensavate
    La qualità della mia vita oscura,
    Sicchè mi giunse nello cor paura
    Di dimostrar cogli occhi mia viltate.

§ XXXVI. Then sometime after, forasmuch as I was in a place where I was recalling the time that was past, I stood very pensive and with thoughts so sorrowful that they made me appear outwardly with semblance of dreadful dismay. Wherefore, perceiving my travail, I lifted mine eyes to see if any beheld me. Then saw I a gentle lady, young and most fair, who gazed at me from a window very compassionately, so far as it appeared, so that all compassion seemed gathered in her. Wherefore, inasmuch as when the wretched behold compassion for them in another, they are the sooner moved to tears, as though having compassion for themselves, I then felt mine eyes begin to desire to weep: and therefore, fearing lest I should betray my abject state, I departed from before the eyes of this gentle one and said then within myself: It cannot be but that most noble Love is with that compassionate lady. And therefore I purposed to compose a sonnet, wherein I might speak to her and comprehend therein all that is related in this discourse, and since this sonnet is plain enough I will not divide it.

Mine eyes beheld what great compassion was
    shown forth in your countenance when you
    gazed on the features and presence, which
    oft-times were mine through grief.

Then I perceived that you were thinking on the
    nature of my life of gloom, so that fear entered
    my breast lest I should betray my faint-
    heartedness by mine eyes.

E tolsimi dinanzi a voi, sentendo
  Che si movean le lagrime dal core,
  Ch' era sommosso dalla vostra vista.

Io dicea poscia nell' anima trista :
  Ben è con quella donna quello amore,
  Lo qual mi face andar così piangendo.

§ XXXVII. Avvenne poi che ovunque questa
donna mi vedea, si facea d' una vista pietosa e
d' un color pallido, quasi come d' amore : onde
molte fiate mi ricordava della mia nobilissima
donna, che di simile colore mi si mostrava.   E
certo molte volte non potendo lagrimare nè
disfogare la mia tristizia, io andava per vedere
questa pietosa donna, la quale parea che tirasse
le lagrime fuori delli miei occhi per la sua vista.
E però mi venne anche volontade di dire parole,
parlando a lei ; e dissi questo sonnetto, che
comincia *Color d' Amore*, e ch' è piano senza
dividerlo, per la sua precedente ragione.

Color d' amore, e di pietà sembianti,
  Non preser mai così mirabilmente
  Viso di donna, per veder sovente
  Occhi gentili, e dolorosi pianti,

Come lo vostro, qualora davanti
  Vedetevi la mia labbia dolente ;
  Sì che per voi mi vien cosa alla mente,
  Ch' io temo forte non lo cor si schianti.

Io non posso tener gli occhi distrutti
  Che non riguardin voi spesse fiate,
  Pel desiderio di pianger ch' egli hanno :

And I withdrew me from before you, feeling that tears were springing from my heart that was stirred by sight of you.

Then said I in my sad soul: Truly with that lady is that Love which maketh me to go thus weeping.

§ XXXVII. It then befell that whenever this lady beheld me, she grew visibly compassionate and of pallid hue as if of love: wherefore oft-times I remembered me of my most noble lady who was ever wont to show herself of like hue. And certes many times being unable to weep or to ease my sorrow, I went to behold this compassionate lady who seemed to draw tears forth from mine eyes by her aspect. And therefore a further desire came to me to compose words addressed to her; and I composed this sonnet which begins, *Love's hue*, and which is plain without any division because of the discourse that precedeth it.

Love's hue and Pity's semblance ne'er did face of woman take so wondrously, through oft beholding gentle eyes and dolorous tears,

as did yours, what time you beheld before you my sorrowing countenance; so that through you, that cometh to my mind, whereat I sorely fear lest my heart may break.

I cannot withhold my wasted eyes that they gaze not on you many times, for the desire to weep that they have:

E voi crescete sì lor volontate,
  Che della voglia si consuman tutti;
  Ma lagrimar dinanzi a voi non sanno.

§ XXXVIII. Io venni a tanto per la vista di
questa donna, che li miei occhi si cominciaro a
dilettare troppo di vederla; onde molte volte
me ne crucciava nel mio cuore ed avevamene per
vile assai; e più volte bestemmiava la vanità
degli occhi miei, e dicea loro nel mio pensiero:
Or voi solevate far piangere chi vedea la vostra
dolorosa condizione, ed ora, pare che vogliate
dimenticarlo per questa donna che vi mira, e che
non vi mira se non in quanto le pesa della
gloriosa donna di cui pianger solete; ma quanto
far potete, fate; chè io la vi rimembrerò molto
spesso, maledetti occhi: chè mai, se non dopo
la morte, non dovrebbero le vostre lagrime esser
ristate.   E quando fra me medesimo così avea
detto alli miei occhi, e li sospiri m'assaliano
grandissimi ed angosciosi.   Ed acciocchè
questa battaglia, che io avea meco, non riman-
esse saputa pur dal misero che la sentia, proposi
di fare un sonetto, e di comprendere in esso
questa orrible condizione, e dissi questo che
comincia: *L'amaro lagrimar.*

*Questo sonetto ha due parti: nella prima parlo
agli occhi miei siccome parlava lo mio core in me
medesimo; nella seconda rimovo alcuna dubitazione,
manifestando chi è che così parla; e questa parte
comincia quivi:* Così dice. *Potrebbe bene ancora
ricevere più divisioni, ma sarebbe indarno, perchè
è manifesto per la precedente ragione.*

and you quicken so their will, that by the desire
they are utterly consumed; but weep before
you they cannot.

§ XXXVIII. I came to such pass by the
sight of this lady that mine eyes began to delight
over much in beholding her, wherefore many
times I was angry in my heart and held me
therefore exceeding base; and many times did I
curse the inconstancy of mine eyes and said to
them in my thoughts: Come, ye were wont to
make weep such as beheld your grievous state,
and now it seemeth that ye would forget it because of this lady who gazes at you, and gazes
not at you save in so far as she is weighed down
for the glorious lady for whom ye were wont
to weep; but, what ye can, do; for I will
recall her to you very oft, accursed eyes: since
ne'er save after death ought your tears to be
stayed.   And when I had thus said within myself to mine eyes, lo, sighs most heavy and
choking assailed me.   And in order that this
conflict which I had within me should not remain known to the wretch only who suffered it,
I purposed to make a sonnet and to comprehend
in it this dreadful condition, and I composed this
that begins: *The bitter tears.*

*This sonnet hath two parts; in the first I speak
to mine eyes even as my heart spake within myself;
in the second I remove a certain difficulty by setting
forth who it is that thus speaketh; and this part
begins here:* Thus saith.   *It might indeed receive
yet more divisions, but they would be in vain, since
it is made clear by the preceding discourse.*

L' amaro lagrimar che voi faceste,
  Occhi miei, così lunga stagione,
  Facea lagrimar l' altre persone
  Della pietate, come voi vedeste.

Ora mi par che voi l'obliereste,
  S' io fossi dal mio lato sì fellone,
  Ch' io non ven disturbassi ogni cagione,
  Membrandovi colei, cui voi piangeste.

La vostra vanità mi fa pensare,
  E spaventami sì ch' io temo forte
  Del viso d' una donna che vi mira.

Voi non dovreste mai, se non per morte
  La nostra donna, ch' è morta, obliare:
  Così dice il mio core, e poi sospira.

§ XXXIX. Recommi la vista di questa donna
in sì nova condizione, che molte volte ne pensava
come di persona che troppo mi piacesse. E
pensava di lei così: Questa è una donna gentile,
bella, giovane e savia, ed apparita forse per
volontà d' Amore, acciocchè la mia vita si
riposi. E molte volte pensava più amorosamente,
tanto che il core consentiva in lui, cioè nel mio
ragionare. E quando avea consentito ciò, io mi
ripensava siccome dalla ragione mosso, e dicea
fra me medesimo: Deh, che pensiero è questo,
che in così vile modo mi vuol consolare, e non
mi lascia quasi altro pensare! Poi si rilevava un
altro pensiero, e dicea: Or che tu se' stato in
tanta tribulazione perchè non vuoi tu ritrarti da
tanta amaritudine? Tu vedi che questo è uno

The bitter tears ye wept, eyes of mine, so long
  a season, were wont to make other folk to weep
  with pity as ye have seen.

Now methinks ye would forget her, if on my
  side I so recreant were, as not to thwart every
  impulse thereto, by recalling to you her for
  whom ye wept.

Your levity sets me pondering and affrighteth me
  so, that I fear sorely the sight of a lady that
  gazeth upon you.

Ne'er should ye, save through death, forget our
  lady who is dead: thus saith my heart and
  then doth sigh.

§ XXXIX. The sight of this lady brought
me into so strange a state, that many times I
thought of her as of one who pleased me over
much. And thus I thought of her: This is a
gentle lady, fair, young and wise, and hath
appeared perchance by Love's will, in order that
my life may find rest. And many times I had
still more loving thought, so that my heart consented to it, namely, to my pleading. And when
it had consented to this, I bethought me again as
if moved by reason and said within myself: Ah!
what thought is this that in so foul a guise would
console me and scarce suffereth me to think on
aught else! Then uprose another thought and
said: Now since thou hast been in such tribulation, wherefore wilt thou not withdraw thee from
such bitterness? Thou seest that this is an in-

*E

spiramento, che ne reca li desiri d' Amore
dinanzi, ed è mosso da così gentil parte, com' è
quella degli occhi della donna, che tanto pietosa
ti s' è mostrata.   Ond' io avendo così più volte
combattuto in me medesimo, ancora ne volli
dire alquante parole ; e perocchè la battaglia de'
pensieri vinceano coloro che per lei parlavano,
mi parve che si convenisse di parlare a lei ; e
dissi questo sonetto, il quale comincia : *Gentil
pensiero* ; e dissi *gentile* in quanto ragionava di
gentil donna, che per altro era vilissimo.

In questo sonetto fo due parti di me, secondo
che li miei pensieri erano in due divisi.   L' una
parte chiamo *cuore*, cioè l' appetito ; l' altra *anima*
cioè la ragione ; e dico come l' uno dice all' altro.
E che degno sia chiamare l' appetito cuore,
e la ragione anima, assai è manifesto a coloro,
a cui mi piace che ciò sia aperto.   Vero è che
nel precedente sonetto io fo la parte del cuore
contro a quella degli occhi, e ciò pare contrario
di quel ch' io dico nel presente : e però dico,
che anche ivi il cuore intendo per l' appetito,
perocchè maggior desiderio era il mio ancora di
ricordarmi della gentilissima donna mia, che di
vedere costei, avvegnachè alcuno appetito ne
avessi già, ma leggier paresse : onde appare che
l' uno detto non è contrario all' altro.

*Questo sonetto ha tre parti : nella prima
comincio a dire a questa donna come lo mio desiderio
si volge tutto verso lei ; nella seconda dico come
l'anima, cioè la ragione, dice al cuore, cioè all'
appetito ; nella terza dico come le risponde.   La*

spiration which proffers us Love's desires and
springeth from a place so gentle as the lady's
eyes who hath shown such compassion for thee.
Wherefore having thus many times wrestled
within myself, I desired to utter some further
words concerning it; and since they that pleaded
for her, won the battle of thoughts, methought it
were fitting to speak to her and I composed this
sonnet which begins: *A gentle thought*. And I
say *gentle* in so far as it discoursed of a gentle
lady, for otherwise it was most base.

In this sonnet I make of me two parts according
as my thoughts were divided in twain. One
part, to wit, appetite, I call *heart*; the other, to
wit, reason, I call *soul*, and I tell what one saith
to the other. And that the appetite may be
worthily called heart, and reason soul, is very
manifest to those to whom it pleaseth me that
this be plain. True it is that in the preceding
sonnet I take the part of the heart against that
of the eyes, and that seemeth contrary to what I
am saying in the present one; and therefore I
say, that there too I understand by the heart, the
appetite, since greater desire was still mine to
remember my most gentle lady than to behold
this one, albeit some appetite thereto I had
already, but slight it seemed; wherefore it
appeareth that one saying is not contrary to the
other.

*This sonnet hath three parts: in the first I
begin to say to this lady how my desire is wholly
turned towards her; in the second I say how the
soul, that is reason, speaketh to the heart, that is, to
the appetite; in the third I say how he maketh*

seconda comincia quivi : L' amina dice ; *la terza quivi :* Ei le risponde.

Gentil pensiero, che parla di vui,
    Sen viene a dimorar meco sovente,
    E ragiona d' amor sì dolcemente,
    Che face consentir lo core in lui.

L' anima dice al cor : Chi è costui,
    Che viene a consolar la nostra mente ;
    Ed è la sua virtù tanto possente,
    Ch' altro pensier non lascia star con nui ?

Ei le risponde : O anima pensosa,
    Questi è uno spiritel nuovo d' amore,
    Che reca innanzi a me li suoi desiri :

E la sua vita, e tutto il suo valore,
    Mosse dagli occhi di quella pietosa,
    Che si turbava de' nostri martiri.

§ XL. Contra questo avversario della ragione si levò un dì, quasi nell' ora di nona, una forte immaginazione in me ; chè mi parea vedere questa gloriosa Beatrice con quelle vestimenta sanguigne, colle quali apparve prima agli occhi miei, e pareami giovane in simile etade a quella, in che prima la vidi. Allora incominciai a pensare di lei ; e ricordandomene secondo l' ordine del tempo passato, lo mio core incominciò dolorosamente a pentirsi del desiderio, a cui così vilmente s' avea lasciato possedere alquanti dì contro alla costanza della ragione : e discacciato questo cotal malvagio desiderio, si rivolsero tutti i miei pensamenti alla loro

answer to her. *The second begins here :* The soul saith ; *the third here :* He answereth her.

A gentle thought, that speaketh of you, comes to dwell oft with me and discourseth of love so sweetly that it maketh the heart consent thereto.

The soul saith to the heart: Who is he, that cometh to console our mind ; and whose virtue is so puissant that it suffereth none other thought to abide with us ?

He answereth her: O pensive soul, this is a new inspiration of love, that proffereth me his desires :

And his life and all his power, sprang from the eyes of that compassionate one who was perturbed at our torments.

§ XL. Against this adversary of reason there arose one day a mighty vision within me, almost at the hour of noon ; for methought I beheld this glorious Beatrice, in those crimson garments wherein she first appeared to mine eyes, and she seemed to me youthful and of an age like to that in which I first beheld her. Then I began to think of her ; and remembering her according to the sequence of the times that were passed, my heart began to repent grievously of the desire whereby it had so basely allowed itself to be possessed for certain days, counter to the constancy of reason ; and this evil desire being cast forth, all my thoughts turned again to this most

gentilissima Beatrice. E dico che d' allora
innanzi cominciai a pensare di lei sì con tutto il
vergognoso cuore, che li sospiri manifestavano
ciò molte volte; però che quasi tutti diceano nel
loro uscire quello che nel cuore si ragionava,
cioè lo nome di quella gentilissima, e come si
partio da noi. E molte volte avvenia che tanto
dolore avea in sè alcuno pensiero, che io
dimenticava lui, e là dov' io era.

Per questo raccendimento di sospiri si raccese
lo sollenato lagrimare in guisa, che li miei occhi
pareano due cose, che desiderassero pur di
piangere: e spesso avvenia che, per lo lungo
continuare del pianto, dintorno loro si facea un
colore purpureo, quale apparir suole per alcuno
martirio ch' altri riceva: onde appare che della
loro vanità furono degnamente guiderdonati, sì
che da indi innanzi non poterono mirare persona,
che li guardasse sì che loro potesse trarre a
simile intendimento. Onde volendo che cotal
desiderio malvagio e vana tentazione paressero
distrutti sì che alcuno dubbio non potessero
inducere le rimate parole, ch' io avea dette
dinnanzi, proposi di fare un sonetto, nel quale io
comprendessi la sentenza di questo ragione. E
dissi allora: *Lasso! per forza* ec.

*Dissi lasso in quanto mi vergognava di ciò che
li miei occhi aveano così vaneggiato. Questo sonetto
non divido, però che è assai manifesta la sua
ragione.*

gentle Beatrice. And I say that from thence
forward I began to think of her with all my
shamed heart, so that my sighs made it manifest
many times; since well-nigh all uttered in their
passage what was being spoken in my heart, to
wit, the name of that most gentle one and how
she departed from us. And many times it befell
that some thought held so great pain within itself, that I forgot both it and where I was.

Through this rekindling of sighs, the alleviated
tears were rekindled in such wise that mine eyes
appeared two things whose sole desire was to
weep: and oft it befell that through long weeping they became round about of a purple hue,
such as is wont to appear through some torture
that hath been received: wherefore it appears
that they were worthily rewarded for their inconstancy, so that from thenceforth they could
not look on any person who should so gaze upon
them as perchance to draw them to a like intent.
Wherefore being minded that such an evil desire
and vain temptation should seem wholly rooted
out, and that the words in rhyme which I had
composed before should not be productive of any
doubt, I purposed to make a sonnet wherein I
should comprehend the substance of this discourse
and I then composed: *Alas! by dint etc.*

*I said alas, in that I was ashamed thereof, that
mine eyes had thus roved. I divide not this sonnet
because its argument is manifest enough.*

Lasso! per forza de' molti sospiri,
   Che nascon de' pensier che son nel core,
   Gli occhi son vinti, e non hanno valore
   Di riguardar persona che gli miri.

E fatti son, che paion due desiri
   Di lagrimare e di mostrar dolore,
   E spesse volte piangon sì, ch' Amore
   Gli cerchia di corona di martìri.

Questi pensieri, e li sospir ch' io gitto,
   Diventano nel cor sì angosciosi,
   Ch' Amor vi tramortisce, sì glien duole;

Perocch' egli hanno in sè li dolorosi,
   Quel dolce nome di madonna scritto,
   E della morte sua molte parole.

§ XLI. Dopo questa tribolazione avvenne in
quel tempo che molta gente va per vedere quella
imagine benedetta, la quale Gesù Cristo lasciò
a noi per esempio della sua bellissima figura, la
quale vede la mia donna gloriosamente, che
alquanti peregrini passavano per una via, la quale
è quasi in mezzo della cittade, ove nacque,
vivette e morio la gentilissima donna, e andavano,
secondo che mi parve, molto pensosi. Ond'
io pensando a loro, dissi fra me medesimo:
Questi peregrini mi paiono di lontana parte, e non
credo che anche udissero parlare di questa
donna, e non ne sanno niente; anzi i loro
pensieri sono d' altre cose che di queste quì:
chè forse pensano delli loro amici lontani, li
quali noi non conoscemo. Poi dicea fra me
medesimo: Io so che se questi fossero di propin-
quo paese, in alcuna vista parrebbero turbati,

Alas ! by dint of the many sighs that spring
from thoughts that are in the heart, mine
eyes are vanquished and have no power to
look on any that may gaze at them.

And are become such, that they seem two desires
to weep and to show forth anguish ; and many
times weep they so, that Love encircleth them
with a crown of torments.

These thoughts and the sighs that I utter, become so choking within the heart, that Love
pales there, it grieveth him so.

Because they, the sorrowing ones, have the
name of my lady written in them, and many
words anent her death.

§ XLI. After this tribulation it came to pass
at that season when much people go to behold
the blessed image that Jesus Christ hath left
us for ensample of his most beautiful countenance,
which my lady now beholdeth in glory, that
some pilgrims passed by a way, which is almost
in the middle of the city where the most gentle
lady was born, lived and died ; and they went,
as it seemed to me, very pensively. Wherefore
thinking on them, I said within myself : These
pilgrims seem to me to be from a far country
and I believe that they have not even heard speak
of my lady and know naught of her ; rather their
thoughts are of other things than of these here ;
for perchance they are thinking of their distant
friends whom we know not. Then said I
within myself : I know that if these were from
a near country they would appear in some wise

passando per lo mezzo della dolorosa cittade.
Poi dicea fra me stesso: S' io li potessi tenere
alquanto, io pur gli farei piangere anzi ch' egli
uscissero di questa cittade, perocchè io direi
parole, che farebbero piangere chiunque le udisse.
Onde, passati costoro dalla mia veduta, proposi
di fare un sonetto, nel quale manifestassi ciò
ch' io avea detto fra me medesimo; ed acciocchè
più paresse pietoso, proposi di dire come se io
avessi parlato loro; e dissi questo sonetto, lo
quale comincia : *Deh peregrini* ec.

Dissi *peregrini,* secondo la larga significazione
del vocabolo : chè peregrini si possono intendere
in due modi, in uno largo ed in uno stretto. In
largo, in quanto è peregrino chiunque è fuori della
patria sua; in modo stretto non s' intende peregrino, se non chi va verso la casa di santo Jacopo,
o riede: e però è da sapere, che in tre modi si
chiamano propriamente le genti, che vanno al
servigio dell' Altissimo. Chiamansi *palmieri* in
quanto vanno oltremare là onde molte volte
recano la palma; chiamansi *peregrini* in quanto
vanno alla casa di Galizia, però che la sepoltura
di santo Jacopo fu più lontana dalla sua patria che
d' alcuno altro apostolo; chiamansi *romei* in
quanto vanno a Roma, là ove questi ch' io
chiamo peregrini andavano.

Questo sonetto non si divide, pero ch' assai
il manifesta la sua ragione.

troubled on passing through the dolorous city. Then said I within myself: If I could detain them awhile, I would make them too weep ere they issued from this city because I would say words that should make whosoever heard them, weep.　Wherefore, when these had passed from my sight, I purposed to make a sonnet wherein I should show forth what I had said within myself; and in order that it might appear more piteous, I purposed to write as if I had spoken with them; and I composed this sonnet which begins: *Ah! ye pilgrims etc.*

I said *pilgrims* according to the wider meaning of the word; for *pilgrims* may be understood in two ways, one wide and another narrow.　In the wide sense, in so far as whoever is outside his fatherland is a pilgrim; in the narrow sense, none is called a pilgrim save him who is journeying towards the sanctuary of St James, or is returning: and therefore it should be known that there are three ways of properly naming folk who journey for the worship of the Most High. They are called *palmers*, in so far as they journey over the sea, there, whence many times they bring back palm branches; they are called *pilgrims* in so far as they journey to the sanctuary of Galicia, because the tomb of St James was farther from his own country than that of any other apostle; they are called *romers*, in so far as they journey to Rome, where these which I call *pilgrims*, were going.

This sonnet is not divided because its argument makes it manifest enough.

Deh peregrini, che pensosi andate
  Forse di cosa che non v' è presente,
  Venite voi di sì lontana gente,
  Come alla vista voi ne dimostrate?

Chè non piangete, quando voi passate
  Per lo suo mezzo la città dolente,
  Come quelle persone, che neente
  Par che intendesser la sua gravitate.

Se voi restate, per volerla udire,
  Certo lo core ne' sospir mi dice,
  Che lagrimando n' uscirete pui.

Ella ha perduto la sua Beatrice;
  E le parole, ch' uom di lei può dire,
  Hanno virtù di far piangere altrui.

§ XLII. Poi mandaro due donne gentili a me pregandomi che mandassi loro di queste mie parole rimate; ond' io, pensando la loro nobiltà proposi di mandar loro e di fare una cosa nuova, la quale io mandassi loro con esse, acciocchè più onorevolmente adempiessi li loro prieghi. E dissi allora un sonetto, il quale narra il mio stato, e mandailo loro col precedente sonetto accompagnato, e con un altro che comincia *Venite a intender* ec. Il sonetto, il quale io feci allora, è *Oltre lo spera* ec.

Questo sonetto ha in se cinque parti; nella prima dico là ove va il mio pensiero, nominandolo per nome di alcuno suo effetto. Nella seconda dico per che va lassù, cioè chi 'l fa così andare. Nella terza dico quello che vide, cioè una donna onorata

Ah ye pilgrims, that go lost in thought, perchance of a thing that is not present to you, come ye from folk so far away as by your aspect ye show forth?

For ye weep not when ye pass through the midst of the sorrowing city, even as folk who seem to understand naught of her heaviness.

If ye tarry for desire to hear it, certes my heart all sighing tells me, that ye will then go forth in tears.

She hath lost her Beatrice; and the words that a man can say of her, have power to make one weep.

§ XLII. Then two gentle ladies sent to me praying that I might send them some of these my words in rhyme, wherefore, thinking on their nobleness I purposed to send to them, and to write a new thing which I might send with those words, in order that I might more honourably fulfil their prayers. And I then composed a sonnet which tells of my condition and I sent it to them accompanied with the preceding sonnet and with another that begins: *Come and hear etc.* The sonnet that I then made, is: *Beyond the sphere etc.*

This sonnet hath in itself five parts; in the first I say where my thought goeth, naming it by the name of one of its effects. In the second I say why it goeth upward, to wit, who maketh it thus go. In the third I say what it saw, namely, a lady

E chiamolo allora spirito peregrino *acciocchè
spiritualmente va lassù, e sì come peregrino, la
quale è fuori della sua patria. Nella quarta dico
com' egli la vede tale, cioè in tale qualità ch' io non
la posso intendere ; cioè a dire che il mio pensiero
sale nella qualità di costei in grado che il mio intelletto nol può comprendere ; conciossiacosachè il nostro
intelletto s' abbia a quelle benedette anime, come l'
occhio nostro debole al Sole : e ciò dice il Filosofo
nel secondo della* Metafisica. *Nella quinta dico che,
avvegnachè io non possa vedere là ove il pensiero
mi trae, cioè alla sua mirabile qualità, almeno intendo questo, cioè che tutto è il cotal pensare della
mia donna, perchè io sento spesso il suo nome nel
mio pensiero. E nel fine di questa quinta parte
dico* donne mie care, *a dare ad intendere che son
donne coloro cui parlo. La seconda parte incomincia*
Intelligenza nuova ; *la terza* ; Quand' egli è
giunto ; *la quarta* : Vedela tal ; *la quinta* : So
io ch' el parla. *Potrebbesi più sottilmente ancora
dividere, e più fare intendere, ma puossi passare
con questa divisione, e però non mi trametto di più
dividerlo.*

Oltre la spera, che più larga gira,
    Passa il sospiro ch' esce del mio core :
    Intelligenza nuova, che l'Amore
    Piangendo mette in lui, pur su lo tira.

Quand' egli è giunto là dov' el desira,
    Vede una donna, che riceve onore,
    E luce si, che per lo suo splendore
    Lo peregrino spirito la mira.

honoured. And I call it then pilgrim spirit *inasmuch as in a spiritual sense it ascends even as a pilgrim who is outside his fatherland. In the fourth I say how it beholds her such, to wit, in such state, that I cannot comprehend it, which is to say, that my thought riseth to her state in such degree, that my intellect cannot comprehend it; inasmuch as our intellect is related to those blessed souls, as our weak eye is to the sun; and this the Philosopher saith in the second* book of the Metaphysics; *in the fifth I say that albeit I cannot see in that region whereto my thought draweth me, that is to say, her wondrous state, this at least I understand, namely, that such thought is wholly of my lady because I hear her name oft in my thought. And at the end of this fifth part I say:* dear ladies mine, *to give to understand that those to whom I speak are ladies. The second part begins:* A new faculty; *the third;* When it hath reached; *the fourth:* It beholdeth her such; *the fifth:* I know that it speaks. *This sonnet might be yet more subtly divided and made more comprehensible, but with this division it may pass and therefore I do not concern me to divide it further.*

Beyond the sphere, that circleth widest, passeth
    the sigh that issues from my heart: a new
    faculty that weeping Love implants in it,
    draweth it ever upwards.

When it hath reached there whereto it yearns, it
    beholdeth a lady, that receives honour and
    shineth so, that for her splendour the pilgrim
    spirit gazes on her.

Vedela tal, che, quando il mi ridice,
  Io non lo intendo, sì parla sottile
  Al cor dolente, che lo fa parlare.

So io ch' el parla di quella gentile,
  Perocchè spesso ricorda Beatrice,
  Sicch' io lo intendo ben, donne mie care.

§ XLIII. Appresso a questo sonetto apparve
a me una mirabil visione, nella quale vidi cose,
che mi fecero proporre di non dir più di questa
benedetta, infino a tanto che io non potessi più
degnamente trattare di lei. E di venire a ciò io
studio quanto posso, sì com' ella sa veracemente.
Sicchè, se piacere sarà di Colui, per cui tutte le
cose vivono, che la mia vita per alquanti anni
perseveri, spero di dire di lei quello che mai non
fu detto d' alcuna.

E poi piaccia a Colui, che' è sire della cortesia,
che la mia anima se ne possa gire a vedere la
gloria della sua donna, cioè di quella benedetta
Beatrice, che gloriosamente mira nella faccia di
Colui, *qui est per omnia sæcula benedictus.*

It beholdeth her such, that when it re-telleth it
  me, I understand it not, so subtly it speaketh
  to the sorrowing heart that maketh it to speak.

I know that it speaks of that gentle lady, for oft
  it recalleth Beatrice, so that I understand it
  well, dear ladies mine.

§ XLIII. After this sonnet there appeared
to me a wondrous vision, wherein I beheld things
that made me determine to speak no more of
this blessed one until such time as I could treat
of her more worthily. And to attain to this I
study all I may, even as she truly knoweth.
So that if it be the pleasure of him, by whom
all things live, that my life perséver for some few
years, I hope to write of her what hath never
been written of any woman.

And then may it please him who is the Lord
of grace, that my soul may have leave to go and
behold the glory of its lady, to wit, of that blessed
Beatrice who gazeth in glory on the face of him,
qui est per omnia sæcula benedictus.

NOTE ON THE "VITA NUOVA"

To readers who are content to know their Dante in an English dress the matchless translation of the "Vita Nuova" by Rossetti will ever be supreme. But there will always be those who, possessing some acquaintance with Latin or one of the Romance languages, will desire to read the very words of the master in the original; and to such this new and literal rendering is offered.

The current text has been compared with those of Moore, Beck, and Casini, and some emendations have been adopted.

CANZONIERE

§ I. CERTAINLY GENUINE—
      Sonnets I.-XIII.
      Ballads I.-IV.
      Odes I.-XV.

§ II. DOUBTFUL—
    (a) More probably authentic
        Sonnets XIV.-XVI.
        Ballad V.

    (b) More probably spurious
        Sonnets XVII.-XXI
        Ballad VI.

SONETTO I

Chi guarderà giammai senza paura
  Negli occhi d' esta bella pargoletta,
  Che m' hanno concio sì, che non s' aspetta
  Per me se non la morte, che m' è dura ?

Vedete quanto è forte mia ventura,
  Che fu tra l'altre la mia vita eletta
  Per dare esempio altrui, ch' uom non si metta
  A rischio di mirar la sua figura.

Destinata mi fu questa finita
  Dacch' uomo conveniva esser disfatto,
  Perch' altri fosse di pericol tratto :

E però lasso ! fu' io cosi ratto
  In trarre a me 'l contrario della vita,
  Come virtù di stella margherita.

SONNET 1

Who shall e'er gaze without fear in the eyes
of this fair damsel, that have ill-used me so
that I look for naught save the death that is
so dire to me ?

Behold how heavy is my fate, in that my life
was chosen from among the rest, to give
example to others, that no man brave the risk
of looking on her form.

To me this end was destined, since 'twas meet
that one man should be undone that others be
snatched from peril :

and therefore alas ! was I thus swift in drawing
to me life's contrary, even as a gem doth the
virtue of the stars.

SONETTO II

Dagli occhi della mia donna si muove
   Un lume sì gentil che dove appare,
   Si vedon cose, ch' uom non puo ritrare
   Per loro altezza e per loro esser nuove.

E da' suoi raggi sopra 'l mio cor piove
   Tanta paura, che mi fa tremare,
   E dico : Qui non voglio mai tornare ;
   Ma poscia perdo tutte le mie prove :

E tornomi colà, dov' io son vinto,
   Riconfortando gli occhi paurosi,
   Che sentìr prima questo gran valore.

Quando son giunto, lasso ! ed ei son chiusi,
   E 'l desio, che gli mena quivi, è estinto :
   Però provveggia del mio stato Amore.

SONETTO III

Degno favui trovar ogni tesoro
   La voce vostra, sì dolce e latina ;
   Ma volgibile cor ven desvicina,
   Ove stecco d'Amor mai non fe foro.

.o, che trafitto son in ogni poro
   Dal prun che con sospir si medicina,
   Pur trovo la minera in cui s' afina
   Quella virtù per cui mi discoloro.

Non è colpa del Sol, se l'orba fronte
   Nol vede, quando scende e quando poia,
   Ma della condizion malvagia e croia.

S' i' vi vedesse uscir di li occhi ploia,
   Per prova fare alle parole conte,
   Non mi porreste di sospetto in ponte.

SONNET II

From my lady's eyes there breaks a light so
gentle, that where she appeareth things are
beheld, that no man may re-tell because of
their loftiness and of their being rare.

And from their beams fear so great raineth on
my heart that I do quake and say : " Here
will I return never more " ; but soon forget
I all my trials :

and thither I return where I am undone, com-
forting again my fearful eyes that erst have
felt this great power.

Alas ! when I am arrived, lo, they are shut and
the desire that led them there is quenched.
Therefore let Love provide for my state.

SONNET III

Your muse so sweet and pure doth make you
worthy to find every treasure, but the unstable
heart, where barb of Love ne'er made a
wound, estrangeth you therefrom.

I, who am pierced through every pore by the
thorn that with sighs is physicked, find indeed
the mine where that power is refined, because
of which I grow pale.

No fault it is of the sun if the blind forehead
behold him not, when he declines and when he
mounts, but of evil and gross condition.

E'en tho' I beheld tears streaming from your
eyes to give proof to fair speech, you would
not lodge me on the ridge of doubt.

SONETTO IV

Di donne io vidi una gentile schiera
    Quest' Ognissanti prossimo passato,
    Ed una ne venia quasi primiera,
    Seco menando Amor dal destro lato.

Dagli occhi suoi gettava una lumiera,
    La qual pareva un spirito infiammato:
    E i' ebbi tanto ardir, che in la sua cera
    Guardando, vidi un angiol figurato:

A chi era degno poi dava salute
    Con gli occhi suoi quella benigna e piana,
    Empiendo il core a ciascun di virtute.

Credo che in ciel nascesse esta soprana,
    E venne in terra per nostra salute:
    Dunque beata chi l' è prossimana.

SONETTO V

E' non è legno di sì forti nocchi,
    Nè anco tanto dura alcuna pietra,
    Ch'esta crudel, che mia morte perpetra,
    Non vi mettesse amor co' suoi begli occhi.

Or dunque s' ella incontra uom che l'adocchi,
    Ben gli de' 'l cor passar, se non s'arretra;
    Onde 'l convien morir: chè mai non impetra
    Mercè, ch'il suo dever pur si spannocchi.

Deh perchè tanta virtù data fue
    Agli occhi d'una donna così acerba,
    Che suo fedel nessuno in vita serba?

Ed è contro a pietà tanto superba,
    Che s' altri muor per lei, nol mira piue,
    Anzi gli asconde le bellezze sue.

SONNET IV

Of ladies I beheld a gentle company this All
Hallows day last past, and one of them did
come as 'twere the chief, leading Love with
her on her right hand.

From her eyes she cast a light that seemed a
flaming spirit, and such boldness had I, that
gazing in her countenance, I beheld an angel's
form.

To him who was worthy then gave she salutation with her eyes, that lady benign and
lowly, filling the hearts of all with virtue.

I believe that this sovran lady was born in
heaven and came to earth for our weal:
blessed therefore she who neighbours her.

SONNET V

No wood is there of gnarls so tough nor yet any
stone so hard, that this cruel one who com-
passeth my death would not implant love
there with her fair eyes.

Therefore if she encounter a man that glanceth
at her, truly must she pierce his heart if he
retreat not; wherefore he must die; for ne'er
doth he obtain the grace that e'en his due
be reaped.

Oh! why was such power vouchsafed to eyes
of a lady so harsh, that of her lovers suffereth
none to live?

And is so haughty against pity, that if one die
for her she looketh no more on him, rather
doth she hide her loveliness from him

F

SONETTO VI

Guido, vorrei che tu e Lapo ed io
    Fossimo presi per incantamento,
    E messi ad un vascel, ch' ad ogni vento
    Per mare andasse a voler vostro e mio ;

Sicchè fortuna, od altro tempo rio
    Non ci potesse dare impedimento,
    Anzi, vivendo sempre in un talento,
    Di stare insieme crescesse il disio.

E monna Vanna e monna Lagia poi,
    Con quella ch' è sul numero del trenta,
    Con noi ponesse il buono incantatore :

E quivi ragionar sempre d'amore ;
    E ciascuna di lor fosse contenta,
    Siccome io credo che sariamo noi.

SONETTO VII

Io mi credea del tutto esser partito
    Da queste nostre rime, messer Cino ;
    Chè si conviene omai altro cammino
    Alla mia nave, già lungo dal lito :

Ma perch' i' ho di voi più volte udito,
    Che pigliar vi lasciate ad ogni uncino,
    Piacemi di prestare un pocolino
    A questa penna lo stancato dito.

Chi s' innamora (siccome voi fate)
    E ad ogni piacer si lega e scioglie,
    Mostra ch' Amor leggiermente il saetti ;

Se 'l vostro cor si piega in tante voglie,
    Per Dio vi prego che voi 'l correggiate,
    Sì che s'accordi i fatti a' dolci detti.

SONNET VI

Guido, I would that thou and Lapo and I
were taken by enchantment, and put in a
vessel, that with every wind might sail to
your will and mine;

so that tempest, or other ill weather could give
us no hindrance, rather, living ever in one
mind, our desire might wax to abide together.

And that the good magician might place with
us Mistress Vanna and Mistress Lagia, with
her who is number thirty on the roll:

and there ever to discourse of love; and that
each of them were glad even as I believe we
should be.

SONNET VII

I believed me to be wholly parted from these
our rhymes Master Cino. For henceforth
another track is meet for my bark already far
from shore.

But since I have heard of you many a time,
that ye let you be caught by every hook, it
pleaseth me to lend a while my weary fingers
to this pen.

Whoso is enamoured (as ye are) and by every
winsome form is bound and loosed, showeth
that Love doth lightly wound him.

If your heart is swayed by so many desires, for
God's sake I pray you that ye correct it, so that
there be harmony of deeds with sweet sayings.

SONETTO VIII

Io sono stato con Amore insieme
   Dalla circolazion del Sol mia nona,
   E so com' egli affrena e come sprona,
   E come sotto a lui si ride e geme.

Chi ragione o virtù contro gli spreme
   Fa come quei che 'n la tempesta suona,
   Credendo far colà dove si tuona
   Esser le guerre de' vapori sceme.

Però nel cerchio della sua palestra
   Liber arbitrio giammai non fu franco,
   Sì che consiglio invan vi si balestra:

Ben può con nuovi spron punger lo fianco,
   E qual che sia 'l piacer ch' ora n' addestra,
   Seguitar si convien, se l' altro è stanco.

SONETTO IX

O dolci rime, che parlando andate
   Della donna gentil che l' altre onora,
   A voi verrà, se non è giunto ancora,
   Un che direte: Questi è nostro frate.

Io vi scongiuro che non lo ascoltiate
   Per quel signor che le donne innamora;
   Chè nella sua sentenza non dimora
   Cosa che amica sia di veritate.

E se voi foste per le sue parole
   Mosse a venir inver la donna vostra,
   Non vi arrestate ma venite a lei:

Dite: Madonna, la venuta nostra
   È per raccomandare un che si duole
   Dicendo: Ov' è il desio degli occhi miei?

SONNET VIII

I have been with Love together since my ninth
revolution of the sun and do know how he
plyeth curb and spur, and how under him one
laughs and groans.

Whoso urgeth reason or virtue against him doth
like one who in the tempest rings a peal, thinking to make the warring vapours wane, where
thunder rolls.

But within the bounds of his arena, free-will
ne'er was emancipate, so that in vain is counsel
there shot forth :

truly he can with fresh spurs pierce the flanks, and
whatsoever be the passion that now bestrides
us, follow we must if the other be outworn.

SONNET IX

O sweet rhymes that go speaking of the gentle
Lady that bringeth honour to all others, to you
shall come, if he be not yet arrived, one, of
whom ye will say : This is our brother.

I conjure you that ye hearken not to him for
that lord's sake that kindleth love in ladies,
for in his utterance dwelleth nought that is
friend to truth.

And if ye by his words were moved to come
towards your lady, stay ye not but come to
her :

Say : Madonna our coming is to commend one
that sorroweth saying : Where is the desire
of mine eyes ?

Sonetto x

Parole mie, che per lo mondo siete ;
  Voi che nasceste poich' io cominciai
  A dir per quella donna, in cui errai :
  Voi che intendendo il terzo ciel movete,

Andatevene a lei, che la sapete,
  Piangendo sì ch' ella oda i nostri guai.
  Ditele : Noi sem vostre ; dunque omai
  Più che noi semo, non ci vederete.

Con lei non state ; chè non v' è Amore :
  Ma gite attorno in abito dolente,
  A guisa delle vostre antiche suore.

Quando trovate donna di valore,
  Gittativele a' piedi umilemente,
  Dicendo : A voi dovem noi fare onore.

Sonetto xi

Per quella via che la bellezza corre,
  Quando a destare Amor va nella mente,
  Passa Lisetta baldanzosamente,
  Come colei che mi si crede tòrre :

Quand' ella è giunta al piè di quella torre
  Che s'apre quando l'animo acconsente,
  Ode una voce dir subitamente :
  Lèvati, bella donna, e non ti porre.

Chè quella donna, che di sopra siede
  Quando di signoria chiese la verga,
  Com' ella volse, Amor tosto le diede :

Quando Lisetta accomiatar si vede,
  Di quella parte dove Amore alberga
  Tutta dipinta di vergogna riede.

SONNET X

Words of mine, that are about the world; ye
who sprang forth after I began to rhyme
because of that Lady in whom I went astray:
Ye who by understanding move the third heaven,

Go forth to her, whom ye wot of, weeping so
that she may hear our lamentations. Say to
her: We are yours, and so, more than we now
are, ye shall not behold us.

With her tarry not; for love is not there: but
wend around in mourning garb, after the guise
of your sisters of old.

When ye find a lady of worth, fall ye at her
feet humbly and say: To you our devoir is
to do honour.

SONNET XI

By that way that beauty runs, when she goeth
to awaken love in the understanding, Lisetta
passeth exultingly like one who thinks to win
me unto herself.

When she hath reached the foot of that tower
which openeth when the mind consents, she
hears a voice say suddenly: "begone, fair lady,
and trust thee not nigh."

For when that Lady who sitteth above craved
the wand of dominion, even as she willed,
Love quickly gave it her:

When Lisetta beholds herself dismissed, from
that place where Love dwelleth she returneth,
pictured o'er with shame.

SONETTO XII

Poich' io non trovo chi meco ragioni
   Del Signor cui serviamo e voi ed io,
   Convienmi sodisfare il gran desio,
   Ch' io ho di dire i pensamenti buoni.

Null' altra cosa appo voi m'accagioni
   Dello lungo e noioso tacer mio,
   Se non il loco ov' io son ch' è si rio,
   Che il ben non trova chi albergo gli doni.

Donna non c' è che Amor le venga al volto,
   Nè uomo ancora che per lui sospiri ;
   E chi 'l facesse saria detto stolto.

Ahi, messer Cino, com' è il tempo vòlto
   A danno nostro e delli nostri diri
   Da poi che il ben c'è sì poco ricolto !

SONETTO XIII

Suonar bracchetti, e cacciatori aizzare,
   Lepri levarsi, ed isgridar le genti,
   E dai guinzagli uscir veltri correnti,
   Per bella piaggia volgere o 'nboccare,

Assai credo che deggia dilettare
   Libero core e van d'intendimenti.
   Ed io fra gli amorosi pensamenti
   Da un sono schernito in tale affare,

E dicemi questo motto per usanza :
   Or ecco leggiadria di gentil core :
   Per una sì selvaggia dilettanza,

Lasciar le donne e lor gaja sembianza !
   Allor, temendo non lo senta Amore.
   Prendo vergogna, onde mi vien pesanza.

Sonnet XII

Since I none find who may discourse with me
 of the Lord whom we serve, both you and I,
 it behoves me to satisfy the great desire I
 have to tell my good thoughts.

Let nought else arraign me before you for my
 long and irksome silence, save the place where
 I am, which is so evil, that the Good
 finds none who giveth it shelter.

Lady is none to whose countenance Love
 cometh, nor man yet that sigheth for him;
 and he who did so were called foolish.

Ah me! Master Cino, how hath time changed
 to hurt of us and of our rhymes, since Good
 is so little garnered here.

Sonnet XIII

Sound of beagles and spurring of huntsmen,
 starting of hares and hallooing of folk, and
 fleet hounds issuing from the leash to scour the
 fair slopes or seize the prey,

well I ween must it rejoice the heart free and
 void of purpose.   Lo I, mid amorous musings,
 am mocked by one on this score,

and he saith to me this word for familiar jest:
 Now behold the grace of a gentle heart!
 For a pleasure so boorish,

to leave ladies and their joyous semblance! Then
 fearing lest Love may hear it I take on
 shame, whence heaviness cometh upon me.

 *F

BALLATA 1

Deh Violetta che in ombra d' Amore
   Negli occhi miei di subito apparisti,
   Abbi pietà del cor che tu feristi,
   Che spera in te, e desiando muore.

Tu, Violetta, in forma più che umana,
   Foco mettesti dentro alla mia mente
   Col tuo parlar ch' ancide :
   Poi con atto di spirito cocente
   Creasti speme, che 'n parte m' è sana
   Laddove tu mi ride.
   Deh non guardare perchè a lei mi fide,
   Ma drizza gli occhi al gran disio che m' arde ;
   Chè mille donne già, per esser tarde,
   Sentito han pena dell' altrui dolore.

BALLATA II

Io mi son pargoletta bella e nuova,
   E son venuta per mostrarmi a vui
   Dalle bellezze e loco, dond' io fui.

Io fui del cielo, e tornerovvi ancora
   Per dar della mia luce altrui diletto ;
   E chi mi vede, e non se n'innamora,
   D' amor non averà mai intelletto :
   Chè non mi fu in piacere alcun disdetto,
   Quando natura mi chiese a colui,
   Che volle, donne, accompagnarmi a vui.

BALLAD I

Ah! Violetta that in Love's guise suddenly
appeardst in mine eyes, have pity on the
heart thou didst wound, that hopes in thee
and of desire perisheth.

Thou Violetta, in more than mortal form, didst
kindle a fire within my mind with thy speech
that slayeth: then by the power of a flaming
spirit did'st thou create hope, that in part
healeth me whene'er thou smilest on me.
Ah! regard not why I do trust my hope, but
direct thine eyes to the great desire that con-
sumeth me; for a thousand ladies already
through tardiness have felt the smart of others'
grief.

BALLAD II

I am a maiden beautiful and rare and am come to
shew me to you from the loveliness and the
place whence I had my being.

I was of heaven and thither shall return to give
others the joy of my brightness; and whoso
beholdeth me and is not enamoured thereat
ne'er shall have understanding of Love, for to
me no charm was gainsaid when nature craved
me from him who willed, ladies, to companion
you with me.

Ciascuna stella negli occhi mi piove
  Della sua luce e della sua virtute.
  Le mie bellezze sono al mondo nuove,
  Perocchè di lassù mi son venute ;
  Le quai non posson esser conosciute
  Se non per conoscenza d' uomo, in cui
  Amor si metta per piacere altrui.

Queste parole si leggon nel viso
  D' un' angioletta che ci è apparita :
  Ond' io, che per campar la mirai fiso,
  Ne sono a rischio di perder la vita ;
  Perocch' io ricevetti tal ferita
  Da un, ch' io vidi dentro agli occhi sui,
  Ch' io vo piangendo, e non m' acqueto pui.

BALLATA III

Per una ghirlandetta
  Ch' io vidi, mi farà
  Sospirar, ogni fiora.

Vidi a voi, donna, portar ghirlandetta
  A par di fior gentile.
  E sovra lei vidi volare in fretta
  Un angiolel d' amore tutto umìle :
  E 'n suo cantar sottile
  Dicea : Chi mi vedrà
  Lauderà il mio signore.

S' io sarò là, dove un fioretto sia,
  Allor fia ch' io sospire.
  Dirò : La bella gentil donna mia
  Porta in testa i fioretti del mio sire :
  Ma per crescer desire
  La mia donna verrà
  Coronata da Amore.

.Every star sheds into mine eyes of her light
and of her virtue. My beauties are new to
the world because they have come to me from
on high; the which cannot be known save
by the knowledge of one in whom Love
hath implanted himself by another's pleasure.

These words are read in the countenance of a
sweet angel that hath appeared to us, wherefore, I, who to save me gazed steadfastly at
her, am at hazard to lose my life; for I have
received such wound from one that I beheld
within her eyes, that I go a-weeping and have
peace no more.

BALLAD III

Because of a fair garland I have seen, every
flower will make me sigh.

I beheld you lady, wearing a fair garland, your-
self gentle as a flower, and above it I beheld
flying in haste a sweet angel of love all lowly;
and in his mystic song he said: "Whoso
shall behold me will praise my lord."

If I am there where a floweret be, then must I
sigh. I will say: "The fair gentle lady
mine, beareth on her head the flowerets of my
lord: but to increase desire my lady shall
come crowned by love."

Di fior le parolette mie novelle
   Han fatto una ballata;
   Da lor per leggiadria s' hanno tolt'elle
Una veste, ch'altrui non fu mai data:
   Però siete pregata,
   Quand' uom la canterà,
Che le facciate onore.

BALLATA IV

Voi che sapete ragionar d' amore,
   Udite la ballata mia pietosa,
   Che parla d' una donna disdegnosa,
   La qual m' ha tolto il cor per suo valore.

Tanto disdegna qualunque la mira,
   Che fa chinare gli occhi per paura;
   Chè d'intorno da' suoi sempre si gira
   D' ogni crudelitate una pintura:
   Ma dentro portan la dolce figura,
   Che all' anima gentil fa dir: Mercede;
   Sì virtuosa, che quando si vede,
   Trae li sospiri altrui fuora del core.

Par ch' ella dica: Io non sarò umile
   Verso d'alcun, che negli occhi mi guardi;
   Ch' io ci porto entro quel signor gentile,
   Che m' ha fatto sentir degli suoi dardi.
   E certo io credo che così gli guardi,
   Per vederli per sè quando le piace:
   A quella guisa donna retta face
   Quando si mira per volere onore.

Of flowers my tender words and rare have made
a song: therefrom for adornment they have
a vesture ta'en that to none was e'er given;
therefore ye are entreated when one shall sing
it that ye do it honour.

BALLAD IV

Ye that are skilled to discourse of love, hearken
to my piteous song, that speaketh of a scornful
lady, who hath ravished my heart from me by
her power.

Such scorn hath she for whom soe'er looketh
on her, that she maketh eyes to droop through
fear; for around hers ever circleth a picture
of all cruelty: but within they bear the sweet
form that maketh the gentle soul to say,
"mercy," with such power that when it is
beheld, sighs are drawn from every heart.

She seemeth to say: "To none that looketh in
mine eyes will I be gracious for therein I bear
that gentle lord who hath made me feel of
his shafts." And certes I believe that thus
she guards her eyes to behold them herself
when it pleaseth her: in such wise an upright
lady doth when she is gazed on, zealous for
her honour.

Io non spero che mai per sua pietate
  Degnasse di guardare un poco altrui :
  Così è fera donna in sua beltate
  Questa, che sente Amor negli occhi sui.
  Ma quanto vuol nasconda e guardi lui,
  Ch' io non veggia talor tanta salute,
  Perocchè i miei desiri avran virtute
  Contro il disdégno che mi dà Amore.

No hope have I that e'er of her pity she might
deign to look somewhile on one: so fierce a
lady is she in her beauty, she who feeleth
Love within her eyes. But let her, so long
as she will, hide and guard him lest I behold
some time such great salvation; for my
desires shall have power against the scorn
that Love dealeth to me.

CANZONE I

I

Al poco giorno ed al gran cerchio d' ombra
 Son giunto, lasso! ed al bianchir de' colli,
 Quando si perde lo color nell' erba.
 E 'l mio disio però non cangia il verde,
 Sì è barbato nella dura pietra,
 Che parla e sente come fosse donna.

II

Similemente questa nuova donna
 Si sta gelata, come neve all' ombra;
 Chè non la muove, se non come pietra,
 Il dolce tempo che riscalda i colli
 E che gli fa tornar di bianco in verde,
 Perchè gli copre di fioretti e d' erba.

III

Quand' ella ha in testa una ghirlanda d' erba
 Trae della mente nostra ogni altra donna;
 Perchè si mischia il crespo giallo e 'l verde
 Sì bel, ch' Amor vi viene a stare all' ombra:
 Che m' ha serrato tra piccoli colli
 Più forte assai che la calcina pietra.

ODE I

I

To the short day and the great sweep of shadow
have I come, ah me! and to the whitening of
the hills, when colour vanishes from the grass.
And my longing, for all that, changes not its
green, so is it barbed in the hard stone that
speaks and hears as though it were a woman.

II

And in like fashion does this wondrous woman
stand chill like snow beneath the shadow;
for no more moves her than a stone, the
sweet season that warms the hills and brings
them back from white to green, in that it
covers them with flowers and grass.

III

When on her head she bears a wreath of grass,
she banishes from our mind each other
woman; for the waving gold is mingled with
the green, so beauteous that Love comes there
to sojourn in the shadow, who hath riveted me
between the little hills, more fast by far than
calcined stone.

IV

Canz. i. Le sue bellezze han più virtù che pietra,
      E 'l colpo suo non può sanar per erba ;
      Ch' io son fuggito per piani e per colli,
      Per potere scampar da cotal donna ;
      Ed al suo lume non mi può far ombra
      Poggio, nè muro mai, nè fronda verde.

V

Io l'ho veduta già vestita a verde
      Sì fatta, ch'ella avrebbe messo in pietra
      L'amor ch'io porto pure alla sua ombra :
      Ond'io l'ho chiesta in un bel prato d'erba,
      Innamorata com'anco fu donna,
      E chiuso intorno d'altissimi colli.

VI

Ma ben ritorneranno i fiumi a' colli
      Prima che questo legno molle e verde
      S'infiammi (come suol far bella donna)
      Di me, che mi torrei dormire in pietra
      Tutto il mio tempo, ed ir pascendo l'erba,
      Per veder ov' i panni suoi fanno ombra.

VII

Quandunque i colli fanno più nera ombra,
      Sotto un bel verde, la giovane donna
      La fa sparir, com'huom pietra sott'erba.

IV

Her beauty has more virtue than a gem, and Ode i.
her stroke may not be healed by herb; for I
have fled o'er plains and hills, that I might
escape from such like woman; and against
her light availed to give me shadow nor mount
nor ever wall nor leaf of green.

V

Erst have I seen her clad in green, in such guise
she would have planted in a stone the love I
bear even to her very shadow; wherefore I
have wooed her in a beauteous field of grass,
(enamoured as was ever woman) and girt
around with loftiest hills.

VI

But of a truth the rivers will return to the
hills, or e'er this log, sap-full and green,
catch flame (after the wont of fair woman)
from me, who would endure to sleep in
stone all of my life, and go pasturing on
grass, only to look where her garments cast
a shadow.

VII

When the hills cast the blackest shadow, under
a beauteous green the youthful woman makes
it vanish, as one should hide a stone in grass.

CANZONE II

I

Amor, che muovi tua virtù dal cielo,
  Come 'l sol lo splendore,
  Chè là s' apprende più lo suo valore,
  Dove più nobilità suo raggio trova,

E come el fuga oscuritate e gelo,
  Così, alto Signore,
  Tu cacci la viltate altrui del core,
  Nè ira contra te fa lunga prova,

Da te convien che ciascun ben si muova,
  Per lo qual si travaglia il mondo tutto :
  Senza te è distrutto
  Quanto avemo in potenza di ben fare :
  Come pintura in tenebrosa parte,
  Che non si può mostrare,
  Nè dar diletto di color nè d'arte.

ODE II

1

Love who dost launch thy power from the heaven, as doth the sun his splendour ; (for there his worth is apprehended most where his ray most nobility encounters,

And as he puts to flight darkness and chill, so, lofty Sire, dost thou drive baseness from the heart of men, nor can wrath make long stand against thee) :

From thee must every blessing needs arise for which the whole world travaileth : without thee perishes all potency in us of doing well ; e'en as a painting in a darksome place, which may not manifest itself nor give delight of colour nor of art.

II

Canz. ii. Feremi nel cor sempre la tua luce,
Come raggio in la stella,
Poichè l'anima mia fu fatta ancella
Della tua podestà primieramente:

Onde ha vita un disio, che mi conduce
Con sua dolce favella
In rimirar ciascuna cosa bella
Con più diletto quanto è più piacente.

Per questo mio guardar m' è nella mente
Una giovine entrata, che m' ha preso;
Ed ha lì un foco acceso,
Com'acqua per chiarezza fiamma accende:
Perchè nel suo venir li raggi tuoi,
Con li quai mi risplende,
Saliron tutti su negli occhi suoi.

III

Quanto è nell'esser suo bella, e gentile
Negli atti ed amorosa,
Tanto lo immaginar, che non si posa,
L'adorna nella mente, ov' io la porto:

Non che da sè medesmo sia sottile
A così alta cosa,
Ma da gli tua virtù di quel ch' egli osa
Oltra il poter che natura ci ha porto.

È sua beltà del tuo valor conforto,
In quanto giudicar si puote effetto
Sovra degno suggetto,
In guisa ch' è il sol segno di foco,
Lo quale a lui non dà, nè to' virtute;
Ma fallo in alto loco
Nell' effetto parer di più salute.

II

Upon my heart thy light doth ever strike, as Ode ii.
on a star the ray, since when my soul became the handmaiden of thy power at the
first;

Whence hath its life a longing that leadeth me
with its persuasive speech to gaze again upon
each beauteous thing, with more delight in
measure as 'tis winsome.

By power of this my gaze, into my mind a
damsel has entered who has captured me;
and hath kindled there a fire, as water by its
clearness kindles flame: because, when she
approached, those rays of thine, wherewith
thou dost make me glow, all rose up in her
eyes.

III

Even as in her being she is beauteous, and noble
in her features and amorous, so does imagination, resting not, adorn her in the mind wherein I bear her:

Not that its own subtlety suffices for a thing so
lofty, but thy might giveth it of that which
makes it over-dare the power nature hath
proffered us.

Her beauty is thy worth's accreditor, in that
effect may be esteemed upon a worthy subject;
in fashion as the sun is fire's ensign, though
giving not nor reaving from it power, but
making it, in lofty region, reveal more saving
force in its effect.

IV

Canz. ii. Dunque, Signor, di sì gentil natura,
  Che questa nobiltate,
  Che vien quaggiuso, e tutt' altra bontate,
  Lieva principio della tua altezza ;

  Guarda la vita mia, quanto ella è dura,
  E prendine pietate :
  Chè lo tuo ardor per la costei beltate
  Mi fa sentire al cor troppa gravezza,

  Falle sentire, Amor, per tua dolcezza
  Il gran disio ch'io ho di veder lei :
  Non soffrir che costei
  Per giovinezza mi conduca a morte ;
  Chè non s' accorge ancor com' ella piace,
  Nè quant io l'amo forte,
  Nè che negli occhi porti la mia pace.

V

  Onor ti sarà grande, se m' aiuti,
  Ed a me ricco donò
  Tanto, quanto conosco ben ch'io sono
  Là, ov' io non posso difender mia vita :

  Chè gli spiriti miei son combattuti
  Da tal, ch' io non ragiono,
  Se per tua volontà non han perdono,
  Che possan guari star senza finita.

  Ed ancor tua potenza fia sentita
  Da questa bella donna che n' è degna ;
  Che par che si sconvegna   •
  Non darle d'ogni ben gran compagnia,
  Siccome quella, che fu al mondo nata
  Per aver signoria
  Sovra la mente d'ogni uom che la guata.

IV

Then, Sire, of such gentle nature that this Ode ii. nobility which cometh down to us, and all other excellence, taketh its source from thy loftiness;

Have regard unto my life, how hard it is, and take pity on it; for thy burning, by her beauty, maketh me have at heart excess of anguish.

Love, of thy sweetness, make her feel the great yearning that I have to behold her: nor suffer not that she, by glory of her strength, lead me to death; for not yet is she aware how she doth please, nor how mightily I love her, nor how she bears my peace within her eyes.

V

Great honour shall it be to thee if thou aid me, and rich gift to me, in measure as I know full well, who find me at such point where I may not defend my life:

For my spirits are assailed by such an one that I deem not, save I have succour through thy will, that they can keep their stand and perish not.

And thy potency, moreover, shall be felt by this fair lady, who is worthy of it; for it seems it were unfitting not to give to her great store of every good, as one born into the world to hold lordship over the mind of all who look upon her.

CANZONE III

I

Amor, che nella mente mi ragiona
   Della mia donna disiosamente,
   Move cose di lei meco sovente
   Che l' intelletto sovr' esse disvia.

Lo suo parlar sì dolcemente suona,
   Che l' anima ch' ascolta e che lo sente
   Dice: Oh me lassa! ch' io non son possente
   Di dir quel ch' odo della donna mia!

E certo e' mi convien lasciare in pria,
   S' io vo' trattar di quel ch' odo di lei,
   Ciò che lo mio intelletto non comprende,
   E di quel che s'intende
   Gran parte, perchè dirlo non saprei.
   Però se le mie rime avran difetto,
   Ch' entreran nella loda di costei,
   Di ciò si biasmi il debole intelletto,
   E 'l parlar nostro che non ha valore
   Di ritrar tutto ciò che dice Amore.

ODE III

I

Love, that discourses to me in my mind yearn-ingly of my lady, moveth many a time such things with me anent her that my intellect loses its way concerning them.

His discourse soundeth so sweetly that the soul that heareth him and feeleth, cries; 'Oh me! that I have not power to tell that which I hear about my lady.'

And verily it behoveth me first to drop, would I treat of that which I hear of her, all that my intellect apprehendeth not: and great part of that which it understandeth, because I should not know to tell it. Wherefore, if defect shall mark my rhymes which shall enter upon her praises, for this let our feeble intellect be blamed, and our speech, which hath not power to tell again all that Love speaketh.

II

Canz. iii. Non vede il sol, che tutto 'l mondo gira,
   Cosa tanto gentil quanto in quell' ora
   Che luce nella parte ove dimora
   La donna, di cui dire Amor mi face.

  Ogn' intelletto, di lassù la mira:
   E quella gente che qui s'innamora,
   Ne' lor pensieri la trovano ancora,
   Quando Amor fa sentir della sua pace.

  Suo esser tanto a quei che gliel dà piace.
   Ch' infonde sempre in lei la sua virtute
   Oltre il dimando di nostra natura.
   La sua anima pura,
   Che riceve da lui questa salute,
   Lo manifesta in quel ch' ella conduce,
   Chè sue bellezze son cose vedute;
   E gli occhi di color dov' ella luce
   Ne mandan messi al cor pien di disiri,
   Che prendon aere e diventan sospiri.

II

The sun, who circleth all the world, seeth not a Ode iii. thing so gentle as in that hour when he shineth on the place where sojourneth the lady of whom Love constraineth me to speak.

Every supernal intellect gazes upon her, and such folk as are here enamoured find her still in their thoughts when love maketh them feel of his peace.

Her being is so pleasing to him who gives it her that he ever poureth his power into her, beyond what our nature asketh. Her pure soul, which receiveth this salvation from him, maketh it show forth in that which she doth guide; for her beauties are things clear to view, and the eyes of those in whom she shineth send messages thereof to the heart filled with longings, which gather air and turn to sighs.

III

Canz. iii. In lei discende la virtù divina,
       Siccome face in angelo che 'l vede ;
       E qual donna gentil questo non crede
       Vada con lei e miri gli atti sui.

       Quivi dov' ella parla si dichina
       Uno spirto dal ciel, che reca fede
       Come l' alto valor ch' ella possiede
       È oltre a quel che si conviene a nui.

       Gli atti soavi ch' ella mostra altrui
       Vanno chiamando Amor, ciascuno a prova,
       In quella voce che lo fa sentire.
       Di costei si può dire :
       Gentil è in donna ciò che in lei si trova ;
       E bello è tanto, quanto lei simiglia.
       E puossi dir che il suo aspetto giova
       A consentir ciò che par maraviglia
       Onde la fede nostra è aiutata ;
       Però fu tal da eterno ordinata.

III

On her descendeth the divine power, as it doth Ode iii.
upon an angel who beholdeth it; and whatsoever gentle lady not believeth this, let her
go with her and mark well her bearing.

Where she speaks, there cometh down a spirit
from heaven who gives us faith that the lofty
worth which she possesses transcends all that
consorts with our nature.

The sweet inflections she reveals to others go
calling upon Love, each vying with the other,
in that voice which maketh him to hear. Of
her it may be said: *Gentle is that in lady which
in her is found; and beauteous is so much only
as is like to her.* And affirm we may that to
look on her gives help to accept that which
seems a miracle; whereby our faith is aided;
therefore from eternity such was she ordained.

G

IV

Canz. iii. Cose appariscon nello suo aspetto,
              Che mostran de' piacer del Paradiso;
              Dico negli occhi e nel suo dolce riso,
              Chè le vi reca Amor com' a suo loco.

              Elle soverchian lo nostro intelletto,
              Come raggio di sole un fragil viso:
              E perch' io non le posso mirar fiso,
              Mi convien contentar di dirne poco.

              Sua beltà piove fiammelle di fuoco,
              Animate d' un spirito gentile,
              Ch' è creatore d' ogni pensier buono:
              E rompon come tuono
              Gl' innati vizi che fanno altrui vile.
              Però qual donna sente sua beltate
              Biasmar per non parer queta ed umile,
              Miri costei ch' è esemplo d' umiltate.
              Quest' è colei ch' umilia ogni perverso:
              Costei pensò chi mosse l' universo.

IV

Things are revealed in her aspect which show
us of the joys of Paradise ; I mean in her eyes
and in her sweet smile, for Love assigns them
there as to their true abode.

They transcend our intellect, as the sun's ray the
feeble vision : and, because I may not gaze
fixedly upon them, needs must I content me
with scant speech of them.

Her beauty rains down flamelets of fire, made
living by a gentle spirit which is the creator
of every good thought : and they shatter like
thunder the inborn vices that make folk vile ;
wherefore whatsoever lady heareth her beauty
blamed for not seeming tranquil and humble, let
her gaze on her, who is the pattern of humility.
It is she who humbleth each perverse one : of
her was he thinking who set the universe in
motion.

v

Canz. iii. Canzone, è par che tu parli contraro
     Al dir d' una sorella che tu hai ;
     Chè questa donna, che tant' umil fai,
     Ella la chiama fera e disdegnosa.

    Tu sai che 'l ciel sempr' è lucente e chiaro,
     E quanto in sè non si turba giammai :
     Ma li nostr' occhi per cagioni assai
     Chiaman la stella talor tenebrosa ;

    Così quand' ella la chiama orgogliosa,
     Non considera lei secondo 'l vero,
     Ma pur secondo quel che a lei parea :
     Chè l' anima temea,
     E teme ancora sì che mi par fero
     Quantunque io veggio dov' ella mi senta.
     Così ti scusa, se ti fa mestiero ;
     E, quando puoi, a lei ti rappresenta,
     E di' : Madonna, s' ello v' è a grato,
     Io parlerò di voi in ciascun lato.

v

Ode ! it seemeth that thy speech is counter to Ode iii.
the utterance of a sister whom thou hast ;
for this lady, whom thou makest to be humble,
she calleth cruel and disdainful.

Thou knowest that the heaven is ever shining
and clear, and as concerns itself is disturbed
never ; but our eyes, for many a cause, call
the star clouded, time and time again,

So when she calleth her orgulous, she considereth
her not according to the truth, but only according as to her she appeared ; for the soul
was in terror, aye and is in such terror yet
that it seemeth me a dire thing whensoever
I look where she perceiveth me. Thus plead
thy excuse if thou have need ; and, when thou
canst, present thyself to her, and say : 'My
lady, if it be acceptable to thee, I will discourse of thee on every side.'

CANZONE IV

I

Amor, dacchè convien pur ch' io mi doglia,
  Perchè la gente m' oda,
  E mostri me d' ogni virtute spento,

Dammi savere a pianger come voglia.
  Sì che 'l duol che si snoda
  Portin le mie parole come 'l sento.

Tu vuoi ch' io muoia, ed io ne son contento:
  Ma chi mi scuserà, s' io non so dire
  Ciò che mi fai sentire?
  Chi crederà ch' io sia omai sì colto?
  E se mi dai parlar quanto tormento,
  Fa, signor mio, che innanzi al mio morire,
  Questa ria per me nol possa udire:
  Chè, se intendesse ciò ch' io dentro ascolto,
  Pietà faria men bello il suo bel volto.

ODE IV

I

Love, since I needs must make complaint, for
folk to hear, and show myself bereft of every
virtue,

Grant me the skill to wail even as I would,
that the woe which is shot out may be
borne forth on my words even as I feel it.

Thou wilt have me die, and I am satisfied; but
who shall pardon me, if I have not skill to
tell that which thou makest me to feel? Who
shall believe that I am now so smitten?
And, if thou grant me speech in measure with
my torment, see to it, O my liege, that e'er I
die she who is guilty may not hear it through
me; for should she understand that which I
feel within, pity would make less beauteous
her beauteous face.

II

Canz. iv   Io non posso fuggir ch'ella non vegna
       Nell'immagine mia,
       Se non come il pensier che la vi mena.

L'anima folle, che al suo mal s'ingegna,
       Com' ella è bella e ria,
       Così dipinge, e forma la sua pena :

Poi la riguarda, e quando ella è ben piena
       Del gran desio, che dagli occhi le tira,
       Incontro a sè s'adira,
       C'ha fatto il foco, ov'ella trista incende.
       Quale argomento di ragion raffrena
       Onde tanta tempesta in me si gira ?
       L'angoscia che non cape dentro, spira
       Fuor della bocca sì, ch'ella s'intende,
       Ed anco agli occhi lor merito rende.

III

La nimica figura, che rimane
       Vittoriosa e fera,
       E signoreggia la virtù che vuole,

Vaga di sè medesma andar mi fane
       Colà, dov'ella è vera,
       Come simile a simil correr suole.

Ben conosco che va la neve al sole ;
       Ma più non posso : fo come colui
       Che nel podere altrui
       Va co' suoi piedi al loco ov'egli è morto.
       Quando son presso, parmi udir parole
       Dicer: Via via ; vedrai morir costui !
       Allor mi volgo per veder a cui
       Mi raccomandi : e intanto sono scorto
       Dagli occhi che m'ancidono a gran torto.

II

I may not flee so that she come not within my fantasy, no more than I may flee the musing that brings her there.

The mad soul, which plies its wit to its own ill, depicts her, beauteous and injurious as she is, and forges its own torture.

Then gazes on her, and when right full of the great yearning it draws through the eyes, falls into rage against itself for having made the fire wherein all dismally it burns. What argument of reason draws the rein on that whence so great tempest whirls within me? The anguish, that may not be contained within, breathes so through the mouth as to grow articulate and give, to boot, their merit to the eyes.

III

The hostile figure that remains, victorious and cruel, and that lords it o'er the power that wills,

Enamoured of itself, bids me to go where, in verity, is she herself, since like to like still rushes.

Well know I that 'tis snow seeking the sun: but, having no more strength, I do as he who, in another's power, goes with his own feet to his place of death. When I draw nigh meseems that I hear words which cry: 'Quick! quick! and thou shalt see him die.' Then I turn to see to whom I may commend me; and am marshalled on, the while, by the eyes that slay me with grievous wrong.

*G

IV

Canz. iv. Qual'io divegno sì feruto, Amore,
          Sai lo tu, non io,
          Che rimani a veder me senza vita:

E se l'anima torna poscia al core,
Ignoranza ed oblio
Stato è con lei mentre ch' ella è partita.

Com'io risurgo, e guato la ferita,
Che mi disfece quando io fui percosso,
Confortar non mi posso
Sì, ch'io non tremi tutto di paura,
E mostri poi la faccia scolorita
Qual fu quel tuono che mi giunse addosso;
Che, se con dolce riso è stato mosso,
Lunga fiata poi rimane oscura,
Perchè lo spirto non si rassicura.

V

Così m'hai concio, Amore, in mezzo l'Alpi,
Nella valle del fiume,
Lungo il qual sempre sopra me sei forte.

Qui vivo e morto, come vuoi, mi palpi;
Mercè del fiero lume,
Che folgorando fa via alla morte.

Lasso! non donne qui, non genti accorte
Vegg'io, cui me lamenti del mio male.
Se a costei non ne cale,
Non spero qui da altrui aver soccorso:
E questa, sbandeggiata di tua corte,
Signor, non cura colpo di tuo strale:
Fatto ha d'orgoglio al petto schermo tale,
Ch'ogni saetta lì spunta suo corso;
Per che l'armato cuor da nulla è morso.

IV

And what, so wounded, I become, O Love, Ode iv. thou know'st, not I, thou who dost stay to look on lifeless me:

And though the soul thereafter come again to the heart, nescience and oblivion have been her comrades whilst she was away.

When I arise again and look upon the wound which undid me when I was struck, I may not so assure myself but that I tremble all for fear; and my discoloured face declares what was the thunder bolt that leaped upon me; for, though 'twas a sweet smile that launched it, long time thereafter it abides darkened, in that the spirit cannot trust itself.

V

Thus hast thou dealt with me, O Love, amongst the alps, in that river's vale on whose banks thou ever hast been strong upon me.

Here, living or dead, at thy will thou handlest me in virtue of that fierce light that makes a thunder-crashing path for death.

Woe's me! no ladies here, nor folk of skill, can I perceive, to whom I may lament me of my woe. If she heed it not, I hope not here for succour from another: and she, banned from thy court, my liege, marks not thine arrow's stroke: such mail of pride hath she forged for her breast that every shaft there breaks its point and course, for her armed heart by nought is bitten.

VI

Canz. iv O montanina mia canzon, tu vai ;
          Forse vedrai Fiorenza, la mia terra,
          Che fuor di sè mi serra,
          Vota d' amore e nuda di pietate :
          Se lì vai dentro, va dicendo : Omai
          Non vi può fare il mio fattor più guerra
          Là ond'io vegno, una catena il serra
          Tal che, se piega vostra crudeltate,
          Non ha di ritornar più libertate.

VI

Oh mountain song of mine, thou goest on thy
way, mayhap to see my city Florence, who
bars me out from her, void of love and stripped
of pity. If thou enter in, go crying: 'Now
no longer can my maker war upon you; there,
whence I come, a chain clips him, such that,
should thy cruelty give way, he has no longer
freedom to return.'

Ode iv.

CANZONE V

I

Amor, tu vedi ben che questa donna
   La tua virtù non cura in alcun tempo,
   Che suol dell' altre belle farsi donna.
   E poi s' accorse ch' ell' era mia donna,
   Per lo tuo raggio che al volto mi luce,
   D' ogni crudelità si fece donna:
   Sicchè non par ch' ell' abbia cuor di donna,
   Ma di qual fiera l' ha d' amor più freddo.
   Chè per lo tempo caldo e per lo freddo
   Mi fa sembianti pur com' una donna,
   Che fosse fatta d' una bella pietra
   Per man di che meglio tagliasse in pietra.

II

Ed io che son costante più che pietra
   In ubbidirti per beltà di donna,
   Porto nascoso il colpo della pietra,
   Con la qual tu mi desti come a pietra
   Che t' avesse noiato lungo tempo:
   Talchè mi corse al core, ov' io son pietra.
   E mai non si scoperse alcuna pietra
   O da splendor di sole o da sua luce,
   Che tanta avesse nè virtù nè luce
   Che mi potesse atar da questa pietra,
   Sicch' ella non mi meni col suo freddo
   Colà dov' io sarò di morte freddo.

ODE V

I

Love, thou perceivest that this lady heeds not thy power at any season, which is wont to make itself the mistress of the other fair ones. And when she perceived that she was my mistress, by thy ray that shines on my face, she made herself the mistress of all cruelty ; so that it seems not she has the heart of woman, but of whatever beast has heart most chilled of love. For, through the warm season and through the chill, she shows me the semblance of a woman who should be made of beauteous stone, by hand of such as should best carve in stone.

II

And I who am unshaken more than rock in obeying thee, for the beauty of a woman, bear concealed the stroke of the stone with which thou didst smite upon me, as on a stone that had offended thee long season, in such guise as to reach my heart, where I am stone. And never was discovered any gem, or by splendour of the sun or by his light, which had so much of virtue or of light as to have power to aid me against that stone, so that it should not lead me with its chill to where I shall be dead with chill.

III

Canz. v. Signor, tu sai che per algente freddo
            L' acqua diventa cristallina pietra
            Là sotto tramontana, ov' è il gran freddo;
            E l' aer sempre in elemento freddo
            Vi si converte sì, che l' acqua è donna
            In quella parte, per cagion del freddo;
            Così dinanzi dal sembiante freddo
            Mi ghiaccia sovra il sangue ad ogni tempo:
            E quel pensier che m' accorcia il tempo
            Vi si converte tutto in corpo freddo,
            Che m' esce poi per mezzo della luce;
            Là ond' entrò la dispietata luce.

IV

In lei s' accoglie d' ogni beltà luce:
            Così di tutta crudeltate il freddo
            Le corre al core, ove non va tua luce:
            Perchè negli occhi sì bella mi luce,
            Quando io la miro, ch' io la veggio in pietra,
            E poi in altro ov' io volga mia luce.
            Dagli occhi suoi mi vien la dolce luce
            Che mi fa non caler d' ogni altra donna:
            Così foss' ella più pietosa donna
            Ver me, che chiamo di notte e di luce,
            Solo per lei servire, e luogo e tempo;
            Nè per altro desio viver gran tempo.

III

Sire, thou knowest that by freezing chill the Ode v.
water turns to crystal rock, there under the
north where is the great chill; and the
atmosphere ever so converts itself there into
the element of chill that water is mistress in
that region, by reason of the chill. So,
before the semblance chill, freezing comes
o'er my blood in every season: and that
thought which shortens my life is all con-
verted into substance chill, which issues then
through the midst of the eye, by which there
entered the dispiteous light.

IV

In her is gathered all beauty's light; and in like
fashion all cruelty's chill runs to her heart,
whither pierces not thy light. Wherefore in
my eyes so beauteous does she shine, when I
look on her, that I see her in the rock,
and then wheresoever else I turn my sight.
From her eyes there comes to me the sweet
light that makes me heedless of each other
woman. Ah would that she were a more
piteous lady towards me, who seek, in darkness and in light, only for serving her the
place and season, nor for aught else desire to
live long season.

V

Canz. v. Però, Virtù, che sei prima che tempo,
           Prima che moto e che sensibil luce,
           Increscati di me, c' ho si mal tempo.
           Entrale omai in cor, chè ben n' è tempo,
           Sicchè per te se n' esca fuora il freddo
           Che non mi lascia aver, com' altri, tempo :
           Chè se mi giunge lo tuo forte tempo
           In tale stato, questa gentil pietra
           Mi vedrà coricare in poca pietra
           Per non levarmi, se non dopo il tempo ;
           Quando io vedrò se mai fu bella donna
           Nel mundo, come questa acerba donna.

VI

      Canzone, io porto nella mente donna
           Tal, che con tutto ch' ella mi sia pietra,
           Mi dà baldanza onde ogni uom mi par freddo :
           Sicchè m' ardisco a far per questo freddo
           La novità che per tua forma luce,
           Che non fu mai pensata in alcun tempo.

V

Wherefore, O Power who art earlier than time, Ode v earlier than motion or than sense-felt light, take pity upon me who have such evil season. Enter now into her heart, for in truth 'tis season, so that by thee there pass forth from her the chill which suffers me not, like others, to have my season: for if thy strong season overtake me, in this such state, that noble rock will see me lying in a narrow stone never to raise me till time is no more. And then shall I see if ever was fair lady in the world like unto this bitter lady.

VI

Ode, I bear in my mind a lady, such that, for all she be to me of stone, she giveth me such hardihood that meseems every man is chill; so that I dare to make for this chill the new thing that, through thy form, gives light which never was conceived in any season.

CANZONE VI

I

Così nel mio parlar voglio esser aspro,
   Com' è negli atti questa bella pietra
   La qual ognora impietra
   Maggior durezza e più natura cruda:

E veste sua persona d' un diaspro
   Tal, che per lui, o perch' ella s' arretra,
   Non esce di faretra
   Saetta, che giammai la colga ignuda.

Ed ella ancide, e non val ch' uom si chiuda,
   Nè si dilunghi da' colpi mortali;
   Che, com' avesser ali,
   Giungono altrui, e spezzan ciascun'arme;
   Sicch' io da lei non so nè posso aitarme.

II

Non trovo scudo ch' ella non mi spezzi,
   Nè luogo che dal suo viso m' asconda;
   Ma come fior in fronda,
   Così della mia mente tien la cima.

Cotanto del mio mal par che si prezzi
   Quanto legno di mar che non leva onda:
   Lo peso che m' affonda
   È tal che non potrebbe adeguar rima

Ahi! angosciosa e dispietata lima,
   Che sordamente la mia vita scemi,
   Perchè non ti ritemi
   Di rodermi sì il core, scorza a scorza,
   Com' io di dire altrui chi ten dà forza?

ODE VI

I

As harsh in my discourse would I fain be as in
her bearing is that beauteous stone whom,
every hour, more hardness and more cruel
nature petrify:

And she clothes her person in an adamant such
that for it, or for that she arrests her, there
issues not arrow from quiver that can ever
catch her naked.

But she slays; and it avails not for a man to case
him, nor to flee from the mortal blows; for,
as had they wings, they light on folk and
shatter every armour; wherefore to protect
me from her I have nor wit nor power.

II

I find no shield she may not shatter for me, nor
place to hide me from her vision; but as the
flower on the spray so does she hold the
summit of my mind.

She seems as much to heed my misery as a craft
does a sea that uplifts no wave: the weight
that sinks me is such as no rhyme may hold
in poise.

Oh agonising and unpitying file, that dumbly
scrap'st away my life, how is it that thou
shrinkest not from gnawing thus my heart,
coat within coat, as I from telling folk who
he is that gives thee power thereto?

III

Canz. vi. Chè più mi trema il cor, qualora io penso
      Di lei, in parte ov' altri gli occhi induca,
      Per tema non traluca
      Lo mio pensier di fuor si che si scopra,

      Ch' io non fo della morte, che ogni senso
      Colli denti d' amor già mi manduca:
      Ciò è che il pensier bruca
      La lor virtù sì che n' allenta l' opra.

      El m' ha percosso in terra, e stammi sopra
      Con quella spada ond' egli ancise Dido,
      Amore, a cui io grido,
      Mercè chiamando, ed umilmente il priego:
      Ed ei d' ogni mercè par messo al niego.

IV

      Egli alza ad or ad or la mano, e sfida
      La debole mia vita esto perverso,
      Che disteso e riverso
      Mi tiene in terra d'ogni guizzo stanco.

      Allor mi surgon nella mente strida;
      E 'l sangue, ch' è per le vene disperso,
      Fuggendo corre verso
      Lo cor che 'l chiama; ond' io rimango bianco.

      Egli mi fiede sotto al lato manco
      Sì forte che 'l dolor nel cor rimbalza;
      Allor dico: S' egli alza
      Un' altra volta, morte m' avrà chiuso
      Anzi che 'l colpo sia disceso giuso.

III

For my heart more trembles when I think of
her, in such region that folk may thither
direct their eyes, for fear my thought shine
through externally and be discovered,

Than I do at death, who already crunches every
sense with the teeth of love: to wit my
musing scorches so their powers that it allays
their working.

He has smitten me to earth and stands over
me, with that same sword wherewith he
slaughtered Dido, Love, to whom I cry and
call for grace and humbly pray; and he seems
set to refuse all grace.

IV

He ever and anon uplifts his hand and defies
this my weak life, in his perversity; and he
pins me to the earth, outstretched and over-
thrown, exhausted past a quiver.

Then rise up shrieks within my mind, and the
blood, all scattered through the veins, flees
running towards the heart that summons it,
and I am left all bleached.

He smites me under the left side so rudely that
the pain re-echoes through my heart; then
do I cry: 'Should he uplift one other time,
death will have closed me in e'er down his
blow descends.'

v

Canz. vi.   Cosi vedess' io lui fender per mezzo
       Lo core a quella crudel che 'l mio squatra ;
       Poi non mi sarebb' atra
       La morte, ov' io per sua bellezza corro!

     Ma tanto dà nel sol quanto nel rezzo
       Questa scherana micidiale e latra.
       Oimè! perchè non latra
       Per me, com' io per lei, nel caldo borro?

     Che tosto griderei: Io vi soccorro;
       E farel volentier, siccome quegli,
       Che ne' biondi capegli,
       Ch' Amor per consumarmi increspa e dora,
       Metterei mano e piacerei le allora.

vi

S' io avessi le belle treccie prese
     Che fatte son per me scudiscio e ferza,
     Pigliandole anzi terza
     Con esse passerei vespro e le squille :

E non sarei pietoso nè cortese,
     Anzi farei com' orso quando scherza.
     E se Amor me ne sferza,
     Io mi vendicherei di più di mille ;

Ancor negli occhi ond' escon le faville
     Che mi fiammano il cor, ch' io porto anciso,
     Guarderei presso e fiso,
     Per vendicar lo fuggir che mi face:
     Poscia le renderei con amor pace

V

So might I see him to the centre cleave the cruel Ode vi.
one's heart who quarters mine! Then were
the death to which I hasten through her
beauty no longer black to me.

But she smites as hard in sun as shade, this
murderous assassin and robber. Oh me, that
she howls not for me, as I for her, in the hot
caldron.

For swiftly would I cry: 'I succour thee,' and
eagerly would do it, e'en as one who upon
those fair locks, that Love has crisped and
goldened to consume me, would set my hand
and then would do her will.

VI

Had I seized the fair locks that have become
my scourge and lash, laying hold of them
ere tierce I would pass with them vesper
and evening bells:

And would be nor pitiful nor courteous, but
were rather as the bear taking his sport.
And, if Love scourges me therewith, I would
take more than thousand vengeance.

Still on those eyes, whence issue forth the sparks
which set on flame the heart I carry slain,
close would I gaze and fixedly, to avenge me
for that he makes me flee: and then would I
render her peace with love.

VII

Canz. vi. Canzon mia vatten dritto a quella donna
          Che m' ha feruto e morto, e che m'invola
          Quello ond' io ho più gola :
          E dàlle per lo cor d' una saetta ;
          Chè bell' onor s'acquista in far vendetta.

VII

My ode, take thou thy way straight to that Ode vi.
lady who hath smitten me and slain, and who
robs from me that for which most I thirst,
and with an arrow drive thou at her heart;
for fair honour is acquired in accomplishing
revenge.

CANZONE VII

I

Doglia mi reca nello core ardire,
  A voler ch' è di veritade amico :
  Però, donne, s' io dico
  Parole quasi contro a tutta gente,
  Non ven maravigliate,

Ma conoscete il vil vostro desire ;
  Chè la beltà, ch' amore in voi consente,
  A virtù solamente
  Formata fu dal suo decreto antico,
  Contra 'l qual voi fallate.

Io dico a voi, che siete innamorate ;
  Che se beltate a voi
  Fu data, e virtù a noi,
  Ed a costui di due potere un fare,
  Voi non dovreste amare,
  Ma coprir quanto di beltà v' è dato ;
  Poichè non c' è virtù, ch' era suo segno.
  Lasso ! a che dicer vegno ?
  Dico, che bel disdegno
  Sarebbe in donna, di ragion lodato,
  Partir beltà da sè per suo commiato.

ODE VII

I

Grief furnishes my heart with daring for a wish
that is truth's friend; wherefore, ladies, if I
utter words almost against all mankind, marvel
not at it,

But recognise your base desire; for beauty, which
love concedes to you, was formed for virtue
only, by his decree of old, against which ye
offend.

You I address who are enamoured; for if to us
virtue was given, and to you beauty, and to
him power to make one the two, ye should not
love at all, but hide away whatever beauty
hath been granted you; because there is no
virtue, which was its targe. Woe's me! what
do I go about to say? I say that to sever
beauty from herself, by dismissal, were act of
fair disdain in woman, and were praised of
reason.

II

Canz. vii Uomo da sè virtù fatta ha lontana,
            Uomo non ma la bestia ch' uom somiglia :
            O Dio, qual maraviglia,
            Voler cadere in servo di signore !
            Ovver di vita in morte !

            Virtute al suo fattor sempre è sottana,
            Lui obbedisce, a lui acquista onore,
            Donne, tanto ch' Amore
            La segna d' eccellente sua famiglia
            Nella beata corte.

            Lietamente esce dalle belle porte,
            Alla sua donna torna,
            Lieta va e soggiorna :
            Lietamente opra suo gran vassallaggio.
            Per lo corto viaggio
            Conserva, adorna, accresce ciò che trova :
            Morte repugna sì che lei non cura.
            O cara ancella e pura,
            Colt' hai nel ciel misura !
            Tu sola fai signore ; e questo prova
            Che tu se' possession che sempre giova.

II

Man has made virtue distant from himself.   Man? Ode vii.
no! but the beast that bears man's semblance;
Oh God, what marvel to choose to decline to
slave from master, or from life to death!

Virtue is still supporting to her doer, him she
obeys, to him acquires honour, ladies, so much
that love stamps him of his chosen household
in the blessed court.

Joyously she issues from the beauteous gates of
her mistress, and returns: joyously she goes
and sojourns, joyously she does her great
service.   Through the short journey preserves,
adorns, increases what she finds: to death
she is so counter that she heeds him not.
Oh dear handmaid and pure, in heaven hast
thou taken measurement!   Thou alone givest
mastery; and this is proved by that thou art
a possession always of avail.

III

Canz. vii. Servo, non di signor ma di vil servo,
    Si fa, chi da cotal serva si scosta.
    Volete udir se costa,
    Se ragionate l' uno e l' altro danno,
    A chi da lei disvia?

Questo servo signor tanto è protervo
    Che gli occhi, ch' alla mente lume fanno,
    Chiusi per lui si stanno,
    Sicchè gir ne conviene a colui posta
    Ch' adocchia pur follia.

Ma, perchè lo mio dire util vi sia,
    Discenderò del tutto
    In parte, ed in costrutto
    Più lieve, perchè men grave s' intenda;
    Chè rado sotto benda
    Parola oscura giunge allo 'ntelletto;
    Per che parlar con voi si vuole aperto.
    Ma questo vo', per merto
    Per voi non per me certo,
    Ch' aggiate a vil ciascuno ed a sospetto;
    Chè simiglianza fa nascer diletto.

III

Slave not of a master but of a base slave he Ode vii
makes himself who departs from such a handmaid. Would you know if it be costly,
reckoning one against the other loss, to him
who wanders from her?

This slavish master is so arrogant that the eyes
which make light for the mind are closed for
him, so that he needs must walk at prompting
of one who hath his eye only on folly.

But, that my speech may serve you, I will
descend from the whole to the detail, and that
in sentences more easy, that it be less hardly
understood; for rarely underneath the veil
does a dark saying reach the understanding;
wherefore there is need of open speech with
you; but this I will, for the behoof of you
and verily not me : that ye hold vile all men
and in contempt, for it is likeness that breeds
delight.

H

IV

Canz. vii. Chi è servo come quello ch' è seguace
Fatto a signore, e non sa dove vada,
Per dolorosa strada ;
Come l' avaro seguitando avere,
Ch' a tutti signoreggia ?

Corre l' avaro, ma più fugge pace
(O mente cieca, che non puoi vedere
Lo tuo folle volere !)
Che numero, con oro passar bada,
Che infinito vaneggia.

Ecco, giunta colei che ne pareggia,
Dimmi, che hai tu fatto,
Cieco avaro disfatto ?
Rispondimi, se puoi altro che nulla.
Maledetta tua culla,
Che lusingò cotanti sogni invano :
Maledetto lo tuo perduto pane,
Che non si perde al cane ;
Che da sera e da mane
Hai ragunato, e stretto ad ambe mano,
Ciò che si tosto ti si fa lontano.

IV

Who is a slave like him who followeth a liege Ode vii.
in haste, and knoweth not whither he goeth,
along the dolesome path ; as doth the miser,
hurrying after wealth which plays the tyrant
over all.

The miser runs, but peace more quickly flees
(Oh blind mind that may not see thy mad
desire !) for he looks to catch up with his
gold the sum that infinitely gapes.

Lo, when she has come who levels us, tell me
what hast thou wrought, blind undone miser ?
Answer me, if thou canst give other reply than
nought. A curse upon thy cradle which
lulled so many dreams in vain ! A curse
upon thy wasted bread, which is not wasted
on the dog ! For at eve and morn thou hast
amassed and clutched with either hand that
which so swiftly draws away from thee.

ꝟ

Canz. vii. Come con dismisura si raguna,
   Così con dismisura si ristringe ;
   E quest' è quel che pinge
   Molti in servaggio ; e s' alcun si difende
   Non è senza gran briga.

  Morte, che fai ; che fai, fera Fortuna ;
   Che non solvete quel che non si spende :
   Se 'l fate, a cui si rende ?
   Nol so ; posciachè tal cerchio ne cinge,
   Che di lassù ne riga.

  Colpa è della ragion, che nol castiga.
   Se vuol dire : Io son presa ;
   Ah ! com' poca difesa
   Mostra signore a cui servo sormonta !
   Qui si raddoppia l' onta,
   Se ben si guarda là, dov' io addito.
   Falsi animali, a voi ed altrui crudi :
   Che vedete ire nudi
   Per colli e per paludi
   Uomini, innanzi a cui vizio è fuggito ;
   E voi tenete il vil fango vestito.

v

As without measure it is gathered so without **Ode vii.**
measure is it hugged ; and this it is that thrusts
many into slavery : and should any defend
himself, it is not save with mighty conflict.

Death, what art thou doing, dire Fortune, what
art doing, that ye dissipate not that which is
not spent ?   But, if ye did, to whom to render
it ?   I know not, since such a circle rings us,
compassing us from above.

It is the blame of reason, who doth not correct
it.   If she would say : 'I am captive,' ah
how sorry a defence does the master show
whom a slave overcomes !   Here shame is
doubled, if that to which I point be well con-
sidered.   False animals, cruel to yourselves
and others !   For ye see, going naked o'er
hills and marshes, men before whom vice takes
to flight ; and ye keep the vile mire clad.

VI

Canz. **vii.** Fassi dinanzi al avaro volto
  Virtù, che i suoi nemici a pace invita,
  Con materia pulita,
  Per allettarlo a sè ; ma poco vale ;
  Che sempre fugge l' esca.

  Poichè girato l' ha, chiamando 'l molto,
  Gitta 'l pasto ver lui, tanto glien cale ;
  Ma quei non v' apre l' ale.
  E se pur viene, è quando ell' è partita ;
  Tanto par che gl' incresca.

  Come si possa dar, sicchè non esca
  Del benefizio loda,
  Intendo ciascun m' oda :
  Chi con tardare, e chi con vana vista,
  Chi con sembianza trista
  Volge il donare in vender tanto caro.
  Quanto sa sol chi tal compera paga.
  Volete udir se piaga ?
  Tanto chi prende smaga,
  Che 'l negar poscia non gli pare amaro
  Cosi altrui e se concia l' avaro.

VI

Before the miser's face virtue displays herself, **Ode vii.**
who invites her very foes to peace, with
polished matter to entice him to her; but
little it avails, for he ever flees the bait.

When she has swung it round, summoning him
aloud, she flings the food towards him, so great
her care for him; but he spreads not his wings
at it.   And if at last he come, it is when she
is gone , so seemeth it to irk him.

How one may give so as to make all praise
vanish from benefit, I mean all men to hear
from me : one by delaying, and one by vain display, and one by gloomy semblance, turns the
gift into a sale so dear as he knows only who
pays such purchase.   Would you hear whether
it wounds ? So dismayed is he who receives
that henceforth refusal seems not bitter to him :
so does the miser mutilate himself and others.

VII

Canz vii. Disvelato v' ho, donne, in alcun membro
La viltà della gente che vi mira,
Perchè gli aggiate in ira ;
Ma troppo è più ancor quel che s'asconde,
Perch' a dicer v' è lado.

In ciascuno è di ciascun vizio assembro,
Perchè amistà nel mondo si confonde ;
Chè l' amorosa fronde
Di radice di bene altrui ben tira,
Poi sol simile è in grado.

Vedete come conchiudendo vado :
Che non de' creder quella,
Cui par ben esser bella,
Esser amata da questi cotali :
Ma se beltà fra' mali
Vogliamo annoverar creder si puone,
Chiamando amore appetito di fera.
Oh ! cotal donna pera,
Che sua beltà dischiera
Da natural bontà per tal cagione,
E crede amor fuor d' orto di ragione.

VII

Ladies, in a certain branch have I unveiled to Ode vii. you the baseness of the folk that gaze upon you, that ye may hold them in wrath; but far more yet is that which is concealed because 'tis foul to tell you.

In each one is a gathering of all vices because the world's way is that friendship blends: for the love-some leaf of the root of good draws forth the good from others, for like only pleases.

See how I advance to my conclusion; for she should not believe, who thinks that she is fair indeed, that she is loved by such as these. But if we would enumerate beauty amongst evil things, it might be believed, giving the appetite of a beast the name of love. Oh may such woman perish as dissociates her beauty from natural goodness, on such cause, or believes in love outside of reason's garden.

CANZONE VIII

E' m' incresce di me si duramente,
   Ch' altrettanto di doglia
   Mi reca la pietà quanto 'l martiro:

Lasso ! però che dolorosamente
   Sento contra mia voglia
   Raccoglier l' aer del sezza' sospiro

Entro quel cor che i begli occhi feriro,
   Quando gli aperse Amor con le sue mani,
   Per conducermi al tempo che mi sface.
   Oimè quanto piani,
   Soavi e dolci ver me si levaro,
   Quand'egli incominciaro
   La morte mia, che tanto mi dispiace,
   Dicendo : Nostro lume porta pace.

ODE VIII

I

I have ruth for myself so cruelly that as much
 suffering is furnished me by the pity as by the
 pain:

Ah me! that dolorously I feel, against my will,
 the breath of the last sigh gathering

Within the heart that the beauteous eyes smote,
 when Love opened them with his own hands,
 to lead me to the season that undoes me. Oh
 me! how gentle, tender and sweet did they
 lift themselves upon me, when they began the
 death that is so grievous to me, saying: 'Our
 light brings peace.'

II

'Noi darem pace al cor, a voi diletto,'
   Diceano agli occhi miei
   Quei della bella donna alcuna volta:

Ma poichè sepper, da loro intelletto,
   Che per forza di lei
   M' era la mente già ben tutta tolta

Con l'insegne d'Amor dieder la volta,
   Sicchè la lor vittoriosa vista
   Poi non si vide pur una fiata.
   Ond' è rimasa trista
   L' anima mia, che n' attendea conforto.
   Ed ora quasi morto
   Vede lo core a cui era sposata,
   E partir le conviene innamorata.

III

Innamorata se ne va piangendo
   Fuora di questa vita
   La sconsolata, chè la caccia Amore.

Ella si muove quinci, sì dolendo
   Ch' anzi la sua partita
   L'ascolta con pietate il suo fattore.

Ristretta s' è entro il mezzo del core
   Con quella vita, che rimane spenta
   Solo in quel punto ch' ella sen va via:
   Ed ivi si lamenta
   D'Amor, che fuor d'esto mondo la caccia:
   E spessamente abbraccia
   Gli spiriti che piangon tuttavia,
   Perocchè perdon la lor compagnia.

II

' Peace will we give thy heart, to thee delight,' Ode viii.
  said to my eyes, time was, those of the
  beauteous lady ;

But when, of their intelligence, they learned
  that, by her might, my mind was now reft
  wholly from me,

With love's ensigns they so wheeled about, that
  their victorious spectacle was not beheld by
  me again one single time. Whence is left
  mourning my soul that looked for solace from
  them : and now she beholds the heart well
  nigh dead, to whom she was espoused ; and she
  must needs depart love-smitten.

III

Love-smitten she goes weeping on her way,
  beyond this life, she the disconsolate, for love
  expels her.

She departs thence, so grieving, that, e'er she
  goes, her maker hearkeneth with pity to her.

She hath gathered herself, midmost the heart,
  together with that life which remains
  quenched only at the moment when she
  wends her way : and there utters her complaint of Love, who from this world expels
  her : and many a time embraces the spirits that
  ever weep that they are losing their companion.

IV

Canz.
viii.

L'immagine di questa donna siede
  Su nella mente ancora,
  Dove la pose quei che fu sua guida:

E non le pesa del mal ch' ella vede,
  Anzi vie è più bell' ora
  Che mai, e vie più lieta par che rida:

Ed apre gli occhi micidiali, e grida
  Sopra colei che piange il suo partire,
  Vatten, misera, fuor, vattene omai.
  Questo gridò il desire,
  Che mi combatte così come suole;
  Avvegna che men duole,
  Perocchè 'l mio sentire è meno assai
  Ed è più presso al terminar de guai.

V

Lo giorno che costei nel mondo venne,
  Secondo che si trova
  Nel libro della mente che vien meno,

La mia persona parvola sostenne
  Una passion nuova,
  Tal ch' io rimasi di paura pieno:

Ch' a tutte mie virtù fu posto un freno
  Subitamente sì, ch' io caddi in terra
  Per una luce, che nel cuor percosse.
  E (se' l libro non erra)
  Lo spirito maggior tremò sì forte,
  Che parve ben che morte
  Per lui in questo mondo giunta fosse:
  Ma or n' incresce a quei che questo mosse.

IV

The image of this lady sits yet in my mind, Ode viii.
where he established her who was her guide:

And it irks her not of the woe which she
beholds, nay rather is she far more beauteous
now than e'er before, and far more joyously
she seems to smile:

And opens eyes that slay, and cries over her
who weeps that she must go: 'Get gone,
thou wretch, now get thee gone!' And this
cry is caught up by the yearning which assails
me, after its wont; albeit the smart is less,
for greatly hath the power of feeling waned,
and draweth nearer to the end of woes.

V

The day whereon she came into the world, as
stands recorded in memory's book that wanes,

My infant person sustained a passion never
known, such that I remained fulfilled with
terror.

For on my every power a curb was set so
suddenly that down I fell to earth, by reason
of a light that struck upon the heart. And,
if the book errs not, the main spirit trembled
so mightily that well it seemed as though
death was reached in this world by him.
Now he who set this moving has ruth of it.

VI

Canz. Quando m' apparve poi la gran beltate,
viii.   Che sì mi fa dolere,
             Donne gentili, a cui io ho parlato,

Quella virtù che ha più nobilitate,
     Mirando nel piacere,
     S' accorse ben che' l suo male era nato

E conobbe 'l disio ch' era criato
     Per lo mirare intento ch' ella fece.
     Sicchè piangendo disse all' altre poi :
     Qui giugnerà, in vece,
     D' una ch' io vidi la bella figura,
     Che già mi fa paura ;
     E sarà donna sopra tutte noi,
     Tosto che fia 'l piacer degli occhi suoi.'

VII

Io ho parlato a voi, giovani donne,
     Che avete gli occhi di bellezza ornati,
     E la mente d' amor vinta e pensosa,
     Perchè raccomandati
     Vi sian gli detti miei dovunque sono.
     E innanzi a voi perdono
     La morte mia a quella bella cosa,
     Che men' ha colpa, e mai non fu pietosa.

VI

Then, when the great beauty appeared to me Ode viii.
which so makes me mourn, ye gentle ladies
to whom I have addressed me,

The power that has most nobility, gazing upon
the joy, perceived right well that its affliction
was born :

And recognised the longing that had been
created by the intent gaze that it wrought ;
so that it then said, weeping, to the others :
' Here shall arrive, to hold vicarious sway,
the beauteous form of one whom I have seen,
who even now strikes me with terror, and
shall be lady over all of us, so soon as it shall
be the pleasure of her eyes.'

VII

To you, ye youthful ladies, have I spoken,
whose eyes are adorned with beauty, and
mind vanquished and bemused by love, that
commended be to you my rhymes where'er
they are. And, before you, I pardon my
death to that beauteous being who has the
blame of it to me-wards, and has never pitied.

CANZONE IX

I

Io sento sì d' amor la gran possanza,
  Ch' io non posso durare
  Lungamente a soffrire ; ond' io mi doglio :

Perocchè il suo valor sì pure avanza,
  E 'l mio sento mancare
  Sì, ch' io son meno ognora ch' io non soglio.

Non dico ch' Amor faccia ciò ch' io voglio,
  Chè se facesse quanto il voler chiede,
  Quella virtù che natura mi diede
  Nol sofferia, perocch' ella è finita :
  Ma questo è quello ond' io prendo cordoglio,
  Che alla voglia il poder non terrà fede,
  E se di buon voler nasce mercede,
  Io la dimando, per aver più vita,
  Dagli occhi che nel suo bello splendore
  Portan conforto ovunque io senta amore.

ODE IX

I

So do I feel the mighty power of love that I
may not long endure to support it; which is
grievous to me:

For so does his might keep growing, and mine I
so feel to fail, that hour by hour I am en-
feebled from my wont.

I say not that Love works that which I desire,
for, if he wrought all that my will demands,
such power as nature gave me would support
it not, in that it is finite : and this it is whence
I pluck sorrow, that power will not keep faith
with purpose; and if from goodwill springs
reward, I demand it, for furtherance of life,
of those eyes which in their beauteous
splendour bring comfort whensoe'er I taste
of pain.

II

Canz   **x**   Entrano i raggi di questi occhi belli
        Ne' miei innamorati,
        E portan dolce ovunque io sento amaro:

       E sanno lo cammin, siccome quelli
        Che già vi son passati;
        E sanno il loco dove Amor lasciaro,

     Quando per gli occhi miei dentro il menaro.
        Per che mercè, volgendosi a me, fanno;
        E di colei cui son procaccian danno
        Celandosi da me; poi tanto l' amo
        Che sol per lei servir mi tengo caro:
        E' miei pensier, che pur d' amor si fanno,
        Come a lor segno al suo servigio vanno:
        Per che l' adoperar sì forte bramo,
        Che, s' io 'l potesse far fuggendo lei,
        Lieve saria; e so ch' io ne morrei.

II

The rays of these beauteous eyes enter into mine   Ode ix.
enamoured ones, and bring the sweet whenas
I taste the bitter.

And they know the way, even as such who erst
have traversed it ; and they know the spot
where they left Love,

When through my eyes they led him in.
Wherefore they do mercy when they turn on
me ; and to her whose I am they purchase
loss when they hide themselves from me ;
since so I love her, that only to serve her do
I hold myself dear : and my musings, compact
merely of love, hie them, as to their goal, to
her service : wherefore to perform the same I
long so greatly, that, might I accomplish it
by fleeing her, it were an easy thing to do ;
and I know that I should die thereby.

III

Canz. ix   Ben è verace amor quel che m' ha preso,
       E ben mi stringe forte,
       Quand' io farei quel ch' io dico per lui.

   Che nullo amore è di cotanto peso
       Quanto è quel che la morte
       Face piacer, per ben servire altrui:

   Ed in cotal voler fermato fui
       Si tosto come il gran desio ch' io sento
       Fu nato per virtù del piacimento
       Che nel bel viso d' ogni ben s' accoglie.
       Io son servente: e quando penso a cui,
       Qual ch'ella sia, di tutto son contento;
       Chè l' uom può ben servir contra talento:
       E se mercè convenenza mi toglie,
       Aspetto tempo che più ragion prenda;
       Purchè la vita tanto si difenda.

III

'Tis very love indeed that hath captured me, Ode ix
and mightily indeed he grips me, since I
would do that which I say for him.

For no love is of such weight as is that which
makes death acceptable, for good service of
another :

And in such will was I confirmed so soon as
the great longing, which I feel, was born, by
virtue of the pleasure which gathers from all
good in the fair countenance.   A servant am
I : and when I bethink me whose, and what
she is, I am utterly content ; for a man may
serve well, against good pleasure ; and if grace
withholds all covenant from me, I look to the
time which shall gain more regard ; if but
my life shall hold her own so long.

IV

Quand io penso un gentil desio, ch' è nato
          Del gran desio ch' io porto,
          Ch' a ben far tira tutto il mio potere,

    Parmi esser di mercede oltra pagato ;
          Ed ancor più ch' a torto
          Mi par di servidor nome tenere :

    Cosi dinanzi agli occhi del parere
          Si fa 'l servir, mercè d' altrui bontate ;
          Ma poich' io mi ristringo a veritate,
          Convien che tal desio servigio conti,
          Perocchè, s' io procaccio di valere,
          Non penso tanto a mia proprietate,
          Quanto a colei che m' ha in sua podestate,
          Chè 'l fo perchè sua cosa in pregio monti :
          Ed io son tutto suo ; e così mi tegno,
          Chè Amor di tanto onor m' ha fatto degno.

IV

When I muse upon a noble longing, born of that Ode ix great longing which I bear, that draws all my powers to well-doing.

Meseems that I am overpayed with grace; and yet more than wrongly meseems I bear the name of servant;

So, before the eyes of my seeming, is service transformed, thanks to a not-my goodness. Yet, since I hold me close knit to truth, needs must such longing count as service; because, if I make haste to be of worth, I ponder on what not so much concerns myself as her who hath me in her power; for I so do in order that her cause may be more prized; and I am wholly hers; and so esteem myself, because Love hath made me worthy of so great honour.

▼

Canz. ix. Altri ch' Amor non mi pote far tale
            Ch' io fossi degnamente
            Cosa di quella che non s' innamora,

        Ma stassi come donna a cui non cale
            Dell' amorosa mente,
            Che senza lei non può passare un' ora.

        Io non la vidi tante volte ancora,
            Ch' io non trovassi in lei nuova bellezza ;
            Onde Amor cresce in me la sua grandezza
            Tanto quanto il piacer nuovo s' aggiugne.
            Onde m' avvien, che tanto fo dimora
            In uno stato, e tanto Amor m' avvezza
            Con un martiro e con una dolcezza,
            Quanto è quel tempo che spesso mi pugne,
            Che dura dacch' io perdo la sua vista
            Infino al punto ch' ella si racquista.

v

Other than Love could not have made me such Ode ix.
as to be worthily aught that pertains to her,
the unenamoured,

Who takes her stand as a lady whom the
amorous mind concerns not, that without her
may not pass an hour.

Not yet so many times have I beheld her, but
that new beauty I may find in her; whence
Love makes grow his greatness in me, in
measure as new joy is added. Wherefore it
comes about that so long do I abide in one
state, and so long doth love lime me with one
torment and with one sweetness, as lasts that
season, that so often goads me, which endures
from when I lose the sight of her until the
moment it be won again.

VI

Canzon mia bella, se tu mi somigli,
   Tu non sarai sdegnosa
   Tanto quanto alla tua bontà s' avviene :

Però ti prego che tu t' assottigli,
   Dolce mia amorosa,
   In prender modo e via che ti stea bene.

Se cavalier t' invita, o ti ritiene,
   Innanzi che nel suo piacer ti metta,
   Spia se far lo puoi della tua setta,
   Se vuoi saver qual e la sua persona
   Chè 'l buon col buon camera sempre tiene.
   Ma egli avvien, che spesso altri si getta
   In compagnia che non è che disdetta
   Di mala fama, ch' altri di lui suona.
   Con rei non star nè ad ingegno nè ad arte ;
   Chè non fu mai saver tener lor parte.

[Canzone, à' tre men rei di nostra terra
   Te n' andarai, prima che vadi altrove :
   Li due saluta ; e l' altro fa che prove
   Di trarlo fuor di mala setta in pria.
   Digli ch' è folle chi non si rimove,
   Per tema di vergogna, da follia ;
   Che quegli teme, c' ha del mal paura ;
   Perchè, fuggendo l' un, l' altro assicura.]

VI

My beauteous ode, if thou be like to me, thou
   wilt not be scornful so much as cometh to thy Ode ix.
   excellence :

Therefore I pray thee that thou ply thy wit, my
   sweet amorous one, in culling mode and way
   that shall become thee.

Should cavalier invite thee or arrest, e'er thou
   yield thyself to his pleasure see if thou canst
   make him of thy sect, would'st thou know
   the nature of his person, for the good keeps
   chamber ever with the good.   But it chances
   that one often throws himself into a company
   whence there is nought save smirch of evil
   fame, that men proclaim of him.   With the
   guilty sojourn not by wit nor art ; for never
   was it wisdom yet to hold their side.

[Ode ! to the three least vicious of our city thou
   shalt take thy way e'er thou go otherwhither :
   salute the two : and see to it that thou try
   the third, to draw him first out of ill company.
   Tell him that he is mad who fleeth not, for
   fear of shame, from madness ; for he feareth
   who hath terror of the evil ; therefore, fleeing
   the one, he maketh sure the other.

CANZONE X

I

Io son venuto al punto della rota
    Che l' orizzonte, quando il sol si corca,
    Ci partorisce il geminato cielo,

E la stella d' amor ci sta rimota
    Per lo raggio lucente che la 'nforca
    Sì di traverso che le si fa velo:

E quel pianeta che conforta il gelo,
    Si mostra tutto a noi per lo grand' arco
    Nel qual ciascun de' sette fa poca ombra:
    E però non mi sgombra
    Un sol pensier d' amore, ond' io son carco,
    La mente mia, ch' è più dura che pietra
    In tener forte immagine di pietra.

II

Levasi della rena d' Etiopia
    Lo vento peregrin, che l' aer turba,
    Per la spera del sol ch' or la rescalda;

E passa il mare, onde n' adduce copia
    Di nebbia tal che, s' altro non la sturba,
    Questo emispero chiude tutto, e salda:

E poi si solve, e cade in bianca falda
    Di fredda neve, ed in noiosa pioggia;
    Onde l' aere s' attrista tutto, e piagne:
    Ed Amor, che sue ragne
    Ritira al ciel per lo vento che poggia,
    Non m' abbandona; sì è bella donna
    Questa crudel, che m' è datta per donna.

ODE X

I

I have come to the point of the wheel where
the horizon, when the sun declines, yields up
the twinned heaven;

And the star of love is severed from us by the
shining ray, that enforks her so athwart as to
become her veil:

And that planet that strengthens the cold displays himself to us full on the great circle
wherefrom each of the seven casts shortest
shadow.—And yet my mind discharges not
one single thought of love wherewith I am
laden, for it is harder than a stone in holding
firm the image of stone.

II

Rises from the sand of Ethiopia the alien wind
that troubles the air, by reason of the sun's
sphere that is now burning it;

And passes the ocean, whence it leads us store
of cloud, such that if another baffle it not, it
all closes up and seals this hemisphere;

And then resolves, and falls in white flakes of
chill snow and of grievous shower, whence
the air is saddened all and weeps.—And
Love, who draws back his nets on high by
reason of the beating wind, abandons not me;
so beauteous is the lady, this cruel one, who
is given me for my lady.

III

Canz. x. Fuggito è ogni augel, che'l caldo segue,
    Dal paese d' Europa, che non perde
    Le sette stelle gelide unquemai :

E gli altri han posto alle lor voci triegue
    Per non sonarle infino al tempo verde,
    Se ciò non fosse per cagion di guai :

E tutti gli animali, che son gai
    Da lor natura, son d' amor disciolti,
    Perocchè il freddo lo spirto gli ha ammorta.
    E 'l mio più d' amor porta ;
    Chè gli dolci pensier non mi son tolti,
    Nè mi son dati, per volta di tempo ;
    Ma donna gli mi dà di picciol tempo.

IV

Passato hanno lor termine le fronde,
    Che trasse fuor la virtù del Ariete,
    Per adornare il mondo, e morta è l' erba ;

Ramo di foglia verde non s' asconde,
    Se non in lauro, in pino, od in abete,
    Od in alcun che sua verdura serba :

E tanto è la stagion forte ed acerba,
    Ch' ha morti gli fioretti per le piaggie,
    Gli quai non posson tollerar la brina :
    E la crudele spina
    Amor però di cor non la mi tragge ;
    Ond' io son certo di portarla sempre
    Ch' io sarò in vita, s' io vivessi sempre.

III

Every bird that followeth the heat, hath fled
that region of Europe that loses not the seven
chill stars ever;

And the rest have set a truce upon their voices,
no more to sound them till the green season,
unless it be by cause of wailing;

And all animals that are wanton by their nature,
are discharged from love, because the chill has
deadened their spirit.—And mine beareth the
more of love; for my sweet musings are not
reft from me, nor are not given me, by revolving season; but a lady gives them me of
but short season.

IV

Passed their limit have the leaves, that the virtue
of the Ram drew forth to adorn the world,
and dead is all the grass.

No branch conceals itself in green, save laurel
or pine or fir, and such other as preserves its
verdure:

And so hard and bitter is the season that it
hath slain upon the slopes the flowers that
have not power to endure the frost.—And
Love, for all that, draws not the cruel thorn
from out my heart; and so am I assured ever
to bear it, the while I am in life, although I
lived for ever.

I

V

Canz. x. Versan le vene le fumifere acque,
          Per li vapor che la terra ha nel ventre,
          Che d' abisso gli tira suso in alto ;

Onde cammino al bel giorno mi piacque,
    Che ora è fatto rivo, e sarà, mentre
    Che durerà del verno il grande assalto.

La terra fa un suol che par di smalto,
    E l' acqua morta si converte in vetro
    Per la freddura che di fuor la serra.
    Ed io della mia guerra
    Non son però tornato un passo arretro,
    Nè vo' tornar ; chè, se 'l martiro è dolce,
    La morte de' passare ogni altro dolce.

VI

Canzone, or che sarà di me nell' altro
    Dolce tempo novello, quando piove
    Amore in terra da tutti li cieli ;
    Quando per questi geli
    Amore è solo in me, e non altrove ?
    Sarà di me quel ch' è d' un uom di marmo,
    Se in pargoletta fia per cuore un marmo.

V

The veins pour forth the steaming waters, by Ode x. reason of the vapours earth holdeth in her womb, who draweth them up aloft from the abyss;

Whereby the path that pleased me in fair weather, has now become a river, and will be, whilst the winter's great assault shall last.

The earth makes one seeming-cemented floor, and the dead water turns to glass by reason of the cold that locks it from without.—And I from my warfare have not, for that, drawn back one step, nor would draw back; for, if torment be sweet, death must surpass all other sweetness.

VI

My ode, what now will come of me in the next sweet season of renewal, when love rains upon the earth from all the heavens, if throughout these frosts love is in me alone and no other where? That will come to me which comes to a man of marble, if in the maiden, for a heart, be marble.

CANZONE XI

I

La dispietata mente, che pur mira
  Di dietro al tempo che se n' è andato,
  Dall' un de' lati mi combatte il core ;

E 'l disio amoroso, che mi tira
  Verso 'l dolce paese ch' ho lasciato,
  D' altra parte è con la forza d' amore :

Nè dentro io sento tanto di valore,
  Che lungamente io possa far difesa,
  Gentil madonna, se da voi non vene.
  Però, se a voi convene
  Ad iscampo di lui mai fare impresa,
  Piacciavi a lui mandar vostra salute,
  Che sia conforto della sua virtute.

II

Piacciavi, donna mia, non venir meno,
  A questo punto, al cor che tanto v' ama,
  Poi sol da voi lo suo soccorso attende ;

Chè buon signor mai non ristringe 'l freno,
  Ver lo suo servo se merce gli chiama :
  Che non pur lui, ma 'l suo onor difende.

E certo la sua doglia più m' incende,
  Quand' io mi penso ben, donna, che vui
  Per man d' Amor la entro pinta sete :
  Così e voi dovete
  Vie maggiormente aver cura di lui ;
  Chè quel, da cui convien che 'l ben s' appari,
  Per l' immagine sua ne tien più cari.

ODE XI

I

The torturing memory, that ever looks back to the time that has departed, from the one side assails my heart:

And the amorous longing that draws me towards the sweet country I have left, hath on the other side the might of love.

Nor do I find such strength within as may long make defence, gentle my lady, save it come from thee; wherefore, if it behoves thee for its deliverance e'er to do emprise, may it please thee send thy salutation, to be the heartening of its power.

II

May it please thee, my lady, not to fail, at this point, the heart that so loveth thee; since from thee alone it looks for succour;

For good liege lord ne'er draweth rein when making for his vassal who cries to him for grace, for not him only he defends but his own honour.

And verily its pain afflicts me hotlier when I reflect that thou, my lady, by love's own hand art painted therewithin: and even for that cause shouldst thou also hold it far greatlier in care: for he from whom all good must needs appear, because of his own image holdeth us the dearer.

III

Canz. xi. Se dir voleste, dolce mia speranza,
        Di dare indugio a quel ch' io vi domando,
        Sappiate che l'attender più non posso ;

    Ch' io sono al fine della mia possanza.
        E ciò conoscer voi dovete, quando
        L' ultima speme a cercar mi son mosso:

    Che tutti i carchi sostenere addosso
        De' l' uomo infino al peso ch' è mortale,
        Prima che 'l suo maggiore amico provi ;
        Che non sa qual lo trovi,
        E s' egli avvien che gli risponda male,
        Cosa non è che tanto costi cara ;
        Chè morte n' ha più tosta e più amara.

IV

    E voi pur sete quella ch' io più amo,
        E che far mi potete maggior dono,
        E' n cui la mia speranza più riposa ;

    Chè sol per voi servir la vita bramo.
        E quelle cose che a voi onor sono
        Dimando e voglio ; ogni altra m' è noiosa.

    Dar mi potrete ciò ch' altri non osa,
        Chè 'l sì e 'l no di me in vostra mano
        Ha posto Amore ; ond' io grande mi tegno.
        La fede ch' io v' assegno
        Muove dal portamento vostro umano ;
        Chè ciascun che vi mira in veritate,
        Di fuor conosce che dentro è pietate.

III

If thou shouldst speak, O sweet my hope, of Ode xi.
setting a delay on that which I demand, know
that I may not longer wait on it;

For at the limit of my power I stand: and this
thou shouldst discern, seeing that I have set
me to explore my final hope;

For to bear every load upon his back a man is
bound, up to the mortal weight, e'er he make
trial of his chiefest friend; for how he shall
discover him to stand he knows not, and if it
chance that he respond amiss to him, nought
is there that can cost so dear; for he hath the
swifter and more bitter death thereby.

IV

And whom I chiefliest love art thou, and who
the greatest gift canst give me, and in whom
most my hope reposes;

For only to serve thee do I desire life; and such
things as make for thy honour I demand and
will: all else being grievous to me.

Thou hast the power to give me what no other
may, for all the yea and nay of me hath Love
placed within thy hand; whereat myself I
magnify.   The faith I mete to thee flows from
thy tender bearing; for whoso looks on thee
in verity, knows from without that within there
is pity.

v

Canz. xi. Dunque vostra salute omai si muova,
              E vegna dentro al cor che lei aspetta,
              Gentil madonna, come avete inteso :

        Ma sappia che allo entrar di lui si trova
              Serrato forte di quella saetta
              Ch' Amor lanciò lo giorno ch' io fu' preso ;

        Per che lo entrare a tutt' altri è conteso,
              Fuor ch' a' messi d' Amor, ch' aprir lo sanno
              Per volontà della virtù che 'l serra.
              Onde nella mia guerra
              La sua venuta mi sarebbe danno,
              Sed ella fosse senza compagnia
              De' messi del signor che m' ha in balia.

vi

        Canzone, il tuo cammin vuol esser corto ;
              Che tu sai ben che poco tempo omai
              Puote aver luogo quel per che tu vai.

V

Then let thy salutation now be launched and come into the heart that waits for it, gentle my lady, e'en as thou hast heard: Ode xi.

But know that, at its entrance, it is found strong barred by that same arrow that Love discharged the day I was made captive;

Whereby the entrance is disputed to all other save to the messengers of Love, who know to open it, by will of that same power that barred. Wherefore, in my conflict, its coming were but hurt to me were it without escort of messengers of that liege lord who hath me in his power.

VI

My ode, needs must be brief thy journey; for thou knowest that for short space now that may be brought about for which thou goest.

*1

CANZONE XII

(*Contra gli erranti*)

I

Le dolci rime d' amor, ch' io solìa
    Cercar ne' miei pensieri,
    Convien ch' io lasci; non perch' io non speri
    Ad esse ritornare,

Ma perchè gli atti disdegnosi e feri,
    Che nella donna mia
    Sono appariti, m' han chiuso la via
    Dell' usato parlare.

E poichè tempo mi par d' aspettare,
    Diporrò giù lo mio soave stile,
    Ch' io ho tenuto nel trattar d' amore,
    E dirò del valore
    Per lo qual veramente è l'uom gentile,
    Con rima aspra e sottile
    Riprovando il giudizio falso e vile
    Di que' che voglion che di gentilezza
    Sia principio ricchezza.
    E cominciando, chiamo quel signore
    Ch' alla mia donna negli occhi dimora,
    Per ch' ella di sè stessa s' innamora.

ODE XII

(Against the erring ones)

I

The sweet rhymes of love which I was wont to
  search out in my thoughts, needs must I
  abandon; not that I have no hope of a return to them.

But because the scornful and haughty gestures
  which have appeared in my lady, have closed
  the way of wonted speech to me.

And because meseems 'tis time for waiting, down
  will I lay my tender style, which I have held
  in treating of love, and I will tell of the worth
  whereby a man is truly gentle, with harsh and
  subtle rhyme refuting the judgment false and
  base of such as would have it that of gentlehood the principle is wealth.   And, at the
  outset, I invoke that lord who so dwelleth
  in my ladies eyes that of herself she is
  enamoured.

II

Canz. xii. Tale imperò, che gentilezza volse,
    Secondo 'l suo parere,
    Che fosse antica possession d' avere,
    Con reggimenti belli :

    Ed altri fu di più lieve sapere
    Che tal detto rivolse,
    E l' ultima particola ne tolse,
    Chè non l' avea fors' elli.

    Di dietro da costui van tutti quelli
    Che fan gentili per ischiatta altrui
    Che lungamente in gran ricchezza è stata :
    Ed è tanto durata
    La così falsa opinion tra nui,
    Che l' uom chiama colui
    Uomo gentil che può dicere : I' fui
    Nipote o figlio di cotal valente,
    Benchè sia da niente :
    Ma vilissimo sembra, a chi 'l ver guata,
    Cui è scorto il cammino e poscia l' erra,
    E tocca tal ch' è morto e va per terra.

II

A certain one held empire who would have Ode xii. gentlehood, according as he deemed, to be the ancient possession of wealth, with gracious manners.

And some other was there, of lighter wisdom, who recast such saying, and stripped it of its latter phrase, methinks because he had it not.

After him go all they who make folk gentle because of race which has long abode in great wealth : and so inured is such false thought amongst us, that folk call that man a gentleman, who can aver : ' I was grandson or son of such an one of worth,' though he himself be nought. But basest doth he seem, to whoso looks on truth, who hath been shown the way, and after errs therefrom ; and he hits nigh to who should be a corpse yet walk the earth.

III

Canz. xii. Chi difinisce: uomo è legno animato;
Prima dice non vero,
E dopo 'l falso parla non intero;
Ma più forse non vede.

Similemente fu chi tenne impero
In difinire errato,
Chè prima pone 'l falso, e d' altro lato
Con difetto procede;

Chè le divizie, siccome si crede
Non posson gentilezza dar nè torre;
Perocchè vili son di lor natura:
Poi chi pinge figura,
Se non può esser lei, non la può porre:
Nè la diritta torre
Fa piegar rivo che da lunge corre.
Che sieno vili appare ed imperfette,
Chè, quantunque collette,
Non posson quietar, ma dan più cura
Onde l' animo ch' è dritto e verace
Per lor discorrimento non si sface.

III

He who defines : 'Man is a living trunk,' in Ode xii.
the first place speaks that which is not true,
and further, utters the falsehood in defective
guise ; but haply sees no more.

In like fashion did he who held empire err in
definition, for in the first place he lays down
the false, and on the other hand proceeds
defectively ;

For riches can not (as is held) either give
gentlehood or take away, since in their nature
they are base. Further, who paints a figure,
unless himself can be it, can not set it down :
nor is an upright tower made to lean by a
river that flows far away. That they be base
and imperfect is apparent ; for, how much
soever gathered, they can give no quiet, but
multiply care ; wherefore the mind that is
upright and true is not dismayed by their
dispersion.

IV

Canz. xii. Nè voglion che vil uom gentil divegna,
      Nè di vil padre scenda
      Nazion che per gentil giammai s' intenda :
      Quest' è da lor confesso ;

      Onde la lor ragion par che s' offenda,
      In tanto quanto assegna
      Che tempo a gentilezza si convegna,
      Diffinendo con esso.

      Ancor segue, di ciò che innanzi ho messo.
      Che siam tutti gentili ovver villani,
      O che non fosse all' uom cominciamento.
      Ma ciò io non consento
      Nè eglino altresì, se son Cristiani ;
      Per che a intelletti sani
      È manifesto i lor diri esser vani :
      Ed io così per falsi li riprovo,
      E da lor mi rimuovo ;
      E dicer voglio omai, siccome io sento,
      Che cosa è gentilezza, e da che viene,
      E dirò i segni che gentil uom tiene.

IV

Nor will they have it that a base man can be-   Ode xii.
come gentle, nor that from a base father can
descend a family that ever can be held as
gentle: this is avowed by them.

Wherefore their argument appears to halt, inasmuch as it lays down that time is requisite to
gentlehood, defining it thereby.

Further it followeth from what I have above set
down, that we be all gentle or else simple, or
that man had not an origin: but this I grant
not, neither do they, if they be Christians.
Wherefore to sound intellects 'tis manifest that
what they say is vain, and thus do I refute
the same as false, and therefrom dissociate me.
And now I would declare, as I regard it,
what thing is gentlehood and whence it
comes; and I will tell the tokens that a
gentleman retains.

v

Canz. xii. Dico ch' ogni virtù principalmente
        Vien da una radice,
        Virtute, intendo, che fa l' uom felice
        In sua operazione.

     Quest' è, secondochè l' *Etica* dice,
        Un abito eligente,
        Lo qual dimora in mezzo solamente ;
        E tai parole pone.

     Dico che nobiltate in sua ragione
        Importa sempre ben del suo subietto,
        Come viltate importa sempre male:
        E virtute cotale
        Dà sempre altrui di sè buono intelletto ;
        Perchè in medesmo detto
        Convengono ambedue, ch' èn d' un effetto ;
        Onde convien dall' altra venga l' una,
        O da un terzo ciascuna :
        Ma se l' una val ciò che l' altra vale,
        Ed ancor più, da lei verrà piuttosto :
        E ciò ch' io ho detto qui sia per supposto.

v

I affirm that every virtue in principle cometh Ode xii
from one root, I mean virtue that maketh man
blessed in his doing.

This is (according as the *Ethics* say), 'a
selective habit, which abideth solely in the
mean'; such are the words set down.

I affirm that nobility in its constituent essence
ever implies the goodness of its seat, as baseness ever implies ill.   And such like virtue
always carries the import of good; wherefore
in one same implication the two agree, being
to one effect.   Therefore the one needs must
derive from the other, or both from the same
third.   But if one signifies all that the other
signifies, and more as well, the derivation will
rather be from it.   And let this which I have
now declared be presupposed.

VI

Canz. xii. È gentilezza dovunque è virtute,
      Ma non virtute ov' ella;
      Siccome è 'l cielo dovunque la stella;
      Ma ciò non *e converso.*

    E noi in donne ed in età novella
      Vedem questa salute,
      In quanto vergognose son tenute;
      Ch' è da virtù diverso.

    Dunque verrà, come dal nero il perso,
      Ciascheduna virtute da costei,
      Ovvero il gener lor, ch' io misi avanti.
      Però nessun si vanti,
      Dicendo: Per ischiatta io son con lei
      Ch' elli son quasi dei
      Que' c' han tal grazia fuor di tutti rei;
      Chè solo Iddio all' anima la dona
      Che vede in sua persona
      Perfettamente star, sicchè ad alquanti
      Lo seme di felicità s' accosta,
      Messo da Dio nell' anima ben posta.

VI

Gentlehood is wherever there is virtue, but not Ode xii.
  virtue where she is; even as the heaven is
  wherever is the star, but not conversely.

And in women and in youthful age we perceive
  this saving thing, in so far as they are deemed
  alive to shame, which is diverse from virtue.

Therefore shall be evolved (like perse from
  black) each several virtue out of her, or their
  generic kind which I have expressed above.
  Wherefore let no one vaunt himself and say:
  'I belong to her by race'; for they are
  well-nigh gods who have such grace, apart
  from all the guilty; for God alone presents it
  to the soul which he sees take perfect stand
  within its person; even as to some the seed of
  blessedness draws nigh, despatched by God
  into the well-placed soul.

VII

Canz. xii. L' anima cui adorna esta bontate
Non la si tiene ascosa ;
Chè dal principio ch' al corpo si sposa,
La mostra infin la morte.

Ubidiente, soave e vergognosa
È nella prima etate,
E sua persona adorna di beltate,
Colle sue parti accorte :

In giovinezza temperata e forte,
Piena d' amore e di cortese lode,
E solo in lealtà far si diletta :
E nella sua senetta,
Prudente e giusta, e larghezza se n' ode ;
E in sè medesma gode
D' udire e ragionar dell' altrui prode ;
Poi nella quarta parte della vita
A Dio si rimarita,
Contemplando la fine che l' aspetta ;
E benedice li tempi passati.
Vedete omai quanti son gl' ingannati !

VIII

Contra gli erranti, mia canzon, n' andrai ;
E quando tu sarai
In parte, dove sia la donna nostra,

Non le tenere il tuo mestier coverto.
Tu le puoi dir per certo :
Io vo parlando dell' amica vostra.

VII

The soul whom this excellence adorns, holds it **Ode xii.** not concealed; for, from the first when she weds the body, she shews it forth till death.

Obedient, sweet and alive to shame, is she in the first age; and adorns her person with beauty with well according parts.

In manhood she is temperate and brave, full of love and courteous praises, and delights only in deeds of loyalty. And in old age is prudent and just, and hath a name for open-handedness, rejoicing in herself to hear and to discourse of others' excellence. Then in the fourth term of life to God is re-espoused, contemplating the end that is awaiting her, and blesses the past seasons. See now how many they who be deceived!

VIII

Against the erring ones take thou thy way, my ode, and when thou shalt be in the region where our lady is,

Keep not thy business hid from her: thou may'st securely say to her: 'I go discoursing of a friend of thine.'

CANZONE XIII

I

Poscia ch' Amor del tutto m' ha lasciato,
   Non per mio grato,
   Che stato—non avea tanto gioioso,
   Ma perocchè pietoso
   Fu tanto del mio core,
   Che non sofferse d' ascoltar suo pianto,

Io canterò così disamorato
   Contr' al peccato,
   Ch' è nato—in noi di chiamare a ritroso
   Tal, ch' è vile e noioso,
   Con nome di valore,
   Cioè di leggiadria; ch' è bella tanto

Che fa degno di manto
   Imperial colui dov' ella regna.
   Ella è verace insegna,
   La qual dimostra u' la virtù dimora:
   Perche io son certo, se ben la difendo
   Nel dir com' io la 'ntendo,
   Ch' Amor di sè mi farà grazia ancora.

ODE XIII

I

Since Love has utterly forsaken me,—not at
my will, for never had I been so joyous,—
but because he had so much pity upon my
heart that he might not endure to hearken to
its wailing,

I will sing, thus disenamoured, against the sin
that has arisen in our midst, of counter-calling
such one as is base and irksome by a name
of worth, to wit of gallantry; which is a
thing so fair

As to make worthy of the imperial mantle him
in whom it reigns. A veritable sign it is,
which shows where virtue sojourns; wherefore I am assured that if I well defend it in
speech, even as I conceive it, Love will again
do me grace of himself.

II

Canz.
xiii.

Sono, che per gittar via loro avere
    Credon potere
    Capere—là, dove gli buoni stanno,
    Che dopo morte fanno
    Riparo nella mente
    A quei cotanti c' hanno conoscenza:

Ma lor messione a' buon non può piacere,
    Perchè 'l tenere
    Savere—fora, e fuggirieno 'l danno
    Che s' aggiunge allo inganno
    Di loro, e della gente
    C' hanno falso giudizio in lor sentenza.

Qual non dirà fallenza
    Divorar cibo, ed a lussuria intendere?
    Ornarsi, come vendere
    Si dovesse al mercato de' non saggi?
    Ma 'l savio non pregia uom per vestimenta,
    Ch' altrui sono ornamenta,
    Ma pregia il senno e gli gentil coraggi.

II

There are who by flinging their wealth away Ode xiii.
think to be able to have place where good
men take their stand who after death make
their repair within the mind of such as have
discernment.

But no pleasure may their largesse give the good;
because restraining it had been wisdom, and
they had escaped the loss that is now added
to the error, both of them and of the folk
who pass false judgment in their deeming.

Who will not call it fault to engulf food and
give the mind to wantoning, and deck him as
for sale impending at the fair of fools? But
the wise prizes not a man after his garments,
which are but alien ornaments, but prizes
intellect and noble hearts.

III

Canz.
xiii.

Ed altri son, che, per esser ridenti,
    D' intendimenti
    Correnti—voglion esser giudicati
    Da quei che so' ingannati,
    Veggendo rider cosa
    Che l' intelletto cieco non la vede.

Ei parlan con vocaboli eccellenti:
    Vanno spiacenti,
    Contenti—che dal volgo sian mirati:
    Non sono innamorati
    Mai di donna amorosa:
    Ne' parlamenti lor tengono scede:

Non moverieno il piede
    Per donneare a guisa di leggiadro:
    Ma come al furto il ladro,
    Così vanno a pigliar villan diletto;
    E non però che in donne è sì dispento
    Leggiadro portamento,
    Che paiono animai senza intelletto.

III

And others are there who, by being quick to Ode xiii.
smile, would be supposed of understanding
swift by such as be deceived, seeing them
laugh at aught which the blind intellect
perceives not.

They speak with words elect, go their unpleas-
ing way, content so they be gaped at by the
herd: they are enamoured never of amorous
lady: in their discourse they cleave to mere
grimace.

They will not move the foot to serve a lady
after gallant fashion: but as a robber to his
theft, so do they pace to pluck their base
delight; and it is not that in women all gallant
bearing is so quenched that they seem animals
bereft of intellect.

IV

Ancorchè ciel con cielo in punto sia
Che leggiadria
Disvia—cotanto e più quant' io conto,
Io che le son conto,
Mercè d' una gentile
Che la mostrava in tutti gli atti sui,

Non tacerò di lei, che villania
Far mi parria
Si ria,—ch' a' suoi nemici sare' giunto ;
Per che da questo punto
Con rima più sottile
Tratterò il ver di lei, ma non so a cui.

Io giuro per colui
Ch' amor si chiama, ed è pien di salute,
Che senza oprar virtute,
Nissun puote acquistar verace loda :
Dunque se questa mia materia è buona,
Come ciascun ragiona,
Sarà virtute, o con virtù s' annoda.

IV

Albeit heaven be at such point with heaven that Ode xiii.
gallantry goes erring from its way, as much as
I relate and more, I, who have skill of it,
thanks to a gentle one who showed it forth
in all her utterance,

Shall not be silent of it; for to do so would
appear to me villainy so base that I should
have joined me to its enemies.   Wherefore,
from this point forth, with rhyme more subtle
will I treat of truth about it: but to whom I
know not.

I swear by him whose name is love, and who is
full of saving, that without doing virtue none
may acquire true praise; wherefore, if that
which I am handling be good, as each declares,
it must be virtue, or with virtue linked.

v

Canz. Non è pura virtù la disviata ;
xiii.   Poich' è biasmata,
             Negata,—dov' è più virtù richiesta,
             Cioè in gente onesta
             Di vita spirituale,
             O in abito che di scienza tiene.

        Dunque s' ell' è in cavalier lodata,
             Sarà mischiata,
             Causata—di più cose ; perchè questa
             Convien che di sè vesta
             L' un bene e l' altro male :
             Ma virtù pura in ciascuno sta bene.

        Sollazzo è, che convene
             Con esso amore ; e l' opera perfetta,
             Da questo terzo retta,
             È pura leggiadria.   In esser dura,
             Siccome il sole, al cui esser s' adduce
             Lo calore e la luce
             Con la perfetta sua bella figura.

▼

Not virtue, pure and simple, is this strayed thing ;   Ode xiii.
    for it is blamed, renounced, where virtue is
    demanded most ; that is in seemly folk of
    spiritual life, or garb that holds with study.

Therefore, if it be praised in a cavalier, it must
    be mingled, caused by more things than one ;
    wherefore this same must needs clothe itself
    upon one well another ill ; but virtue, pure
    and simple, becomes every man.

A joyance is it that consorts with love himself :
    and the completed work, directed by this third,
    is very gallantry.   In being it endures, even
    as the sun, to make whose being are conjoined
    the heat and light and his own perfect fair
    form.

K

VI

Al gran pianeta è tutta simigliante,
 Che da levante
 Avante—infino a tanto che il s' asconde,
 Con li bei raggi infonde
 Vita e virtù quaggiuso
 Nella materia sì com' è disposta:

E questa, disdegnosa di cotante
 Persone quante
 Sembiante—portan d'uomo, e non risponde
 Il lor frutto alle fronde,
 Per lo mal c' hanno in uso,
 Simili beni al cor gentile accosta;

Che in donar vita è tosta,
 Con bei sembianti, e con begli atti nuovi
 Ch' ognora par che trovi;
 E virtù per esempio ha chi ben piglia.
 O falsi cavalier, malvagi e rei,
 Nemici di costei,
 Ch' al prence delle stelle s' assimiglia.

VI

To the great planet she is all resemblant, who, **Ode xiii**
from the east forward till he conceals himself,
with his fair rays down pours life and power
below into material, according as it is disposed.

Even as she,—scornful of so many folk as bear
human semblance, but their fruit corresponds
not to their leaves, because of ill which they
have practised,—brings like blessings nigh
the gentle heart;

For she is swift to give life, with fair semblance
and new beauteous acts which every hour she
seems to find: and he has virtue for his
model who lays true hold on her. Oh false
cavaliers, evil and guilty, enemies of her who
is likened to the prince of stars!

VII

Dona e riceve l' uom cui questa vuole,
 Mai non sen duole ;
 Nè 'l sole,—per donar luce alle stelle,
 Nè per prender da elle
 Nel suo effetto aiuto,
 Ma l' uno e l' altro in ciò diletto tragge.

Già non s' induce ad ira per parole,
 Ma quelle sole
 Ricole,—che son buone ; e sue novelle
 Son leggiadre e belle.
 Per sè è car tenuto
 E desiato da persone sagge,

Chè dell' altre selvagge
 Cotanto lode quanto biasmo prezza :
 Per nessuna grandezza
 Monta in orgoglio ; ma quando gl' incontra
 Che sua franchezza gli convien mostrare,
 Quivi si fa laudare :
 Color che vivon, fanno tutti contra.

VII

That man whom she will have, both gives and Ode xiii.
takes, and ne'er it irks him: neither the sun
to give light to the stars nor to take from them
help in working his effect: but one and the
other draws delight therein.

Ne'er is he drawn to wrath by words, but such
only does he gather as be good: and what
things he hath to tell are gallant and are fair.
For his own sake is he held dear and by sage
ones desired,

For from the savage rest he holds or praise or
blame of equal worth; for no greatness doth
he mount up in pride, but where it chances
that it is fitting to display his valour, there he
wins praise. They who are living all work
counterwise.

CANZONE XIV

I

Tre donne intorno al cor mi son venute,
  E seggionsi di fore ;
  Chè dentro siede Amore,
  Lo quale è in signoria della mia vita.

Tanto son belle, e di tanta virtute,
  Che 'l possente signore,
  Dico quel ch' è nel core,
  Appena di parlar di lor s' aita.

Ciascuna par dolente e sbigottita,
  Come persona discacciata e stanca,
  Cui tutta gente manca,
  E cui virtute ne beltà non vale.
  Tempo fu già, nel quale,
  Secondo il lor parlar, furon dilette ;
  Or sono in ira a tutti ed in non cale,
  Queste così solette
  Venute son come a casa d' amico,
  Chè sanno ben che dentro è quel ch' io dico.

ODE XIV

I

Three ladies have gathered round my heart, and
seat themselves without, for within sits Love
who holds seignory over my life.

So beauteous are they and of such power that
the mighty liege, I mean him who is in my
heart, can scarce man himself to speak of
them.

Each one seems grieving and dismayed, as one
cast out and weary, from whom all folk have
fallen, and whom nor virtue doth avail nor
beauty.   Time was wherein, according to
their speech, they were beloved: now they
are held in wrath and in neglect by all.
These, so lonely, have come as to the house
of a friend ; for they know verily that within
is he of whom I speak.

II

Canz.
xiv.

Dolesi l' una con parole molto,
   E'n sulla man si posa
   Come succisa rosa.
   Il nudo braccio, di dolor colonna,

Sente lo raggio che cade dal volto:
   L' altra man tiene ascosa
   La treccia lagrimosa;
   Scinta e discalza, e sol da sè par donna.

Come Amor prima per la rotta gonna,
   La vide in parte che il tacere è bello,
   Pietoso e fello,
   Di lei e del dolor fece dimanda.
   Oh di pochi vivanda!
   (Rispose voce con sospiri mista)
   Nostra natura qui a te ci manda.
   Io, che son la più trista,
   Son suora alla tua madre, e son Drittura;
   Povera, vedi, a fama ed a cintura.

II

Much doth the one of them grieve in her Ode xiv.
words, and on her hand supports her, like a
clipped rose: her naked arm, column of grief,

Feels the ray falling from her face: the other
hand conceals her tear-drenched locks: un-
girt, unsandalled, and only in herself seeming
a lady.

When first Love through her tattered gown
saw her where it were comely not to say, he,
in pity and in wrath, of her and of her grief
made question: 'Oh food of few,' answered
a voice mingled with sighs, 'our nature sends
us here to thee. I, who am saddest, am
sister to thy mother, and am Righteousness:
poor, as thou seest in repute and cincture.'

III

Poichè fatta si fu palese e conta,
Doglia e vergogna prese
Lo mio signore, e chiese
Chi fosser l' altre due ch' eran con lei.

E questa, che fu sì di pianger pronta,
Tosto che lui intese,
Più nel dolor s' accese,
Dicendo: A te non duol degli occhi miei?

Poi cominciò: Siccome saper dei,
Di fonte nasce il Nilo picciol fiume:
Ivi, dove 'l gran lume
Toglie alla terra del giunco la fronda,
Sovra la vergin onda
Generai io costei che m' è da lato,
E che s' asciuga con la treccia bionda.
Questo mio bel portato,
Mirando sè nella chiara fontana,
Generò questa che m' è più lontanta.

III

When she had revealed her and made known, Ode xiv.
grief and shame laid hold upon my lord, and
he demanded who were those other two with
her.

And she who was so eager in her tears, soon as
she understood him, was kindled into hotter
grief, saying: 'On my eyes' behalf, hast thou
not ruth?'

Then she began: 'As thou shouldst know,
from its source springs the Nile, a slender
stream: there, where the great light is
shielded from the earth by the rush-spikes,
over the virgin wave did I bring forth her at
my side who with her fair tresses dries her
tears. This my beauteous birth, gazing on
herself in the clear fountain, brought her forth
who is more distant.'

IV

Fenno i sospiri Amore un poco tardo;
   Poscia con gli occhi molli,
   Che prima furon folli,
   Salutò le germane sconsolate.

E poichè prese l' uno e l' altro dardo,
   Disse: Drizzate i colli:
   Ecco l'armi ch'io volli;
   Per disusar vedete son turbate.

Larghezza e Temperanza, e l' altre nate
   Del nostro sangue mendicando vanno,
   Però, se questo è danno,
   Pianganlo gli occhi, e dolgasi la bocca
   Degli uomini a cui tocca,
   Che sono a' raggi di cotal ciel giunti;
   Non noi, che semo dall' eterna rocca:
   Chè, se noi siamo or punti,
   Noi pur saremo, e pur tornara gente,
   Che questo dardo farà star lucente.

IV

His sighs held Love a little back : then with eyes softened, that before were wild, he greeted the disconsolate kinswomen ;   Ode xiv.

And, having grasped one and the other dart, he cried : 'Uplift your necks : behold the arms which I have chosen ; rusted by disuse, ye see, they are.

Generosity and Temperance, and the others born of our blood, go their way begging ; whereat, if this be loss, let the eyes weep, and the mouth wail, of men, whom it concerns, who have come under the rays of such a heaven: not we, who are of the eternal rock ; for, though we now be thrust at, we shall endure, and folk will come again who shall make this dart abide in brightness.'

v

Canz. Ed io che ascolto nel parlar divino
xiv.   Consolarsi e dolersi
      Così alti dispersi,
      L' esilio, che m' è dato, onor mi tegno:

E se fortuna, o forza di destino,
    Vuol pur che il mondo versi
    I bianchi fiori in persi,
    Cader co' buoni è pur di lode degno.

Ma perocchè degli occhi miei 'l bel segno
    Per lontananza m' è tolto dal viso,
    Che m' have in fuoco miso,
    Lieve mi conterai cio che m' è grave.
    Ma questo fuoco m' have
    Già consumato sì l' ossa e la polpa,
    Che morte al petto m' ha posto la chiave:
    Onde s' io ebbi colpa,
    Più lune ha volto il sol, poichè fu spenta;
    Se colpa muore perchè l' uom si penta.

vi

Canzone; a' panni tuoi non ponga uom mano,
    Per veder quel che bella donna chiude:
    Bastin le parti nude:
    Lo dolce pomo a tutta gente niega,
    Per cui ciascun man piega.
    E s' egli avvien che tu mai alcun truovi
    Amico di virtu, ed el te priega,
    Fatti di color nuovi:
    E mostra gli quel fior, che, bel di fuori,
    Fa desiar negli amorosi cuori.

V

And I, who, in divine discourse, mark comfort   Ode xiv.
and dole bestowed upon such lofty exiles,
count as my glory the banishment wreaked on
me:

And if chance or force of destiny will have the
world convert white flowers into dark, falling
amongst the good is yet worthy praise.

But because the fair signal of my eyes, which
has set me in flame, is reft by distance from
my sight, light should I count that which is
heavy on me.   But this flame has already so
consumed my bone and flesh that death has
put his key unto my breast; for which if I
had fault, many a moon has the sun revolved
since it was quenched, if a fault dies because
a man repents.

VI

Ode, on thy weeds let no man set his hand to
look on that which a fair woman hides; let
the uncovered parts suffice; the sweet apple
to all folk deny for which each one extends
his hand.   But if it chance that ever thou find
one, a friend of virtue, who should pray thee,
make thyself of fresh hues, and reveal to him
the flower, that, beauteous without, wakes
longing in amorous hearts.

CANZONE XV

I

Voi che intendendo il terzo ciel movete
    Udite il ragionar ch' è nel mio core,
    Ch' io nol so dire altrui, sì mi par novo.

Il ciel che segue lo vostro valore,
    Gentili creature che voi siete,
    Mi tragge nello stato ov' io mi trovo.

      Onde 'l parlar della vita ch' io provo,

Par che sì drizzi degnamente a vui:
    Però vi prego che lo m' intendiate.
    Io vi dirò del cor la novitate,

Come l' anima trista piange in lui,
    E come un spirto contra lei favella,
    Che vien pei raggi della vostra stella.

ODE XV

I

Ye who by understanding move the third heaven,
hearken to the discourse which is in my heart,
for I may not tell it to any other, so strange it
seemeth me.

'Tis the heaven which followeth your worth,
gentle creatures that ye be, that draweth me
into the state wherein I find me.

Wherefore the discourse of the life which I
endure,

Meseems were worthily directed unto you.
Therefore I pray that ye give me heed anent
it. I will tell you the wondrous story of my
heart

How the sad soul waileth in it, and how a spirit
discourseth counter to her, that cometh upon
the rays of your star.

II

Canz. xv. Solea esser vita dello cor dolente
 Un soave pensier che se ne gìa
 Molte fiate a' piè del vostro sire ;

Ove una donna gloriar vedia,
 Di cui parlava a me sì dolcemente,
 Che l' anima diceva : I' men vo' gire.

 Or apparisce chi lo fa fuggire ;

E signoreggia me di tal virtute
 Che 'l cor ne trema si che fuori appare.
 Questi mi fece una donna guardare,

E dice : Chi veder vuol la salute,
 Faccia che gli occhi d' esta donna miri,
 S' egli non teme angoscia di sospiri.

III

Trova contraro tal, che lo distrugge,
 L' umil pensiero che parlar mi suole
 D' un' angiola che 'n cielo è coronata.

L' anima piange, sì ancor le 'n duole,
 E dice : Oh lassa me, come si fugge
 Questo pietoso che m' ha consolata !

 Degli occhi miei dice questa affannata :

Qual ora fu, che tal donna gli vide ?
 E perchè non credeano a me di lei ?
 Io dicea : Ben negli occhi di costei

De' star colui che le mie pari uccide.
 E non mi valse, ch' io ne fossi accorta,
 Che non mirasser tal, ch' io ne son morta.

II

Was wont to be the life of my grieving heart a Ode xv
sweet thought that would take its way many
a time to the feet of your sire,

Where it beheld a lady in glory of whom it discoursed to me so sweetly that my soul said
ever: 'Fain would I go thither.'

Now one appears who putteth him to flight,

And lords it over me with such might that my
heart so trembles thereat as to reveal it in
outward semblance. He makes me gaze
upon a lady,

And saith: 'Who would behold salvation, heed-
fully let him look upon this lady's eyes if he
fear not the anguish of sighings.'

III

Findeth such an adversary as destroyeth him, the
humble thought that is wont to discourse to me
of an angelet who is crowned in heaven.

The soul wails, so doth she still grieve thereat,
and saith: 'O wretched me, how fleeth that
tender one who hath consoled me!'

Of my eyes this afflicted one exclaimeth:

'What hour was that wherein such lady looked
upon them! And wherefore did they not
believe me concerning her? I ever said:
Verily in her eyes

Must he needs stand who slays my peers. And
my perceiving it availed me nought against
their gazing upon such an one that I am slain
thereby.'

IV

Canz. xv. Tu non se' morta, ma se' sbigottita,
    Anima nostra, che sì ti lamenti,
    Dice uno spiritel d' amor gentile ;

Chè questa bella donna, che tu senti,
    Ha trasmutata in tanto la tua vita,
    Che n' hai paura, sì se' fatta vile.

    Mira quant' ella è pietosa ed umile,

Saggia e cortese nella sua grandezza :
    E pensa di chiamarla donna omai :
    Chè se tu non t' inganni tu vedrai

Di sì alti miracoli adornezza,
    Che tu dirai : Amor, signor verace,
    Ecco l' ancella tua ; fa' che ti piace.

V

Canzone, i' credo che saranno radi
    Color che tua ragione intendan bene,
    Tanto la parti faticosa e forte :

Onde se per ventura egli addiviene
    Che tu dinanzi da persone vadi,
    Che non ti paian d'essa bene accorte ;

    Allor ti priego che ti riconforte,

Dicendo lor, diletta mia novella :
    Ponete mente almen com' io son bella.

IV

'Thou art not slain, only thou art dismayed, Ode xv.
  O soul of ours who dost so lament thee,'
  saith a little spirit of gentle love;

'For this fair lady, whom thou perceivest, hath
  so transformed thy life that thou art terrified,
  so cowardly hast thou become.

  See how tender she is and humble,

Sage and courteous in her greatness, and think
  henceforth to call her lady: for, if thou
  deceive not thyself, thou shalt see

Adornment of such lofty miracles, that thou
  shalt say: *Love, very lord, behold thy handmaid: do as pleaseth thee.*'

V

Ode! I believe that they shall be but rare who
  shall rightly understand thy meaning, so in-
  tricate and knotty is thy utterance of it:

Wherefore if perchance it come about that thou
  take thy way into the presence of folk who
  seem not rightly to perceive it;

  Then I pray thee to take heart again,

And say to them, O my beloved lastling:
  'Give heed at least how beautiful I am.'

Sonetto xiv

Due donne in cima della mente mia
   Venute sono a ragionar d'amore :
   L' una ha in sè cortesia e valore,
   Prudenza ed onestate in compagnia.

L'altra ha bellezza e vaga leggiadria,
   E adorna gentilezza le fa onore.
   Ed io, mercè del dolce mio signore,
   Stommene a piè della lor signoria.

Parlan bellezza e virtù all' intelletto,
   E fan quistion, come un cuor puote stare
   Infra duo donne con amor perfetto.

Risponde il fonte del gentil parlare :
   Che amar si può bellezza per diletto,
   E amar puossi virtù per alto oprare.

Sonnet xiv

Two ladies in the high chamber of my mind
are come to discourse of love: one hath
within herself courtesy and virtue; prudence
and chastity in her train.

The other hath beauty and winsome grace; and
radiant gentleness doeth her honour. And I,
by favour of my sweet lord, stand at the
footstool of their throne.

Beauty and virtue speak to the understanding and
make question, how one heart can remain between mistresses twain, with perfect love.

The fount of gentle speech respondeth: that
one can love beauty for delight and one can
love virtue for high deeds.

Sonetto xv

Lo re, che merta i suoi servi a ristoro
   Con abbondanza e vince ogni misura,
   Mi fa lasciare la fiera rancura
   E drizzar gli occhi al sommo concistoro.

E qui pensando al glorioso coro
   De' cittadin della cittade pura
   Laudando il creatore, io creatura
   Di più laudarlo sempre m' innamoro.

Chè s' io contemplo il gran premio venturo
   A che Dio chiama la cristiana prole
   Per me niente altro che quello si vuole:

Ma di te, caro amico, sì mi duole
   Che non rispetti al secolo futuro
   E perdi per lo vano il ben sicuro.

Sonetto xvi

Nulla mi parrà mai più crudel cosa
   Che lei, per cui servir la vita smago;
   Chè 'l suo desire in congelato lago
   Ed in fuoco d' amore il mio si posa:

Di così dispietata e disdegnosa
   La gran bellezza di veder m' appago,
   E tanto son del mio tormento vago,
   Ch' altro piacere agli occhi miei non osa.

Nè quella, ch' a veder lo Sol si gira,
   E 'l non mutato amor mutata serba,
   Ebbe quant' io giammai fortuna acerba;

Onde, quando giammai questa superba
   Non vinca, Amor, fin che la vita spira
   Alquanto per pietà con me sospira.

SONNET XV

The king, who rewardeth his servants in full
meed with plenty and surpasses all measure,
maketh me to cease my fierce spite and direct
mine eyes to the high consistory.

And there, thinking on the glorious quire of the
citizens of that pure city, I, his creature, giving
praise to the creator, am ever enamoured of
praising him more.

For if I contemplate the great reward to come,
to which God calls the Christian race, by me
naught else than that is desired.

But for thee, dear friend, it grieves me so, that
thou regardest not the world to come and
dost lose the real for the shadowy good.

SONNET XVI

Naught will e'er seem to me a crueller thing
than she, through serving whom I waste my
life; for her desire is bound in a frozen lake
and mine swathed in flames of love:

So cruel and scornful is she whose great beauty
I cheat me with gazing on, and so do I yearn
for my torment, that no other pleasure dares
mine eyes.

Nor she who turneth her to behold the Sun, and
an unchanged love, by changing, cherisheth,
had e'er so bitter fortune as I.

Wherefore e'en if this proud one, Love, thou
ne'er mayst vanquish, while breath of life endure, somewhat for pity's sake sigh with me.

BALLATA V

In abito di saggia messaggiera
　　Muovi, ballata, senza gir tardando,
　　A quella bella donna a cui ti mando
　　E dìgli quanto mia vita è leggiera.
Comincierai a dir che gli occhi miei
　　Per riguardar sua angelica figura
　　Solean portar corona di desiri :
　　Ora perchè non posson veder lei,
　　Li strugge Morte con tanta paura,
　　C' hanno fatto ghirlanda di martiri.
　　Lasso ! non so in qual parte gli giri
　　Per lor diletto; sì che quasi morto
　　Mi troverai, se non rechi conforto
　　Da lei : onde gli fa dolce preghiera

Ballad v

In the habit of a trusty messenger, hie thee
song, with no laggard gait, to that fair lady to
whom I send thee and tell her how my life is
frail.

Thou shalt begin and say, that mine eyes,
through looking on her angel form, were wont
to wear a crown of desires: now, for that
they cannot behold her, Death wasteth them
with such fear that they have received a garland of tortures. Alas! I know not to what
place I may turn them for their joy ; so that
nigh dead thou shalt find me if thou bring not
comfort from her : for which make sweet
prayer unto her.

SONETTO XVII

Io maledico il dì ch' io vidi in prima
    La luce de' vostri occhi traditori,
    E 'l punto che veniste in sulla cima
    Del core a trarne l' anima di fuori:

E maledico l' amorosa lima,
    C' ha pulito i miei detti, e i bei colori,
    Ch' io ho per voi trovati e messi in rima,
    Per far che il mondo mai sempre v' onori.

E maledico la mia mente dura,
    Che ferma è di tener quel che m' uccide,
    Cioè la bella e rea vostra figura,

Per cui Amor sovente si spergiura
    Sicchè ciascun di lui e di me ride,
    Che credo tor la ruota alla ventura.

SONNET XVII

I curse the day when I first beheld the light of
your traitorous eyes, and the moment when
ye mounted the summit of my heart to draw
thence the soul forth.

And I curse the amorous file that hath burnished
my ditties, and the fair hues that for you I
have invented and set in rhyme, to make the
world honour you evermore.

And I curse my stubborn mind that is fast to
hold that which slayeth me, to wit: yours,
the fair and guilty form

for whom Love oft is foresworn so that all men
do laugh at him and me, who think to wrest
her wheel from fortune.

SONETTO XVIII

Io son sī vago della bella luce
    Degli occhi traditor che m' hanno anciso,
    Che là, dov' io son morto e son deriso,
    La gran vaghezza pur mi riconduce.

E quel che pare, e quel che mi traluce,
    M' abbaglia tanto l' uno e l' altro viso,
    Che da ragione e da virtù diviso
    Seguo solo il disio come mio duce;

Lo qual mi mena tanto pien di fede
    A dolce morte sotto dolce inganno,
    Ch' io lo conosco sol dopo 'l mio danno.

E' mi duol forte del gabbato affanno;
    Ma più m' incresce, ahi lasso! che si vede
    Meco pietà tradita da mercede.

SONETTO XIX

Onde venite voi cosi pensose?
    Ditemel, s' a voi piace, in cortesia:
    Ch' i ho dottanza che la donna mia
    Non vi faccia tornar cosi dogliose.

Deh! gentil donne, non siate sdegnose,
    Nè di ristare alquanto in questa via,
    E dire al doloroso, che disia
    Udir della sua donna, alcune cose;

Avvegnachè gravoso m' è l' udire:
    Si m' ha in tutto Amor da sè scacciato,
    Ch' ogni suo atto mi trae a finire.

Guardate bene, s' io son consumato;
    Ch' ogni mio spirto comincia a fuggire,
    Se da voi, donne, non son confortato.

Sonnet XVIII

So do I yearn for the fair light of traitorous
eyes that have slain me, that there, where I
am destroyed and mocked, the great longing
leads me back again.

And that which visibly appears and that which
illumines me, daze so both my outward and
inward vision, that from reason and virtue
sundered, I follow desire alone as my leader;

who leadeth me all trustful to sweet death
under a sweet beguilement so that I recognise it only after my hurt.

It grieveth me sorely for my suffering mocked;
but more it irks me alas! that in me is
beheld pity betrayed of its reward.

Sonnet XIX

Whence come ye thus pensive? tell me, an it
please you, in courtesy: for I have dread lest
my lady be the cause that ye return thus
sorrowing.

Ah! gentle ladies, be ye not scornful, neither
to tarry awhile by this wayside, and speak to
the sorrowful one, that desireth to hear some
tidings of his lady;

albeit heavy to me be the hearing of it: so
wholly hath Love chased me from him that
his every act draweth me to mine end.

Look ye well how I am consumed; for all my
senses begin to flee, if by you ladies I am not
comforted.

Sonetto xx

Se vedi gli occhi miei di pianger vaghi,
    Per novella pièta che il cor mi strugge,
    Per lei ti priego, che da te non fugge,
    Signor, che tu di tal piacer gli svaghi ;

Con la tua dritta man cioè che paghi
    Chi la giustizia uccide, e poi rifugge
    Al gran tiranno, del cui tosco sugge,
    Ch'egli ha già sparto, e vuol che 'l mondo
        allaghi.

E messo ha di paura tanto gelo
    Nel cuor de' tuoi fedei, che ciascun tace :
    Ma tu, fuoco d' amor, lume del cielo,

Questa virtù, che nuda e fredda giace,
    Levala su vestita del tuo velo ;
    Chè senza lei non è qui in terra pace.

Sonetto xxi.

Voi, donne, che pietoso atto mostrate,
    Chi è esta donna, che giace sì venta ?
    Saria mai quella ch' è nel mio cor pènta ?
    Deh ! s' ella è dessa, più nol mel celate.

Ben ha le sue sembianze sì cambiate,
    E la figura sua mi par sì spenta,
    Ch' al mio parere ella non rappresenta
    Quella, che fa parer l' altre beate.

Se nostra donna conoscer non puoi,
    Ch' è sì conquisa, non mi par gran fatto,
    Perocchè quel medesmo avvenne a noi.

Ma se tu mirerai, al gentil atto
    Degli occhi suoi conosceraila poi :
    Non pianger più, tu sei già tutto sfatto.

SONNET XX

If thou seest mine eyes fain to weep for the new
anguish that wasteth my heart, I pray thee,
Lord, for her sake that fleeth not from thee,
that thou disenchant them of such pleasure ;

that, to wit, thou repay with thy right hand
him who slayeth justice, and then takes refuge
with the great tyrant from whom he sucks the
poison that he hath now scattered, and would
that it o'erwhelm the world.

And such chill of fear hath cast into thy lieges'
hearts that all are mute : but thou, fire of
love, light of heaven,

this virtue, that naked lieth and cold, do thou
raise up, clothed with thy veil; for without
it no peace is here on earth.

SONNET XXI

" Ye ladies that shew a pitying mien, who is this
lady that lieth so vanquished ?   Should it e'er
be she that in my heart is painted ?   Ah ! if
she it is, hide it no more from me.

Truly hath she so changed a semblance, and to
me her form appeareth so spent, that to my
seeming she resembleth not her who maketh
the others appear blest."

" If thou canst not recognise our lady that is so
stricken, 'tis no great marvel methinks, for
that very same did hap to us.

But if thou wilt look, then by the gentle
habit of her eyes thou shalt recognise her :
weep no more, already art thou quite undone."

L

Ballata vi

Donne, io non so di che mi preghi Amore,
  Ch' egli m' ancide e la morte m'è dura,
  E di sentirlo meno ho più paura.

Nel mezzo della mia mente risplende
  Un lume da' begli occhi ond' io son vago,
  Che l' anima contenta ;
  Vero è che ad or ad or d' ivi discende
  Una saetta che m' asciuga un lago
  Dal cor pria che sia spenta.
  Ciò face Amor qual volta mi rammenta
  La dolce mano e quella fede pura,
  Che dovria la mia vita far sicura.

Ballad vi

Ladies, I know not what to entreat of Love, for he slayeth me and death to me is dire; and to feel him less I dread yet more.

In the midst of my mind, a light shineth from the fair eyes whereof I am fain, that maketh glad the soul; true it is that now and again a fiery bolt thence descendeth that dryeth up a lake from my heart ere it be quenched. That, Love doeth, each time he recalleth to me the sweet hand and that pure faith that should make my life secure.

NOTE ON THE CANZONIERE.

The canon of the Canzoniere has been drawn up expressly for this edition by Mr Edmund G. Gardner, who has generously placed his wide acquaintance with the MS. authorities at the disposal of the editors. Two of the lyrics (Sonnets iii. and xiii.) are here included for the first time in any collected edition of Dante's works. The latter is taken from Carl Witte's *Dante Forschungen*, vol. ii.; the former from the version by Pellegrini printed in vol. xxxi. of the *Giornale Storico della Litteratura Italiana*. Any of the minor poems commonly attributed to Dante which are not included in this volume may, in the present state of our knowledge, be regarded as spurious.

The text of the Ballads and Sonnets conforms in the main to that of the last edition of Dr Moore's Oxford Dante. But the text of the Canzoni offered special difficulties. The hope expressed on page 388 of the *Convivio* volume of this series has unfortunately not been realised, since Mr Gardner's authoritative text is not yet published. The current text is notoriously unsatisfactory, and it has therefore been thought best to construct a new text. It is almost exclusively based on the Chigi and Barbarini MSS., both of which are accessible in printed form. It is open to all the objections incident to the narrow basis on which it has been built; but it will at least give the reader some idea of the range and importance of the variants, and will probably be found to have adopted or indicated many of the more striking readings which will ultimately find their place in the definitive text. The translation of the Canzoni is a revision, modified in accordance with the changed conditions, of the version given in the *Convivio* volume of this series. The editors wish specially to acknowledge their obligations, in the notes on the Ballads and Sonnets, to Mr Gardner's article, "Dante's Correspondence with Guido and Messer Cino," reprinted from *The Month*, November 1899.

NOTES.

The page and line references are to those of the Translation.

p. 3, l. 3. "Here beginneth the New Life." *Vita nuova* has sometimes been taken as equivalent to *età nuova* and therefore as meaning no more than "early life." But it is better in every way to follow the more natural interpretation and to take the "new life" as meaning the higher life to which the poet was awakened by love. So another early Italian poet speaks of what "the enamoured spirits see, whom this new life of theirs rejoices."

l. 8. *The heaven of light* is the heaven of the sun, and its "proper revolution" is its annual motion (from west to east), as distinct from the diurnal motion (from east to west) which it shares with all the other revolving heavens.

ll. 12, 13. The phrase *non sapeano che si chiamare* may be taken to mean either "did not know what she was called," in which case it would mean that people who did not know her name called her Beatrice, "the giver of blessing," because of her gracious presence; or, "did not know what they were calling her," in which case it would mean that many who called her by her name "Beatrice" did not realise that they were also describing her as "the giver of blessing." Compare, *D'Ancona, Vita Nuova.* Boccaccio declares that Beatrice was the daughter of Folco Portinari, and his statement is confirmed by some of the manuscript copies of the commentary on the *Comedy* by Dante's

325

son Pietro (see *Dante Primer*, page 8). Folco Portinari was a wealthy and public-spirited citizen, and we know from his will, executed early in 1287, that his daughter Bice was at that time the wife of Simone de' Bardi, a member of the great family of bankers, who afterwards played a part in the political conflicts of Florence. Bice's mother was of the family of the Caponsacchi. In section iii. of his life of Dante, Boccaccio gives a charming picture of the first meeting of Dante and Beatrice, which he says took place at a May meeting in the house of Folco Portinari.

ll. 15-17. The reference is to the celestial phenomenon, first observed by Hipparchus (flourished about 150 B.C.), known to astronomers as the precession of the equinoxes; *i.e.* the apparent slow motion of the fixed stars from west to east, which in Dante's day was estimated to be completed in 36,000 years. The time occupied in the movement along one-twelfth of a degree would therefore be eight years and four months.

l. 24. The "vital spirit" has its seat in the heart, which Aquinas calls the "organ of the passions of the soul," that is of the emotional life. The "animal spirit" is the faculty for sense perception that differentiates animals from plants, and it has its seat in the brain. The "natural spirit" presides over the functions of the organic life; and when Dante locates it in the place "where our food is administered" he does not refer to the mouth and the function of speech, as some have supposed, but to the liver, which Aristotle describes as an organ of the digestion. Compare iv. 1-9.

p. 5, ll. 2, 3. "Behold a God mightier than I who is come to master me."

ll. 8, 9. "Now hath your blessedness appeared."

ll. 13, 14. "Ah! wretch! for henceforth I shall be oft impeded."

ll. 26-28. This, like all other quotations from Homer that occur in Dante's works, is taken at second hand; in this case from the Latin translation of Aristotle. Compare *Convivio*, i. 7. 95 ff.

p. 7, l. 16. The wondrous effects on a lover of his mistress' salutation are described by other contemporary poets, *e.g.* Guinicelli and Cino.

l. 20. *Ninth of that day*, counting from sunrise. Compare *Convivio*, iii. 6 : 12-32.

p. 9, ll. 2, 3. "I am thy master."

ll. 10, 11. "Behold thy heart."

p. 11, ll. 17-20. These disturbing analyses are modelled on the custom of Thomas Aquinas, who opens each section of his commentaries on Aristotle's works by an analysis of the text, setting forth its main divisions, and showing what each contains, and rehearsing the words with which it opens.

l. 23. Guido Cavalcanti, mentioned in *Inf.* x. 63. An answer by Cino of Pistoia is also preserved, and a scornful one by Dante of Maiano. All are translated by Rossetti in the *Early Italian Poets*, T.C. edition, pages 222, 264, 276.

ll. 29-31. The vision, Dante thought, was prophetic of the whole course of his love; of the rapture of his "New Life"; Beatrice's slow awakening to the reality of his devotion (§ xii.); the feelings of constraint and perhaps pain which caused her to withdraw her salutation, and the early age at which she was gathered into the arms of Love and borne to heaven.

p. 13, l. 19. In church, where they were celebrating one of the feasts of Mary.

p. 15, ll. 10-12. The well-known Sonnet vi. (p. 162) was obviously one of the poems written for this lady. The reference in lines 13-15 is explained in § vii.

l. 25. *Serventese.* "Sirventes" was originally a term used by the Troubadours to signify a poem of a political or personal character; as distinct, for example, from a love song; but as used by the Italians the term applies to the metre, not to the subject-matter, of the poem. The Italian *serventese* was characterised by the simplicity of its metrical structure, the basis of which was the couplet, or the quatrain with alternate rhymes. No trace of Dante's *serventese* has been discovered, but poems, by other hands, of a similar nature (perhaps written in imitation of it) are extant. Compare Sonnet vi. 10 (p. 162).

p. 17, ll. 11, 12. *Lamentations*, i. 12. "O all ye that pass by the way, stay and behold if there is any sorrow like unto my sorrow." The "double sonnet," of which this poem and the next but one are specimens, was a recognised form in Dante's time. Two seven-syllable lines are added to each of the quatrains, and one to each of the terzettes, making the whole poem twenty lines. Since the whole tenor of the sonnet, taken naturally, implies that the sweet life with which Love had graced the poet was the life of devotion to the screen lady, and yet Dante declares that he was really thinking of Beatrice when he wrote these two lines, we encounter, thus early, a problem which has long vexed students of Dante, viz., how far he consciously or unconsciously read into his poems meanings that were not originally there. The problem assumes importance in connection with the *Convivio*. See T. C. *Convivio*, Appendix II.

p. 23, ll. 2-4. We are to understand Dante to say that in writing these two last lines he was, in his mind, definitely addressing Beatrice, and meant, 'She is now in heaven, and only those of her companions who, like you, are already sure of heaven, can hope ever to meet her again.'

p. 29, ll. 21, 22. Commentators are agreed that an apostrophe to the absent Beatrice, not a prayer to the Virgin, is meant.

ll. 31, 32. "My son, 'tis time to put aside our counterfeiting." Note throughout the *Vita Nuova* the combination, in the conception of Love, of the characteristics of youth and age. Naïve familiarity and swift alternations of mood harmonise with grave authority and unmeasured experience. When the child visitant addresses Dante as "my son" he at once recognises him.

p. 31, ll. 6, 7. "I am as the centre of the circle to which all parts of the circumference bear a like relation; but with thee 'tis not so."

ll. 8-13. The commentators have not succeeded in dispelling the "darkness" of Love's speech. Is Dante actually recording words which came to him in a dream, which seemed pregnant with ominous meaning, but which he could not comprehend? Or are we to suppose that Love means 'You have been weeping because of your present distress only, but I take a farther view and pity you for sorrows to come that are beyond your ken'? This interpretation is perhaps supported by Love's further words when Dante presses him to be more explicit. 'The sorrows and hopes of the moment are enough. It is well for you that my saying remains dark. Seek not to pierce its meaning.'

p. 33, ll. 15-18. The opening quatrain (or other combination of lines) of a ballad is called the *ripresa*, and should be repeated at the close of the poem. Though this practice is never expressly indicated in the manuscripts, we are told by old metrical writers that it was observed as an immemorial custom. It will be found greatly to add to the beauty and effectiveness of the ballad, of which it is an essential characteristic. After the *ripresa* an indeterminate number of stanzas follows. Their structure is somewhat complicated, and the rules are not always strictly observed; but the present ballad is quite regular. Lines 1-3 form the first section, to which the second section, 4-6, corresponds, line for line; then follows the last section, corresponding in the number of lines and syllables to the *ripresa*, and taking up the last line of the second section in its first rhyme. It will be seen that this structure is closely allied to that of the canzone. It is only at the end of the whole poem, not at the end of each stanza, that the *ripresa* is repeated.

p. 37, l. 29. "Names are consequential to things

named." The source of this aphorism has not been traced.

p. 39, ll. 2-6. Dante had exhorted the preceding ballad not to go into Beatrice's presence, except in company with Love; and in lines 56-65 of Ode xi. (which, though not included in the *Vita Nuova*, seems to belong to the same context as the ballad), he had declared that unless Love (as well as pity) came back again in company with the salutation which he implored Beatrice to restore, the salutation itself would come in vain. He is now humiliated to think how much too high he had ventured to place his claim; but he is not yet sufficiently humbled to be prepared to appeal to pity only. In the following sonnet he has thrown away all such reservation, and appeals passionately to the lady's pity, on which he places all his hope and bases his only claim.

p. 41, ll. 6-18. We gather from certain books of etiquette in Dante's time that ten friends of the bride and fourteen of the bridegroom might be invited to the wedding feast, to be held in the new home; but every invited guest was entitled to bring with him one or more uninvited companions, according to his quality and status. A sumptuary law of 1355 reduces the number to six friends of the bride and ten of the bridegroom.

The gratuitous suggestion has been made that Beatrice herself was the bride. If we remember that Dante had openly appealed to her to restore her salutation, and now met her for the first time since he had done so, we shall not think that his agitation is in such excess of what he felt on other occasions as to call for any such improbable hypothesis.

p. 43, ll. 2-14. 'Although I was beside myself (since my eyes were no longer organs of vision but only the seat of a blind yearning), yet I was conscious of what my powers of sight were suffering in not being able to enjoy the loveliness of Beatrice.'

p. 51, ll. 11, 12. Compare Canzone viii., page 234.

p. 55, ll. 11-14. 'If it be true that thy felicity lies in words that praise thy lady, why didst thou indite sonnets of woe and lamentation, rehearsing thine own condition and not her praises?' Compare Dante's own reflections in the lines that immediately follow.

p. 58. Canzone. Carducci and other eminent critics dwell on the evidently immature art and lack of imagination in the early poems of the *Vita Nuova* and on the beauty and originality displayed in the *nuove rime* which this canzone initiates. There is contemporary MS. evidence of the rapid and widely-spread interest evoked by the poem. Compare *Purg.* xxiv. 51 and *De Vulg. Eloq.* ii. 8: 67-79.

The structure of the *Canzone* or Ode is dealt with elaborately in the *De Vulgaria Eloquentia.* See T.C. volume of *Dante's Latin Works,* pp. 121-123. Some attempt has been made to observe the articulation of the stanza in printing the canzoni at the end of this volume.

p. 59, ll. 8-12. If he contemplates his task in its highest aspect he is so appalled as to shrink from making the attempt at all. He must therefore be content not even to aim at more than the lower ranges of his exalted theme.

l. 13. Authorities differ as to the reading and interpretation of this line. Casini and others favour the reading, *Angelo clama il divino intelletto,* and interpret: "The angel host call on, or entreat, God, the divine Intelligence." But Dante, even when he wrote the *Vita Nuova,* would know that "substances sejunct from matter, to wit Intelligences, which are vulgarly called angels" (*Conv.* ii. 5, 6-8), do not entreat with audible voice but in virtue or act of their divine intelligence. Compare *Conv.* ii. end of 6 and beginning of 7, and iii. 6, and *De Vulg. Eloq.* i. 2: 13-16.

ll. 24, 25. These lines have often been interpreted as implying that some conception of the *Comedy*, and specifically the *Inferno*, was already in Dante's mind at this period; but it is difficult to give any definiteness or precision to such an interpretation. It seems more likely that they belong to the same order of thought as the concluding lines of the sonnet (p. 22). Only those who are sure of heaven can hope for the company of the blessed souls eternally. Dante himself is not of such, but even should his lot be with the damned he will boast amongst them that when on earth he looked on one for whom heaven itself was cherishing a longing hope. God in his mercy accords him this privilege, for a season, at the expense of heaven.

p. 67, l. 11. Guido Guinicelli of Bologna. The poem referred to is the canzone: *Al cor gentil ripara sempre amore*. It is translated by Rossetti in *The Early Italian Poets*, T.C. edition, pp. 21 ff. Compare *Inf.* v. 100; *Conv.* iv. 20: 61-69; *De Vulg. Eloq.* i. 9: 30, and ii. 5: 41; and compare the whole sonnet with Guido's doctrine of love.

See *Conv.* iii. 3 for an amplification of Dante's views on the philosophy of love.

ll. 25-27. On the scholastic terms " potentiality " and "actuality," etc., consult T.C. *Convivio*, pp. 123, 200.

p. 69, l. 28. The commentators take this line to mean that Dante himself was generally commended for having already discerned the wondrous power of Beatrice when she was only a child. All the world felt it afterwards.

p. 71, l. 32. Folco Portinari, whom Boccaccio declares to have been Beatrice's father, died Dec. 21, 1289. He was a man of high public spirit and made many charitable foundations.

p. 89, l. 6. In *Par.* xxvii. 67 ff., as here, Dante speaks with beautiful effect of blessed spirits raining up into heaven, obeying the law of spiritual gravitation as snow-flakes that rain down on earth obey the law of material gravita-

tion. Here they are compared to the white and
frost-like manna because of its heavenly quality.

p. 91, l. 34. The mistress of Guido Cavalcanti.
Compare Sonnet vi. (p. 162).

p. 93, ll. 19, 20. "I am the voice of one crying in
the wilderness, Prepare ye the way of the Lord."

p. 95, l. 5. Italian scholars say that (though maiden
ladies may be *addressed* as 'Madonna'), only
married women can be *described* as 'monna.'
Beatrice therefore was now a married woman.

ll. 28-31. The translation here paraphrases the
scholastic terms "substance" and "accident."
A "substance" is anything that exists in-
dependently, on its own account, such as a
stone, a tree, a lion, an angel, a disembodied
soul, or a living man. An angel or a disembodied soul would be an "intellectual" or
"intelligent" substance or being, but only
man still in the flesh would be both an intelligent and corporeal substance. An "accident" is that which exists only as an attribute
or experience of a substance, such as whiteness
weight, shape, or any of the emotions or
sensations. Love then is an accident, and can
have no independent existence, still less a corporeal existence.

p. 97, l. 5. "The Philosopher" is Aristotle; but it
will be noted that Dante does not profess to be
quoting any particular passage. His statement
is strictly correct; for Aristotle constantly implies, or asserts by implication, that nothing but
a physical and sensible body is capable of independent motion. A *quality*, such as redness, or
an experience, such as love, could only be said to
move in dependence upon a body of which it is an
attribute or with which it is conjoined. The
local movement of a body is primary or *essential*;
nothing else can move locally except *incidentally*. Many passages might be cited in confirma-
tion of this; but perhaps the nearest approach to
an explicit statement occurs in chapter ii. of the
"Little First" book of the *Metaphysics*: "We

are compelled to conceive that there is matter in anything that moves."

l. 8. On speech as proper to man (not shared by devil, beast, or angel; nor indeed by the Deity himself) see the curious passage *De Vulg. El.* i. 2. Aristotle remarks incidentally in the 3rd book of the *De Partibus Animalium*, chap. x., that man is the only laughing animal; and Boethius and the schoolmen take up the idea. Aquinas is careful to point out that though man may be defined as a laughing animal, yet such a definition is not *essential*. That is to say, laughter is not necessary to the conception, or essence, of humanity. See further Epistle x. (to Can Grande) § xxvi. lines 501-506, and *note*.

l. 12 ff. The interest of this passage is twofold, inasmuch as it throws light on Dante's conception of the relation of the vernaculars to the "grammars," and of the history of vernacular literature, and also indicates the conservative views with which Dante entered upon his own literary career. He constantly departed further and further from these views, but was haunted by survivals of them to the last.

We must note, then, in the first place, that Dante regarded such languages as Latin and Greek as artificial and conventional creations, deliberately instituted for the twofold purpose of arresting the natural changes to which spoken language is liable, and enabling nations with different vernaculars to communicate with each other. Compare *De Vulg. El.* i. 1: 28-41; i. 9: 47-107; and *Conv.* i. 5: 45-106, together with the *notes* on these passages in the T.C. edition. These artificial languages or "grammars" were supposed to be the proper vehicles of all literature; that is, of all utterances intended to have a significance and a life beyond the immediate purpose which called them forth. All poets, therefore, wrote originally either in Latin or in some other "grammar." But towards the middle of the twelfth century,

Dante declares, one who wished to give
literary form to his addresses to his lady
love adopted the artifice of "rhyming" as
a vernacular equivalent to the quantitative
measures of the Latin poets; and though this
did not fully entitle him to the name of poet,
which was reserved for writers in "grammar"
(they alone being "regular poets." Cf. *De Vulg.
El.* ii. 6: 79, 11: 56), yet it placed him, in a certain
sense, in a position analogous to theirs, and justified him in claiming their privileges. His adoption of the unstable vernacular, however, in
place of the stable language of literature, could
only be justified by the necessity of making
himself intelligible to his lady love; and for
anyone to "rhyme" instead of "poetising" for
other purposes than those of love was therefore
illegitimate.

But Dante's history is at fault. As the commentators well remark, the earliest extant
Provençal poem is of a didactic character, and
the earliest considerable French poems are epic,
and both literatures open notably earlier than
the date given by Dante. Even the lyric poetry
of Provence began earlier than Dante supposes;
for the earliest troubadour of whom we possess
any remains, William of Poitou, the great-
grandfather of our Richard Cœur de Lion, died
about 1127. But it appears from the *De Vulg. El.*
i. 10: 20-25 that Dante was not acquainted with
any Troubadours earlier than Peter of Auvergne
(flo. 1150-1180) and his contemporaries.

Of more interest, perhaps, to readers of the
Vita Nuova than Dante's views of history will
be his own practice. We note that he gradually
expanded his conception of the range of vernacular literature. His *Canzoni*, which mark the
next stage of his literary work after the *Vita
Nuova*, cover a variety of subjects; but he is
careful to bring even those which are of philosophical, ethical, satirical, or personal character
(ii., iii., vii., ix., xii., xiii., xiv.) into some con-

nection with the theme of love. In the *De Vulg. El.* ii. he extends the legitimate sphere of vernacular poetry so as to include War and Virtue, still formally confining it, however, to Odes (Canzoni), Ballads, and Sonnets. All other poems being "illegitimate and irregular," ii. 3: 10. In the *Convivio* he gives us a very elaborate apology, in book i. chapters. v.-xiii., for writing a prose treatise, of miscellaneous contents, in the vernacular. He begins by taking advantage of the form of a commentary, which connects the work with the *Canzoni*. But in the later chapters he openly avows his longing to vindicate the worth of Italian prose. Lastly, when he altogether broke with the tradition and adopted the "illegitimate and irregular" form of the *Comedy*, he had to defend himself against the astonished expostulations of his contemporaries (compare his correspondence with Del Virgilio, T.C. *Latin Works*, pp. 371-385). He himself apparently felt that explanation and excuse were necessary (compare Boccaccio's *Life of Dante*, § 15) and was careful to claim for the work only the humble title of *Comedy* (see *Epistle* x., to Can Grande, § 10), whereas the more elaborate and dignified style of the *Canzoni* had repeatedly been described as "tragic." *De Vulg. El.* ii. 4: 37, 12: 11, 13: 102. Compare *Inferno*, xx. 113.

l. 26, 27. The tongues of Provence (Languedoc) and of Italy.

p. 99, ll. 2-5. Compare *Purg.* xi. 91-99; xxiv. 49-63; xxvi. 124-126; *De Vulg. Eloq.* xiii. 13: 7, ii. 6: 85-89; together with the *notes*.

l. 13. Compare p. 101, line 20. "Colour" is a technical term of the Latin writers on rhetoric, which survives in our phrase to "put a new colour upon a thing." Browning's "The Ring and the Book" is a perfect example of "colours."

l. 29. "Æolus, for to thee," etc.

ll. 30, 31. "Thy task, O queen, to weigh what thou desirest," etc.

l. 33. "Ye hardy Trojans!" etc.

p. 101, ll. 1, 2. In the passage from Lucan, as given by Dante, Rome is apostrophised as owing the privilege of Nero's reign to the civil wars: "Yet much, O Rome, thou owest to civil arms." But the reading is false. *Debes* should be *debet*. The passage occurs in an apostrophe to Cæsar (Nero).

l. 7. The opening lines of the *Odyssey* are paraphrased by Horace in the *Ars Poetica*:—"Tell me, muse, of the man who, after the fall of Troy, saw the manners and cities of many men."

l. 10. Ovid opens his poem on the *Remedies of Love* thus:—"When Love had read the title and name of this book he cried: *Wars, I perceive, wars are in store for me.*"

p. 103, l. 28. "Note, reader, a delicate sense in the words *umiltà, umile, umiliare*, used by Dante in his little work: to wit peace, quietude, tranquillity of the affections, cessation of every appetite." Edd. Pesaresi quoted by D'Ancona.

p. 109, ll. 11, 12. *Lamentations* i. 1. "How doth the city sit solitary that was full of people! How is she become a widow, she that was great among the nations!"

l. 23. The second reason needs no explanation, but both the first and third reasons present difficulties. (1) Apparently Dante regarded the details of Beatrice's death as having no direct bearing upon the proper subject of the *Vita Nuova*, to wit, the praises of his lady and the record of his own love. But this interpretation is not very satisfactory, nor does it harmonise well with the following attempt to solve the problem raised by the third reason. (3) In *Conv.* i. 2, Dante gives at length his reasons for disapproving of a man speaking of himself, whether in praise or blame; and in *Purg.* xxx. 55-63, he apologises for introducing his own name into the *Comedy*. But how could his narrating the particulars of Beatrice's death have involved his own praises? The question has fairly baffled the commentators. May it be suggested that Beatrice, on her death-bed, had expressed some interest in Dante's future? Such a suggestion would explain his subsequent conviction that she had actually watched over him and endeavoured to restrain him when he was wandering into unworthy ways (*Purg.* xxx. 127-135), and that when he persisted in his evil course she had broken her heavenly peace to save him (*Inf.* ii. 52-117; *Purg.* xxx. 139-141). It would also explain the anguish of shame with which he meets Beatrice's reproaches in the Earthly Paradise. Compare *Convivio*, iv. 21: 59-68, 92-99, and many other passages in Dante's works.

p. 111, ll. 12-17. We learn from this passage that Beatrice died on 8th June 1290, within an hour after sunset; for Alphraganus, an Arabic astronomer whom Dante studied carefully, tells us that the *Syrian* ninth month, Haziran, corresponds to the Roman June; and also that the *Arabs* began the day at sunset. The first hour of the Arab ninth day would therefore be the first hour after sunset of the Roman eighth. Tisrin I. (October) was followed by Tisrin II. (November).

l. 21. The perfect number is 10. Compare *Convivio*, ii. 15: 28-34.

p. 115, l. 2. This is to be taken as a dedication of the work to Guido Cavalcanti, not as indicating that it was written for his eye alone.

p. 117, ll. 21, 22. According to the medieval physicians health was maintained by the balance of the four qualities or humours of the body—hot, cold, wet, and dry.

p. 121, l. 13. *Thy sisters.* Previous poems. *Canzone* and *ballata* are feminine, *sonnetto* masculine, but all are personified as maidens.

p. 123, l. 21. It is impossible to render adequately by an English word the meaning of *salute*—spiritual health or perfection—used sometimes in a passive, sometimes in an active sense.

p. 129, l. 12. The empyrean or heaven of peace. Compare note to p. 103

p. 131, l. 1 ff. The episode of the Lady of the Window
has given rise to much speculation. Dante himself, in the second book of the *Convivio*, comment-
ing on Ode xv. (which falls perfectly into the
context of the first lines of this section), gives it
an allegorical turn, and makes the Lady of the
Window represent Philosophy. See especially
Conv. ii. 2 : 1-48, and 16 : 98-103. But it is very
difficult to resist the impression that the poem,
which seems to rise out of a very real and human
experience, was originally meant literally, and
that the allegorising is an afterthought. Compare
T.C. *Convivio*, Appendix ii., especially pp. 432-
434. It is unfortunate that three such well-known
commentators as Rossetti, Fraticelli, and Scartaz-
zini, should all have adopted the unhappy con-
jecture that this lady was Gemma Donati, Dante's
future wife. It is impossible to make this idea
harmonise either with the literal narrative of
the *Vita Nuova* or with the allegory of the
Convivio, and there is nothing of any weight or
precision to urge in its favour.

p. 137, l. 14 ff. Compare Ode xv., the canzone of
Conv. ii. and *Conv.* ii. 13 : 30-81.

p. 141, l. 19. *L'ora di nona*, though rendered
"ninth hour" by Rossetti, and "*neunten stunde*"
by Beck, undoubtedly means "hour of noon."
Compare *Purg.* xxvii. 4. There is, however, a
covert allusion intended to the sacro-sanct number nine, inasmuch as the canonical ninth hour
nona (nones) is sounded immediately after the
expiration of the secular sixth hour *nona* (noon).
Conv. iv. 23 : 127-160.

p. 145, l. 17. The likeness of Jesus here referred to
is the one known as the "Veronica." There
are many versions of its story. According to
the Golden Legend (T.C. Edition, i. 83),
Veronica was an aged and devout widow
who was intimate with Jesus. She desired to
have a likeness of him wherein to find solace
when he should be no more on earth. She had
procured a canvas for this purpose, but Jesus,

learning her wish, pressed it upon his face
and left his likeness upon it. After his death
Veronica was brought to Rome with it, to cure
Tiberius of a mysterious disease that could only be
relieved by the wondrous physician whom Pilate
had slain. The miracle led to Pilate's disgrace
and death. Compare *Par.* xxxi. 106-108.

p. 145, l. 14. The old editions have the reading
"andava," "at the time when many folk went,"
etc.; and this was taken to refer to the year of
Jubilee, 1300, during which the Veronica was
constantly exhibited. Hence the current idea
that the *Vita Nuova* was written in 1300. But
if, with the modern editions, we read "va," the
reference will be not to a special year but to the
season of the year. Now the Veronica was, and
still is, regularly exhibited at the New Year
and at Easter. So we may take the passage as
probably indicating Easter as the season at which
the pilgrims passed through the city, and as
giving no indication of year. We may therefore
suppose that the *Vita Nuova* was completed not
very long after the first anniversary of Beatrice's
death, say in 1292.

p. 147, l. 20. The shrine of St James at Compostella
in Spain.

p. 151, l. 10. In the first chapter of the "Little First"
book of the *Metaphysics* we read that probably
the greatest and most comprehensive truths,
which are hardest to us, may really in themselves
be simplest of all. "In as much as difficulty is
of two kinds, its cause may lie not in the things,
but in us; for as the eyes of bats are to the light
of day so is the perception of our soul towards
things which, in the order of nature, are the
clearest of all."

l. 25. The crystalline heaven or sphere of the
primum mobile. Compare *Conv.* ii. 4; *Par.*
ii. 112-114, xxvii. 99, xxx 38, 39, and many
other passages.

p. 153, l. 8. Compare *Purg.* xxx. 133-135.

l. 21. "Who is blessed through all ages."

Sonnet I. One of the poems of philosophic love, in which Dante applies the imagery and the traditional conceits of love poetry to the passion of the often baffled but always fascinated devotee of learning and philosophy. Compare Ballads ii. and iv., Odes ii., iii., ix., and the disquisitions in books ii. and iii. of the *Convivio*.

> l. 14. Compare *Conv.* iv. 20: 61-69, and Guido Guinicelli's great ode (T.C. *Early Italian Poets*, p. 21).

Sonnet II. A poem of the *Vita Nuova* cycle. Compare *Vita Nuova*, §§ xv., xvi.

Sonnet III. Composed in reply to Cino da Pistoia's sonnet, *Cercando di trovar minera in oro*, wherein Cino confesses that as he sought to find a mine of gold an evil thorn has pierced his heart. Cino was one of the chief masters of the *dolce stil nuovo*, and is often referred to in the *Vulg. Eloq.* There can be no doubt that he is the "dearest brother" to whom Epistle iv. was written (compare *Latin Works*, p. 306), and who wrote an answer to Dante's first sonnet in the *Vita Nuova*.

Sonnet IV. Of the *Vita Nuova* cycle. With line 4 compare *Vita Nuova* and p. 19, lines 32, 33, and p. 95, ll. 9, 10; and with lines 12-14, compare lines 7, 8 of the sonnet in *Vita Nuova*, § xxvi., and the concluding lines of stanza iii. of the Ode in *Vita Nuova*, § xix.

Sonnet V. A poem of the "Pietra" group, to which belong Odes i., v., vi., x. Compare T.C. *Convivio*, Appendix ii., especially pp. 430-432.

Sonnet VI. To Guido Cavalcanti, Dante's "primo Amico." See *Vita Nuova*, §§ iii., xxiv., xxxi., pp. 10, 90, 112. Compare *Inf.* x. 63. This sonnet is the opening of a tenzone or poetical contest between Dante and Guido, of which four sonnets exist by the latter, who first deprecates his own worthiness, and then is even more doubtful of Lapo's qualifications.

> Lapo Gianni was another of the little group of poets which included Dante, Guido, and Cino. He is mentioned in the *De Vulgari*

Eloquentia (i. 13) with Guido and Cino as having recognised the excellence of the Italian vernacular. See T.C. *Latin Works*, p. 44. Lapo Gianni's protocol of June 15, 1300, is the only document extant concerning Dante's priorate of Florence. It confirms the sentence of fine or mutilation passed by the former priors against the three traitors who conspired to betray their city to Pope Boniface VIII.

ll. 9, 10. A comparison with *Vita Nuova*, § vi., shows that in this sonnet we have one of the *certe cosette* written by Dante in honour of the first " screen lady " of *Vita Nuova*, § v.

For a long time the name of Bice was substituted for that of Lagia, the now accepted reading in line 9. Who Lagia was we cannot yet say.

Sonnet VII. This is regarded by Mr Edmund Gardner as probably the very last of Dante's lyrical poems. It was answered by Cino's—

Poi ch' io, fui, Dante, del mio natal stilo.

Sonnet VIII. To Cino, in answer to his sonnet, " Dante quando per caso s'abbandona." Compare *Latin Works*, *Epistle* iv., *note* p. 306.

Sonnet IX. 4. *Un*, a sonnet, of which this is apparently a recantation. It would be unsafe in the present state of our knowledge to attempt an identification or interpretation; but the general tone of the poem, and a comparison with Ode iii., stanza v. (p. 196), suggest that it may belong to the philosophic cycle.

Sonnet X. This poem appears to close the series inspired by the " Lady of the Window " (*Vita Nuova* §§ xxxvi.-xxxix.), to which series Ode xv. (placed at the beginning of *Convivio*, ii.) belongs.

Sonnet XI. 5-11. For the imagery compare *Convivio*, ii. 2 : 31, 32; and Ode xi. st. v. *ll.* 4-9. Who " Lisetta " was cannot at present be determined; but the tone of this poem, especially when compared with that of the preceding sonnet, seems

to preclude the suggestion that she was the
"Lady of the Window."

Sonnet XII. Cino's noble answer, "Dante io non
so in quale albergo suoni," still exists. (T.C.
Early Italian Poets, p. 218.) He prays his
friend to hold fast by the Good, and urges
that the more Evil seems to triumph the
greater need is there for just men to witness for
righteousness. Even if all the world has turned
from truth, let his beloved brother, though
swathed with pain, cling to Faith for Beatrice's
sake.

Sonnet XIII. In this sonnet Dante indulges in gentle
sarcasm against himself. He felt that he had laid
himself open to the charge of shunning the hearty
and natural indulgence of high spirits, as though
it were hardly compatible with his "dedicated"
character as a lover. It is the only authentic
poem in which Dante assumes this half sportive
tone of self-mockery, and it is the true justifica-
tion of Wordsworth's assertion (based, no doubt,
in his own mind on a false ascription to Dante
of the insignificant sonnet, *Messer Brunetto,
questa pulzelletta*, see T.C. *Early Italian Poets*,
p. 208)—

> "The Sonnet glittered a gay myrtle leaf
> Amid the cypress with which Dante crowned
> His visionary brow."

Ballad I. On the ballad form, see note on p. 329.
Violetta has not been identified.

ll. 11-14. 'Do not ask whether my hope is
presumptuous and unfounded, but consider the
ardour of my affection; for many ladies e'er
now have had cause to rue, too late, their in-
credulous and cold disdain.'

Ballad II. A poem of philosophic love (*cf.* note on
p. 341), forming a companion specially to
Ballad iv.

l. 10. All the virtues and the higher truths
are "ladies," and so are all souls, both of men
and women. Moreover, in the high and mystic

regions of emotion, all noble love ot women is closely related to love of truth, of goodness, of beauty, and of God.

l. 17. *By another's pleasure, i.e.* By divine dispensation.

Ballad III. Mr Gardner thinks that this ballad was inspired by one which Guido Cavalcanti addressed to Dante, beginning, "Fresca rosa novella." In that case it is a "May-day fancy" without personal application. Guido's poem is erroneously ascribed to Dante himself in the Oxford Dante and elsewhere.

l. 21. It was a Troubadour tradition to claim praise for novel and even paradoxical literary forms. Compare Ode v. st. vi. *l.* 5.

Ballad IV. A poem of philosophic love. Compare note to Sonnet i. This poem is retracted in the Tornata of Ode iii. (*Convivio*, book iii.).

l. 9. *The sweet form, i.e.* the form of Love.

ll. 15, 16. She has felt the flame of love herself; and, knowing that she is not invincible, stands upon her guard and will not surrender at a word.

l. 18. Philosophy delights in self contemplation. See Ode xii. st. i. lines 19, 20, and the commentary on them in *Convivio*, iv. 2. 150-162 (T.C. edition, p. 237).

ll. 19, 20. *i.e.* When a right-minded lady is stared at, she assumes a reserved bearing, for her honour's sake.

ll. 21-28. See the modern parallel cited in the T.C. *Convivio*, p. 191.

Ode I. (vii. in the T.C. *Convivio*). Of the Pietra group. See note to Sonnet v. On the structure of the *Sestina*, see T.C. *Convivio*, p. 396, *note* 4.

i. 1. Midwinter.

i. 4. *changes not its green* = loses not its vigour.

ii. The lady is no more melted by spring than the poet is chilled by winter. Hence she is *nuova, i.e.* unlike other women, "wondrous."

iii. 5. The *piccoli colli* of this stanza have become

altissimi in stanza v. It is hard to say what, if any, significance there may be in this change.

v. 5. The very grass was love-laden, and the promptings of love issued from it as from a beauteous woman; but in vain.

v. 6. *Girt* agrees with "field," not "grass."

Ode II. (iv. in T.C. *Convivio*). A poem of philosophic love. See note to Sonnet i.

i. 13-15. *e'en as a painting*, *i.e.* all good is but a latent potency till evoked by love; and therefore without love it perishes.

ii. 2. *the ray.* The sun's ray, from which all stars derive their light. *Cf. Par.* xx. 6.

ii. 8. The heart smitten with love, loves all lovely things in proportion to their love-worthiness. *Cf. Par.* xxvi. 64-66.

ii. 12. *as water*, *i.e.* when a glass sphere, filled with water, is used as a burning glass.

iii. 2. *atti* = features, facial expression, attitude, bearing, or gestures.

iii. 5. *its*, *i.e.* the mind's. The humble student distrusts his intellectual powers, but dares greatly; for his great zeal will supplement his small capacity.

iii. 9-15. The sun does not create the power of fire, but reveals it; so this maid the power of love. It is only in a fitting subject that any natural or spiritual power can display its full virtue.

Ode III. (*Convivio*, book iii.). A poem of philosophic love. See note on Sonnet i. This poem is fully explained in book ii. of the *Convivio*.

ii. 14. *that which she doth guide*, *i.e.* the body. Compare Ode vii. st. ii. *l.* 16, and Ode xii.st. vii. *ll.* 7, 8.

v. See Ballad iv.

Ode IV. A poem of earthly love. See T.C. *Latin Works*, pp. 301-4.

ii. 11, 12. *that whence*, *i.e.* 'What argument can control the passion that makes a tempest in my heart?'

ii. 13-15. The words that express his anguish at the same time administer a merited rebuke to his eyes.

iv. 13. *launched it*, i.e. the "bolt."

iv. 14. *it abides darkened*, i.e. "my face," referring back to *l.* 11.

v. 7. *folk of skill*, i.e. skill in love. Compare Sonnet xii., p. 168.

Ode V. (viii. in T.C. *Convivio*). Of the Pietra group. See note on Sonnet v. This composition, which is a modification of the *Sestina*, is built upon the five endings, *donna, tempo, luce, freddo, pietra*. No attempt has been made in the translation to preserve uniformity of rendering for all the different meanings in which these words are used.

iii. 4. *the element of chill* = "water."

iii. 10. *substance chill* = "water."

v. 7. *thy strong season* = "spring."

v. 9. *a narrow stone* = "a sarcophagus."

v. 10-12. Till the resurrection, when all beauty can be seen and compared.

vi. 3. Compared with me no lover or poet has any daring.

vi. 4. *this chill* = "the cold lady."

vi. 5, 6. Compare Ballad iii. 21, and *De Vulg. Eloq.* ii. 13. 85-96.

Ode VI. (vi. in T.C. *Convivio*). Of the Pietra group. See note on Sonnet v. A comparison of *Convivio*, iv. 26: 64-70 with stanza iii. 10 of this Ode (compare also *Conv.* iii. 10: 33-41 with stanza ii. 2) makes it clear that this poem must have been the contemplated text of the seventh treatise of the *Convivio*. Compare T.C. *Convivio*, p. 364, *note* on *l.* 67, and p. 194, *note* on *l.* 41.

i. 6-8. 'No arrow can ever find an unprotected place, because she is cased in proof, and because she never passively awaits attack or offers herself as a mark.'

iii. 8. *their powers* = the powers of the senses.

vi. 7. *therewith.* See vi. 2, but the reading is doubtful.

vi. 12. *he* = Love.

vii. 5. Since she has scorned Love, the quarrel is his.

Ode VII. (xiv. in T.C. *Convivio*). One of the ethico-

satirical Odes. The others are **xii.** (*Convivio,*
book iv.) and **xiii.** A comparison of *Conv.* **i. 8:**
128-132, and *Conv.* **iii. 15:** 140-145, with stanza
vi. of this poem will make it clear that it was
to have formed the text of the fifteenth and last
treatise of the *Convivio.*

i. 6. For beauty to love anything but virtue is base.

i. 14. *to him,* i.e. to Love.

ii. 12. *her mistress,* i.e. the virtuous soul. Compare
iii. 2.

ii. 16. *what she finds,* i.e. the natural accomplishments
of body and soul. Compare Ode xii. st. vii.
ll. 7, 8; and Ode iii. st. ii. *l.* 14.

ii. 19. She has fixed the values of things by heavenly
standards.

ii. 21. To possess her is always to be master, never
slave, of the situation.

iii. 2. *Handmaiden.* Italian *serva,* corresponding to
the *servo* translated "slave" in the preceding
line. But it is here used, without contempt, of
"virtue," the handmaid of the soul. Compare
ii. 12.

iii. 18, 19. Dante here repudiates the inference that
he regards himself as a model of virtue, and is
pleading his own cause. Compare *Epistle* x.
557-569 (§ xxviii.), T.C. *Latin Works,* p. 360;
and passages elsewhere.

iv. 11. *she who levels us* = Death.

v. 6 *Fera* = dire. The MS. authority is conclusively
in favour of *buona,* which must be understood as
an appeal: "dear fortune." But it is extremely
difficult to believe that so startling and impressive
a reading as the current *fera* can have arisen by a
copyist's error. It is provisionally retained, but
with much hesitation.

v. 9. *such a circle,* i.e. the influence of the heavens
(as in Ode xiii. st. iv. *ll.* 1-3, and Ode xiv.
st. iv. *l.* 14). But compare *Purg.* xvi. 58-84.

vi. 6. *swung it round.* Like a falcon's lure.

vii. 4-21. 'It is hard, without offence, to hint that
whatever in you excites desires in the foul hearts
of your lovers must in itself be evil. Good in you

would attract nothing but good, and would leave such natures unmoved. If they love you, you are not truly beautiful.'

Ode VIII. (x. in the T.C. *Convivio*). Of the *Vita Nuova* cycle. This poem and Ode xi. seem to belong to the period (treated with extreme conciseness in the *Vita Nuova*) between Beatrice's first refusal of her salutation, § x., and the memorable rebuke of § xviii. The ladies of this latter paragraph had all of them witnessed "many" of those "discomfitures," only one of which has been related in the text.

ii. 13. *She beholds the heart.* "She" is the soul, personified here and throughout the next two stanzas.

iii. 4. *thence,* i.e. "from this life," referring back to *l.* 2.

iii. 8, 9. The soul, having a moment's respite granted by the creator's pity, rallies the flickering powers of life that will not be finally quenched till the actual moment of her departure.

iv. 3. *Where he established,* etc. Where Love brought the image of my lady and fixed it.

iv. 8. *her who weeps,* etc. = the soul.

iv. 9. *Get gone, thou wretch.* Note that it is the image of his lady in the poet's mind, not his lady herself, who addresses his soul with this imperious familiarity.

iv. 10. The lady herself, Love, the image of the lady in the poet's mind, and now his own yearning towards her, are successively regarded as the power that exiles his soul, *i.e.* that slays him.

v., vi. Stanzas v. and vi. (which are a variant on *Vita Nuova,* § ii.) disturb the context. The *tornata* (stanza vii.) links itself naturally to the close of stanza iv., and it is noteworthy that stanza v. is omitted from the Barbarini MS. But it is difficult to believe that these lines (whether in place or not) come from any hand but Dante's. The statements in stanza v., taken literally, are irreconcilable with the data of the *Vita Nuova,* and it has been urged that this throws

discredit on the story of the *Vita Nuova* itself.
But it may equally well be maintained that this
poem was rejected when the *Vita Nuova* was
written just because it embodied a heightened
poetic idealisation of the facts, which Dante
desired to set forth in literal sincerity in his
confession.

v. 14. *The main spirit.* = The vital spirit. Compare
Vita Nuova, p. 3, *ll.* 23, 24, and note on p. 326.

v. 17. *He who set this moving,* i.e. Love.

vi. 4. *The power*, etc., *i.e.* the sight.

vi. 8. *It wrought.* "It" is the "power," viz. sight.

vi. 9. *The others, i.e.* the other powers or spirits of
the senses, whose chief and leader it (sight) has
hitherto been.

Ode. IX. (v. in the T.C. *Convivio*). A poem of
philosophic love. See note on Sonnet i. p. 341.

i. 3. *Which is grievous to me.* Because if it kills him
he will no longer be able to serve his lady.

iii. 13. *Against good pleasure, i.e.* Against the good
pleasure of her whom he serves.

iii. 14. *Convenenza.* The usual reading is *giovinezza*,
and the passage is taken to mean 'if my youth
and immaturity in study rob me as yet of my
lady's grace, I look forward to the time when
I shall be a more reasonable being, and more
worthy of her favour.' But it seems very difficult
to accept *giovinezza* in this sense, though it must
be confessed that the adoption of the Barbarini
MS. reading *convenenza*, with the interpretation
given in the text, is a somewhat desperate
remedy.

iv. 1. *A noble longing, i.e.* the desire himself to become
more worthy, born of his love of study.

iv. 8. *Thanks to a not-my goodness.* It is not his
own goodness, but his lady's, that transforms the
service itself into lavish payment.

iv. 14. 'My very desire to become more worthy is
itself a service rendered to her, since it is only
for her credit, not for my own good, that I
cherish it.'

v. 5, 6. 'Though the enamoured mind cannot live

an hour without its lady, yet she concerns herself not with its longings.'

v. 16. The winning of a new flash of insight makes him see new beauties, and then his former state (both of torment and rapture) is changed for another.

vi. The lofty meaning of this Ode might naturally clothe it in the pride of conscious superiority; but the humble poet urges it not to presume thereon, but carefully to choose its company.

Alternative Tornata, *l.* 1. There is no clue to determine who these "three least vicious" are.

5-8. The text of these lines is doubtful and the meaning obscure. The translation takes them to mean 'To keep to a bad cause, when you know it to be bad, for fear of infamy, is in fact infamous. If then you really fear infamy you must shun it indeed, not only appear to shun it; so that, by actually deserting the evil cause, you may set your terror of infamy at rest, for infamy has lost all real hold on you.'

Ode X. (ix. in the T.C. *Convivio*). Of the *Pietra* group. See note to Sonnet v., p. 341.

i. 1-3. The sign of the Twins rises at sunset. It is midwinter.

i. 4-6. Venus is too near the sun to be visible.

i. 7. Saturn.

i. 8, 9. The *great circle*, etc., is the meridian. Note that *quando il sol si corca* (line 2) governs the whole context. At sunset the constellation of Gemini is on the eastern horizon, Venus is invisible, and Saturn is on the zenith.

i. 9. *the seven, i.e.* the seven planets.

ii. 3. It being midsummer there, in the southern hemisphere; but note that Dante's usual view is that practically all the dry land lies in the northern hemisphere. See *Conv.* iii. 5: 71-75.

iii. 16. 'A youthful lady.'

iv. 1-3. 'The leaves that spring brought out are now dead and fallen.'

Ode XI. (xii. in the T.C. *Convivio*). Of the *Vita Nuova* cycle. See note to Ode viii.

i. 5.   The special circumstances here referred to cannot be recovered.

ii. 7.   *Its pain, i.e.,* the heart's.

ii. 10-13.   'As God loves us because we bear his
image, so shouldst thou love my heart.'

v. 11.   *Its coming, i.e.* the salutation's.   On the whole
passage compare Sonnet xi. and *note.*

Ode XII. (*Convivio* iv.).   Of the ethico-satirical group
(see note on Ode vii.), but connected by stanza i.
with the poems of philosophic love (see note on
Sonnet i., p. 341).   The poem is fully explained
in the fourth book of the *Convivio.*   The title
" *Contra gli erranti* " is given in obedience to
Dante's express direction, *Convivio,* iv. 30: 24-
30.

Ode XIII. (xi. in the T.C. *Convivio*).   Of the ethico-
satirical group, and connected by stanza i. with
the poems of philosophical love.   See notes to
Ode vii. and to Sonnet i.

i 12.   " Gallantry " is but a makeshift translation of
leggiadria, which includes elegance, grace, and
refined charm.   It is applicable to women as well
as men.

ii. 8.   They lose good money and get nothing for it;
and this in addition to misleading themselves and
others by the semblance of generosity.   So they
would have been wiser not to give at all.

iii. 17-19.   Here Dante expressly rules out the conclusion which he is driven to indicating in
Ode vii. stanza vii.

iv. 1-9.   'The unpropitious relations of the heavens
make gallantry swerve out of her orbit (compare
note on Ode vii. st. v. *ll.* 9, 10), but were I to hold
my peace till better celestial conditions bring her
back to it, I should be faithless, even to the point
of treachery; for I have been made her familiar
and her appointed champion by the friendship of
a gracious lady in whom she is embodied.'   This
beautiful tribute to the unknown lady suggests
the kind of relation indicated in *Purg.* xxiv
37-48 as destined to spring up between Dante
and the Lucchese Gentucca.

iv. 17. *That which I am handling*, *i.e.* my theme, viz. gallantry.

v. 15. *This third*, *i.e.* love, who, with virtue and joyance (solazzo) under his leadership, constitutes gallantry; just as heat (analogous to love) and light (analogous to joyance) united by and in the perfect sphere (as of love) make up the being of the sun.

vii. 3. *Neither the sun*, *i.e.* neither does it irk the sun.

vii. 6. *One and the other*. The sun and the gallant man.

Ode XIV. (xiii. in the T.C. *Convivio*). This beautiful Ode stands by itself and belongs to no group. From *Convivio*, i. 12: 71-89, and iv. 27: 100-103. we learn that the text of the fourteenth and penultimate book of the *Convivio* was to treat of Justice; and further from ii. 1: 34-36, that the same book was to embrace an express treatment of the origin (and presumably the nature) of allegory. We are, therefore, perfectly safe in assuming that this Ode would have been commented on in book xiv. of the completed *Convivio*.

ii. 5. *The ray*, *i.e.* the glancing tear.

ii. 17. *Sister to thy mother*. All the virtues are sisters (compare stanza iv. *ll.* 4, 9), and therefore Love, conceived as a virtue (carità), is feminine and is the sister of Righteousness. But, conceived as a power, Love (amore) is masculine, and is therefore represented as the son of Carità.

iii. 8. 'Hast thou no compassion for the grief that the recital must renew in me?'

iii. 9-18. Apparently the daughter and granddaughter of Righteousness are civil and canon law! Or, more broadly, the maintenance of civic rights, and the establishment of human relations of helpfulness and affection that spring up under their protection. This would nearly coincide with the ideas of law and gospel. But, even if this be accepted, the details of the allegory remain obscure.

iv. 5. *One and the other dart*. Chivalrous love and high friendship?

iv. 14. Compare note on *Ode* vii. st. v. *ll.* 9, 10.

v. 7. *Convert white flowers into dark*, *i.e.* blame the innocent, overturn the moral order and invert the moral perspective of things. There is no need to see a reference to the *bianchi* and *neri* factions, which at the very most would only have indirectly suggested the imagery.

v. 9-12. The reading of the first line is doubtful and the whole passage is obscure. Perhaps it means, 'Since my city and my home are reft from me, I should count all the merely incidental miseries of my exile as nothing.'

v. 16-18. This half confession of offences that penitence should long ago have obliterated, recalls Leonardo Bruni's assertion that before Henry's expedition into Italy (A.D. 1310) Dante had begun to assume a humble tone towards Florence in hope of propitiating her and being recalled.

Ode XV. (*Convivio*, book ii.). Of the *Vita Nuova* cycle. *Vita Nuova*, § xxxix., gives the context of this poem; and the second book of the *Convivio* explains it in detail. On Dante's allegorical explanation of the Lady of the Window as Philosophy, see T.C. *Convivio*, Appendix ii. The Ode is interesting metrically as distinguishing (alone of Dante's Odes) both the *feet* and the *verses* of *De Vulg. El.* ii. 10: 33-38.

Sonnet XVI. 10. Clytie. Compare Ovid, *Metamorphoses* iv. 270. Vertitur ad solem, mutataque servat amorem.

Sonnet XVII. 6. See note to p. 99, l. 13.

Sonnet XVIII. 5. Probably external impressions on the senses and inward spiritual illumination.

Sonnet XX. Apparently of political import.

6. Clement V.

7. Philip le Bel.

12. The power or virtue of the Holy Roman Emperor.

M

APPENDIX.

IN order to give technical completeness to the
Temple Classics translation of Dante (see Editorial
note at the end of this volume), we here add an
English version of a few poems, which, in justice
to Dante, should not be regarded as in any sense
claiming to be serious literature, or to take a
place in the formal canon of his "works," although
the evidence that he actually wrote them appears in
one case to be irresistible, and in the other to reach
a high degree of probability. They consist of:—

1. A series of sonnets, constituting Dante's side of
a metrical correspondence between himself and Forese
Donati, in which each of the friends attacks the other
with a penetrating acidity of insinuation which the insight of friendship can often achieve with a more finished
malice than is possible to the blindness of enmity. The
whole correspondence is probably sportive, but it is
bitter sport. The details of the jargon in which these
poems are written have been deciphered with patient
skill by Del Lungo in his "*Dante ne' Tempi di Dante*"
(Bologna, 1888), to which we must refer any readers
who desire to understand the correspondence, and the
biographical interest of its bearing on *Purgatorio*, xxiii.
115 *sqq.*, and the great scene of Dante's meeting with
Beatrice in the Earthly Paradise. Compare Temple
Classics *Convivio*, Appendix ii. pp. 428 *sqq.*, and *Latin
Works*, pp. 302 *sqq.*

We insert a verbal translation, but as the poems
have no artistic value, we have not thought it necessary
either to explain them or to give the original text.

2. A curious composition (which the manuscripts
consistently assign to Dante) barbarously combined

354

of Provençal, Latin, and Italian lines. The first three
lines run—

> Ai fals ris! per qua traitz avetz
> Oculos meos, et quid tibi feci,
> Che fatto m' hai così spietata fraude.

This is a species of composition which Dante's mature
judgment would conclusively reject, and though it has
some interest for the student of Italian metrical forms,
it has no artistic value whatever; and, indeed, such
merit as it has is stripped of a disguise rather than
robbed of an ornament, when a straightforward translation into any one language is substituted for the
motley dress with which its author chose to clothe
it. The text (as is not unnatural) is very doubtful;
and in the second stanza (which is obscure) we have
departed from the traditional interpretation; but the
general drift of the poem is clear.

I.

THREE SONNETS TO FORESE.

i

Whoso should hear coughing the ill-fated spouse
of Bicci, dubbed Forese, would say that she had
wintered in the land of ice.

In mid-August thou findest her chilled; conceive then
what she must do in every other month! And
naught availeth that she sleeps smothered up, thanks
to the Cortona quilt she hath.

The cough, the cold, and other ill condition, come to
her, not from corrupt humours, but from the lack
she feeleth in the nest.

Her mother weeps, that hath more than one grief,
saying: Alas! that for a handful of dry figs I might
have married her into the house of Count Guido!

ii

Truly, Bicci Novello, the partridge breasts will make
for thee a Solomon's knot, but worse shall be the
mutton chine; for thy hide shall penance do for
the flesh.

So that thou shalt stand ever near St Simon's, if thou
procure thee not means to fare thence; and thou
dost understand that to flee the evil morsels would
now be a tardy remedy.

But, in sooth, 'tis told me thou knowest an art
whereby, if true it be, thou canst recover thyself,
for 'tis of very great gain;

And is practised in times when there is fear of flesh:
no need hast thou to stand idle; but truly ill-hap
thereby fell on Stagno's sons.

iii

Bicci Novel, a son of whom I know not, except I were
to ask thereof Mistress Tessa, so much substance is
wasted down his gullet, that perforce it behoveth
him to steal from others.

And already folk who have purse at girdle are on
their guard against him, when he draweth nigh,
saying: This fellow that hath the scurvy face is a
common thief by his very mien.

And one who belongeth to him, as much as Joseph
to Christ, lies sad in bed because of him, fearing
lest he be caught a-stealing.

Of Bicci and his brethren I can tell, that by taint of
blood they are skilled to play their wives false with
ill-gotten gain.

II.

A MACARONIC ODE.

i

Ah treacherous smile! wherefore hast thou betrayed mine eyes, and what have I done unto thee,
that thou hast wrought on me such pitiful wrong?

The very Greeks might now have heard my plaint!
All other women know, and thou art conscious, that
no deceiver merits any praise.

Thou knowest how rejoiceth

His wretched heart who waits and longs! I hope
on ever, and she takes no thought of me, I ween.
Oh God, what misery and what disastrous tempest is

his lot who wastes expectant days in longing, and never grasps the freshness of the flower!

ii

My foremost plaint, soft heart, is against thee; because, for one mad glance of eyes, thou should'st not have been ousted from thy right!

Yet, for all that, as I smite down the weeds with stroke of hoe, it doth rejoice me to see them still rise up against me from the slime. Whence I am slain, and (by the faith I own)

Much doth it grieve poor me

That I am punished, guiltless all of wrong. Nor does she even say ''Tis ill with him.' On this I base my plaint; for well she knows that if my heart should tremble to the love of any other, leaving her, the false thing would bear heavy suffering.

iii

Truly she needs must have a heart of ice, like to an asp that (by my faith) is deaf, if she should take no pity on her slave.

Right well love knoweth that, if I have not speedy rescue, I meet an evil death, all for her sake; nor can hope longer hold my life together.

Woe to my every nerve,

If she, of her true feeling, suffer not that I gain access to her propitious looks. Ah God, how perfect are they! But I distrust me anent it, so deep my pain therein. Her amorous care to me-ward still is less than is the rooted strength of hope in me.

iv

My song thou hast free course through all the world for I have uttered thee in language trine, so that my grievous thorn may become known throughout the world, and felt of every man. Then she perchance shall have ruth of it, who doth torment me.

The Temple Classics Dante (the only complete edition of Dante's works in any modern language), begun by the issue of the "Paradiso" (1899), is completed by this volume (1906). Mr Thomas Okey is responsible for both text and translation, except those of the Canzoni, which are contributed by Mr Philip H. Wicksteed.